D1497966

CONTEMPORARY APPROACHES TO CREATIVE THINKING

ATHERTON PRESS 70 FIFTH AVENUE, NEW YORK 1967

CONTEMPORARY APPROACHES TO CREATIVE THINKING

A SYMPOSIUM HELD AT THE UNIVERSITY OF COLORADO

Edited by Howard E. Gruber •
Glenn Terrell • Michael Wertheimer

CONTEMPORARY APPROACHES TO CREATIVE THINKING

Edited by Howard E. Gruber, Glenn Terrell & Michael Wertheimer

Library of Congress Catalog Card Number: 62-19403
Printed in the United States of America

FIRST PRINTING: AUGUST 1962
SECOND PRINTING: APRIL 1963
THIRD PRINTING: MAY 1964
FOURTH PRINTING: JANUARY 1967

To

KARL F. MUENZINGER

57008

PREFACE

What is creative thinking? What are its conditions, and how can it be fostered? In the spring of 1958, six eminent scientists gathered at the University of Colorado to consider these questions in a symposium. The participants were Jerome S. Bruner of Harvard, Richard S. Crutchfield of the University of California, Mary Henle of the New School for Social Research, Robert B. MacLeod of Cornell, David C. McClelland of Harvard, and Herbert A. Simon of the Carnegie Institute of Technology. Each day, for three days, two papers were presented, leaving ample time (if time is ever ample) for discussion of each. The discussions were recorded, transcribed, and then circulated among the participants for whatever use they cared to make of them in revising their papers. This volume is the result.

Contemporary Approaches to Creative Thinking is a sequel to an earlier symposium, published as *Contemporary Approaches to Cognition* by Harvard University Press in 1957. In that symposium the entire range of cognitive processes was examined by Jerome S. Bruner, Egon Brunswik, Leon Festinger, Fritz Heider, Charles E. Osgood, and David Rapaport. One of the participants in the earlier conference was asked to participate again—not only because his work is highly relevant but also in the hope of maintaining some continuity between the symposia.

The study of creativity, as no other subject, brings into

ix

a single arena the many characters of psychology, biography, literature, and art. In trying to understand how man's greatest achievements come about, the initial focus is often properly upon the creative product—such as great works of art or science. The products of human creativity are staggeringly diverse, as one delightedly rediscovers on seeing the rich assortment of case materials referred to in these pages.

The study of creativity need not limit itself to the eminent, the extraordinary. There are kinships between the small and the great and perhaps even between the creativity of everyday life and that of a great scientist or artist. If we include "everyday creativity" in our study, we may be in danger of making our conception of it meaningless; but if we exclude it, perhaps we trap ourselves in a "great-man theory" that leaves us no way of moving between the commonplace and the sublime. Even if we are interested both in superior accomplishments and in more modest products, it may be wise to emphasize the superior—and not only because of its greater intrinsic appeal. When a variable is maximized, we are more likely to discover characteristics which are also present, though perhaps in hidden form, in the usual range of the variable. Furthermore, since creativity is at best hard to define, it is only at the extreme that we can be reasonably sure that we are talking about it.

Creativity varies in degree and in kind. The essential continuity is found not in the *product* but in the creative process. Perhaps that is why this symposium centers on the process more than on its products. Simon, for example, in his discussion of computing machines that simulate human thought, is not trying to replace man with a machine that does a better job; he is trying to understand the nature of thought by attempting to duplicate some of its essentials. A machine that outstrips man would be of little use in this scientific endeavor if designing and building it gave us no new insights into the characteristics of human thought processes.

The participants in this symposium have approached the problem of creativity primarily as a problem for scientific understanding. This is not to say that any one of them would forego striving for the other two conventional goals of scientific endeavor, prediction, and control, but these are secondary. They are the tangible media through which we move toward understanding and by which we test it.

To study something, one must begin somewhere. Creative products can be examined, with a view to discovering similarities among them or among the processes leading to them. Process and product both can be considered in a variety of disciplines—painting, music, science. Or the field of study can be differentiated according to the kind of person or organism investigated. As everybody knows, psychologists too often have been guilty of confining their attention to those convenient laboratory animals, the college sophomore and the rat; our symposiasts have gone further afield. McClelland concentrates on physical scientists, Bruner on an inventive "trouble-shooting" group, and Crutchfield on military officers, college alumnae, and research workers. Henle is concerned with theologians, philosophers, and other people from all walks of life, and Simon with computers—one of which (or whom?) even had a paper rejected by a scholarly journal. Taken as a whole, the symposium contains a wide sample of great and humble representatives of the creative process from almost every field of endeavor. Each author, while focusing on a particular subgroup, has amplified his material with allusions and parallels drawn from many sources.

Bruner, for example, has dwelt at length on a team of inventors who carry on much of their creative work in the form of group discussions. It is clear that Bruner's intent is not just to describe this unusual group but to use it to fulfill his own injunction that in the study of thinking the first step is to externalize the behavior. If we are interested in the individual's "internal cast of characters," one way to find out more about it is to study individuals in whom the internal drama has become, as in Bruner's group of inventors, external.

That there are other ways of approaching the same general problem is manifest in the historical and experimental material that Henle draws on for her treatment of the internal discussion. Examining first the general character of the creative process, she pays detailed attention to the way in which these characteristics unfold as the process proceeds. Her rich illustrations vividly convey the involuted and perpetually turbulent nature of the inner struggle that marks the course of creative effort.

McClelland's choice of subject is the scientist, primarily the empirical physical scientist. In tracing the development and testing of his own hypotheses about the familial origins of the creative scientist's personality, McClelland has given us directly a fascinating display of the creative process at work. Especially notable is the blending of commitment and detachment (which Henle and Bruner explicitly describe) with which he goes about his thinking when his first hypotheses go wrong. His paper is so much a case study of the unfolding of a thought process as to include some data collected after the initial presentation of the paper in order to deal with questions that arose in the discussion.

In Crutchfield's paper we actually encounter the sophomore. But the sophomore is not treated in isolation. The experiments reported deal with the general question of conformity pressures in group situations; the behavior of sophomores is compared with that of other groups. The main point of the paper is to examine the relation between conformity and creative thinking. But as a useful by-product we get an important hint about one specific way in which psychologists may make mistaken inductions if they rely too heavily on the study of college sophomores.

It is not particularly facetious to say that the creature Simon has chosen to study is the computer. He in fact does approach the computer as an experimental subject, and in various guises he (or *she,* MacLeod tells us) takes various names, such as Logic Theorist or Chess Player. In some important respects the computers seem to behave like real, creative persons. Designing programs for them yields new levels of precision in simulation and, hence, in the description of creative *human* problem-solving behaviors.

Although MacLeod's role in the symposium was defined primarily as synthesizer and historian, his own creative thoughts on creativity crept through between the lines of history and synthesis. In particular his all-too-brief remarks on the phenomenology of creative thinking are clearly based on the introspections of a sophisticated psychologist. They are provocative and might well be considered the starting point for a fresh and disciplined attack on the way creative thinking looks and feels "from the inside."

There are wide differences in the vocabularies used by the participants, but this should not be permitted to hide essential similarities in the various authors' points of view. The language of computers can sometimes be translated into the language of poetry, metaphor, and intuition; and vice versa. Such translation may some day be routine, although now it often is rather difficult. To give some hint of the kind of translation which the reader might wish to try for himself, consider Bruner's internal cast of characters. These might be described as a set of alternative computer programs, and the way in which they enrich the individual's thought might then be ascribed to a process whereby the results of one program's activity become the inputs for others. Or consider the criteria of creativity offered by almost all participants: they may not be as dissimilar as the linguistic differences might imply.

Obvious though it is, we wish to emphasize that a symposium of only six papers must inevitably omit many important kinds of contributions. The reader who is concerned with the scientific study of creativity will have his own sharpest regrets. There are so many other approaches that it is perhaps better not to mention any. As is manifest in this volume, no single method will elucidate the entire creative process. Many researchers, many methods, many sources of material must be involved. Scientific psychological understanding of creativity moves forward in much the same way as in other scientific fields: laboriously, unevenly, with occasional grand surges. The flash of inspiration which frequently seems to epitomize creativity is only a sometime outcome of prolonged attention. Bruner has alluded to the myth of Perseus slaying the Gorgon Medusa by looking at her reflection in a polished shield rather than directly at her. The meaning of this myth, that the impersonal apparatus of justice permits us to deal with evil without being contaminated by it, might perhaps be extended a trifle: in the study of creativity, let us try many shields. Who knows which one will provide the most illuminating reflection?

PREFACE

In arranging the present symposium we have been fortunate to have had the encouragement and support of many individuals. We would particularly like to acknowledge the help given us by Vice Presidents W. F. Dyde and Eugene Wilson of the University of Colorado in making available funds necessary for the conference itself. We also thank the University's Council on Research and Creative Work for granting funds needed for final preparation of the manuscript. Other individuals who contributed to the success of the symposium were Walter Mischel and the other members of the University of Colorado's Department of Psychology.

Lastly, it is fitting that we record here our great sorrow at the passing of Karl F. Muenzinger, who was to have given the opening address at the symposium but was too ill to do so. He was a creative spirit and an important contributor to scientific psychology and to the backdrop of interest in cognitive processes that gave rise to this symposium. That is why this volume is dedicated to him.

HOWARD E. GRUBER
GLENN TERRELL
MICHAEL WERTHEIMER

Boulder, Colorado

XIV

CONTENTS

1

THE CONDITIONS
OF CREATIVITY

JEROME S. BRUNER
Harvard University

I

We have been asked to address ourselves to the subject of creativity. It is a serious subject indeed, yet I find myself unsolemn at the prospect. For there is something antic about creating, though the enterprise be serious. And there is a matching antic spirit that goes with talking about it. I am amused to be talking about it, for if ever there was a silent process it is the creative one. Antic and serious and silent. It is like the beautiful lines of a poem of William Butler Yeats (1940): *

* A publication date in parentheses indicates a complete bibliographical entry listed in alphabetical order at the end of each chapter.

1

> She thinks, part woman, three parts a child,
> That nobody looks; her feet
> Practice a tinker shuffle
> Picked up on a street.
> Like a long-legged fly upon the stream
> Her mind moves upon silence.[1]

She creates. There is good reason to inquire about creativity as we have been asked to do, a reason beyond practicality, for practicality is not a reason but a justification after the fact. The reason is the ancient search of the humanist for the excellence of man; the next creative act may bring man to a new dignity.

There is, alas, a shrillness to our contemporary concern with creativity, and of this I would like to say a little. Man's search for the sources of his dignity changes with the pattern of his times. In periods during which man saw himself in the image of God, the creation of works *ad majorem Dei gloriam* could provide a sufficient rationale for the dignity of the artist, the artisan, the creative man. But in an age whose dominant value is a pragmatic one and whose massive achievement is an intricate technological order, it is not sufficient to be merely useful. For the servant can pattern himself on the master—and so he did when God was master and man His servant creating works in His Glory—but the machine is the servant of man, and to pattern one's function on the machine provides no measure for dignity. The machine is useful, the system in terms of which the machines gain their use is efficient, but what is man?

The artist, the writer, and to a new degree the scientist seek an answer in the nature of their acts. They create or they seek to create, and this in itself endows the process with dignity. There is "creative" writing and "pure" science, each justifying the work of its producer in its own right. It is implied, I think, that the act of one creating is the act of a whole man, that it is this almost rather than the product that makes it good and worthy. So whoever seeks to proclaim his wholeness turns to the new slogan. There is creative advertising, creative engineering,

[1] From *Last Poems and Plays* by W. B. Yeats. Macmillan, 1940. Reprinted with the permission of The Macmillan Company, Macmillan & Co. Ltd., Bertha Georgie Yeats, and A. P. Watt & Son.

creative problem solving—all lively entries in the struggle for dignity in our time. We, as psychologists, are asked to explicate the process, to lay bare the essence of the creative. Make no mistake about it: it is not simply as technicians that we are being called, but as adjutants to the moralist. Perhaps my antic spirit rises in self-defense! My advice to you, in the midst of the seriousness, is to keep your eye on the part-girl, part-woman, practicing the tinker shuffle.

II

We had best begin with some minimum working definition that will permit us at least to look at the same set of things. An act that produces *effective surprise*—this I shall take as the hallmark of a creative enterprise. The content of the surprise can be as various as the enterprises upon which men are engaged. It may express itself in one's dealing with children, in making love, in carrying on a business, in formulating physical theory, in painting a picture. I could not care less about the person's intention, whether he intended to create. The road to banality is paved with creative intentions. Surprise is not easily defined. It is the unexpected that strikes one with wonder or astonishment. What is curious about effective surprise is that it need not be rare or infrequent or bizarre and is often none of these things. Effective surprises, and we shall spell the matter out in a moment, seem rather to have the quality of obviousness to them when they occur, producing a shock of recognition, following which there is no longer astonishment. It is like this with great formulae, as in the formula for the conservation of energy or for the brilliant insight that makes chemistry possible, the conservation of mass. The stunning condensation of all falling bodies into Galileo's $S = \frac{1}{2} gt^2$ is of this order. It is also a self-evident surprise, after Agamemnon awards the arms of Achilles to Odysseus and not to Ajax, that Ajax's effort to kill himself on his own sword should be thwarted at first by the refusal of his sword to impale him. The maddened hero must thrust it into his heart through his vulnerable armpit.

3

Perhaps we can specify more closely the formal properties of surprise by reference to an interesting critique that George Miller has made of a paper of mine in which I argue that one of the guiding strategies of perceptual development is the minimization of environmental surprise. Such environmental surprise is reduced in essence by the construction of a model or code or map for representing the contingent and transitional event-structure of the environment. Now, it is clearly not a sufficient condition for surprise or its minimization, Miller argues, merely to have a model that represents the probability of occurrence of events singly or in sequence. He illustrates by reference to bridge hands. A middling mixed hand, a Yarborough so-called, is as probable or improbable as a hand containing cards all of the same suit. Yet the latter surprises and the former does not. Improbability may be a necessary condition, but it is not a sufficient one. An improbable event—or better, an unexpected event—must somehow be related to something that matters in order for it to be surprising. The sequence of words from T. S. Eliot (1917), "I have measured out my life with coffee spoons," is interestingly surprising, but the sequence made of the same elements, "Spoons I coffee have with measured life out my," is neither interesting nor surprising. Perhaps surprise requires *unexpectedness* (i.e., not a feature of the model by which we predict the environment) and *interest* (i.e., relation to some enterprise in a person's life). And it may be, simply, that improbability is not a condition for surprise in any direct sense at all but only in the indirect sense that the improbable that matters most often constitutes what we consider to be unexpected. The trivially unexpected, very likely, we do not notice. The conclusion to the line of thought we have been pursuing is that surprise is the privilege only of prepared minds—minds with structured expectancies and interests. If one asks, then, "Who is surprised by effective surprise?" the answer must be, "Those who are prepared to be." For it takes preparation—be it in mathematics, science, or art—to discern what is trivial improbability and what is effective surprise.

I think it is possible to specify three kinds of effectiveness, three forms of self-evidence implicit in surprise of the kind we have been considering. The first is *predictive effectiveness*. It is the kind of surprise that yields high predictive value in its wake—as in the instance of the formula for falling bodies, or in any good theoretical reformulation in science. One may well argue that predictive effectiveness does not always come through surprise, but out of the slow accretion of knowledge, and urge, like Newton, *hypothesis non fingo*. I will reply by agreeing and specifying simply that whether the result of intuitive insight or of slow accretion, I will accept it within my definition. The surprise may only come when we look back and see whence we have come.

A second form of effectiveness is best called *formal*, and its most usual place is in mathematics and logic—possibly in music. One of the most beautiful descriptions of the phenomenon is to be found in Hardy's engaging *A Mathematician's Apology* (1941). It consists of an ordering of elements in such a way that one sees relationships that were not evident before, groupings that were before not present, ways of putting things together not before within reach. Consistency or harmony or depth of relationship is the result. One of the most beautiful and penetrating essays ever written on the subject is, of course, Poincaré's—in his *Science and Hypothesis* (1905). He speaks of making combinations that "reveal to us unsuspected kinship between . . . facts, long known, but wrongly believed to be strangers to one another." It was this kinship that he found on the famous trip he and his unconscious took from Caen to Coutances upon arrival at which there was the surprise of finding the continuity of transformations in Fuchsian functions and those in non-Euclidean geometry.

Of the final form of effectiveness in surprise it is more difficult to write. I shall call it *metaphorical effectiveness*. It, too, is effective by connecting domains of experience that were before apart, but with the form of connectedness that is art.

It is effective surprise that produces what Melville (1850) celebrated as the shock of recognition. Jung (1933) speaks of art that can produce such metaphoric connectedness as "visionary" in contrast to the merely psychological. It is, for example, Eliot's achievement in bringing into a single compass the experience of

5

compassion and contempt in his *Prufrock* (1917), or in the achievement of the unknown Renaissance sculptor whose *Santa Maria Alba* brings to a single expression in sculpture the faces of woman as virgin, strumpet, flirt, daughter, wife, and mother. It is the connecting of diverse experiences by the mediation of symbol and metaphor and image. Experience in literal terms is a categorizing, a placing in a syntax of concepts. Metaphoric combination leaps beyond systematic placement, explores connections that before were unsuspected.[2]

III

I propose that all the forms of effective surprise are the resultant of combinatorial activity—a placing of things in new perspectives. But it is somehow not simply that, not a taking of known elements and running them together by algorithm into a welter of permutations. One could design a calculator to do that, but it would be with some embarrassment, for this is stupid even for a calculator, and Simon can show us much more interesting computer models than that.[3] "To create consists precisely in not making useless combinations and making those which are useful and which are only a small minority. Invention is discernment, choice." If not an algorithm, then it must be a

[2] Herbert Simon points out quite rightly that there is an interesting parallel between the three forms of effectiveness I have noted and the three modes of evaluating symbol systems proposed some years ago by Charles Morris (1938): formal effectiveness being the province of syntactics, predictive effectiveness the domain of semantics, and metaphoric effectiveness being closely related to pragmatics. The parallel is anything but trivial. The formal, the empirical, and the aesthetic—these are the three principal expressions of cognitive functioning and each generates its own criterion of effectiveness, even of truth. It is worth a note in passing that the three modes have at least one thing in common: at the frontiers of their respective excellence, they all seem to fit a common criterion of beauty.

[3] J. T. Culbertson has elucidated the interesting, if stupidly inefficient, properties of such an algorithmic computing problem-solver, and if the reader is interested in pursuing the matter, he is referred to Culbertson's paper in *Automata Studies* (1956).

heuristic that guides one to fruitful combinations. What is the heuristic? Poincaré (1905) urges that it is an emotional sensibility: "the feeling of mathematical beauty, of the harmony of numbers and forms, of geometric elegance." It is this that guides one in making combinations in mathematics. But this is surely not enough. One hears physicists speak of "physical intuition" as distinguishing the good theorist from the mere formalist, the mathematician. I suspect that in each empirical field there is developed in the creating scientist a kind of "intuitive familiarity," to use a term that L. J. Henderson was fond of, that gives him a sense of which combinations are likely to have predictive effectiveness and which are absurd. What precisely this kind of heuristic consists of is probably difficult to specify without reference to the nature of the field in question, which is not to say that the working models are utterly different in different areas of empirical endeavor, for there is obviously some generality, too.

The heuristic neither of formal beauty nor of intuitive familiarity, it would seem, could serve for the artist, the poet, and the playwright. What genius leads a Faulkner to create and combine a Temple Drake and a Popeye in *Sanctuary* (1932)? How does El Greco hit upon the particular combination of piety and pride in his cardinals? How does Picasso choose which objects to include in a painting? Picasso says to Christian Zervos (1932):

> What a sad thing for a painter who loves blondes but denies himself the pleasure of putting them in his picture because they don't go well with the basket of fruit! What misery for a painter who detests apples to have to use them all the time because they harmonize with the tablecloth! I put in my pictures everything I like. So much the worse for the things—they have to get along with one another.

However maddening such a remark may be from a painter, it does point up the essentially emotive nature of the painter's work and his criterion for judging the fitness of combination. So Yeats (1935) may write:

7

> God guard me from those thoughts men think
> In the mind alone,
> He that sings a lasting song
> Thinks in a marrow bone.[4]

But marrow bones are not enough for lasting songs. For if it is true, as Picasso says (Zervos, 1932), that "a picture lives only through him who looks at it," then the artist must speak to the human condition of the beholder, if there is to be effective surprise. I, for one, find myself compelled to believe that there are certain deep sharings of plight between human beings that make possible the communication of the artist to the beholder, and while I object to the paraphernalia that Jung (1933) proposes when he speaks of the collective unconscious, I understand why he feels impelled to proffer the idea. The artist—whatever his medium—must be close enough to these plights in himself so that they may guide his choice among combinations, provide him with the genuine, and protect him from the paste. Later I shall further discuss this obscure matter, in considering the nature of internal drama, but for the moment we may leave it as is— hoping that we have not obscured its vast darkness.

The triumph of effective surprise is that it takes one beyond common ways of experiencing the world. Or perhaps this is simply a restatement of what we have been meaning by effective surprise. If it is merely that, let me say only it is in this sense that life most deeply imitates art or that nature imitates science. For creative products have this power of reordering experience and thought in their image. In science, the reordering is much the same from one beholder of a formula to another. In art, the imitation is in part self-imitation. It is the case, too, that the effective surprise of the creative man provides a new instrument for manipulating the world—physically as with the creation of the wheel, symbolically as with the creation of $E = mc^2$, or metaphorically as when one grasps the significance of Perseus slaying the Gorgon Medusa by the aid of her reflection in a polished shield.

[4] From Preface to *The King of the Great Clock Tower* by W. B. Yeats. Macmillan, 1935. Reprinted with the permission of The Macmillan Company, Macmillan & Co. Ltd., Bertha Georgie Yeats, and A. P. Watt & Son.

I now find myself in the embarrassing position of having built my fences too strongly, having been at some pains to distinguish among formal, predictive, and metaphoric effectiveness. For it is plain, I think, that the three forms of effectiveness are discernible in creative enterprise of all kinds. The poet, the novelist, the painter have formal requirements to challenge them. There is a formal integrity in maintaining a set of painting planes, in balancing the imagery and lyricism of the poem, in plotting a novel with economy and force. Greek sculpture represents a set of formally effective, surprise-producing innovations as truly as it does an aesthetic advance. The same can be said of the advance made by Giotto over his predecessors in the art of painting. These are not simply advances in "technique." If I may quote a remark of Simon's:

> I think we could argue that the twentieth century is peculiarly a century of formal heuristic, or creativity that pays attention to the internal demands of structure, the forms of symmetry of the objects being created. We see this theme repeated through the movement of mathematics toward abstraction, the axiomatic method. We see it in the movement of physics, in the conviction that nature must have a feeling for form, that if a law can be stated that has good properties of symmetry, good properties of invariance under transformation, it must somehow turn out to be a valid law of nature. We see it in music in the movement toward atonality and independence from naturally given harmonies; and we see it in non-representational painting.

It may well be that ours is a century of formal heuristic, yet I would also urge that in all creative activity there has always been the requirement of formal effectiveness.

So, too, in the matter of predictive effectiveness. The great formal advances in physics and astronomy have not been without consideration of the predictive yield to be gained from powerful and elegant formal simplicity. Kepler, Copernicus, and Newton were concerned not simply with the aim of devising beautiful, consistent, and internally ordered descriptions of the movements of heavenly bodies. The impulsion of the age was in the direction of getting astronomy to the point where the arts of navigation—predictive arts par excellence—could be served fully. It was perhaps the nineteenth century as much as any that governed its evaluation by the empirical heuristic. Was it not in that century that Gladstone, visiting Faraday's laboratory, asked, "Of what use is the generator?" Faraday's reply today would have been, "Basic research." In that time and place he countered with, "Of what use is a baby?" Even geometry, that most formal of activities, seems to require something approaching a predictive effectiveness to guide its creative acts. Why else would the geometer make use of diagrams, but to see whether his formal manipulations were making common empirical sense? And insofar as most of the arts have in some measure at some times demanded not so much "representation" as verisimilitude, is it not the case, too, that the artist must stay not too far removed from the empirical heuristic?

The status of the metaphoric as a ubiquitous heuristic is not so clear. Its status in science, it has been argued, is in making possible the leap from magic to the rudiments of scientific thinking. In the poem of Lucretius, *De Rerum Natura* (trans. 1946), it is *as if* one might conceive of the world as divisible into infinitesimal atomic particles—so, too, among the Ionic natural philosophers who were using the metaphor of atomism to describe the constitution of matter. But as science advances, a concerted effort is made to rid its concepts and its laws of metaphoric taint. As at least one eminent physicist has put it, to think of indeterminacy in physics as a general principle of life or of human affairs is to be guilty of punning. Yet there is something arrestingly contradictory about this aseptic urge among scientists. For it appears to be the case that in developing the theoretical frontiers of science, the wide reach of the metaphor is still an enormous aid. Niels Bohr has said, for example, that the idea of complementarity in physics came to him first in metaphoric form: that one could not know somebody simultaneously in the light of love and the light of justice. But what is required, for the metaphoric reach to be effective, is that it be translated and tamed—rendered into a set of equations or an experiment susceptible of being executed. The *product* that we call science—its corpus of laws—is not metaphoric. But in a significant sense, its

10

process seems rather shot through with metaphor at critical moments in the history of science.

One final point about the combinatorial acts that produce effective surprise. They almost always succeed through the exercise of technique. Henry Moore, who is unusually articulate both as craftsman and as artist, tells us (Ghiselin, 1952) that he was driven to the use of holes in his sculpture by the technical problem of giving a sense of three dimensionality to solid forms—"the hole connects one side to the other, making it immediately more three-dimensional," a discovery made while fretting over the puzzle of how to avoid relief carving on brittle material like stone. Consider Joseph Conrad and Ford Madox Ford, sitting before a scene, trying to describe it to each other in the most economical terms possible; Katherine Ann Porter on a campstool before a landscape trying to jot down everything before her—and finally deciding that she could not train her memory that way; Poincaré's endless struggle with his Fuchsian transformations. My young daughter once skated up to Dick Button, the great figure skater, who had just been doing some beautiful free figures on the Harvard rink, and asked him how she could learn to do that. His answer was as correct as it was sweet: "Janey, practice, practice, practice, practice!" Technique, then, and how shall we combine it eventually with the doctrine of inspiration?

IV

Let me now examine some of the conditions that affect the creative process. I have two objects in view. The first is to explore. More directly, however, I should like later to apply whatever notions we may come upon to a group of inventors whose behavior I studied for a year, participating with them as a member of an Invention-Design Group at a famous firm of consulting engineers.

As soon as one turns to a consideration of the conditions of creativity, one is immediately met by paradox and antinomy. A "determinant" suggests itself, and in the next pulse its opposite

11

is suggested. I shall honor these antinomies and what I will have to say will, as a result, seem at times paradoxical.

Detachment and Commitment. A willingness to divorce oneself from the obvious is surely a prerequisite for the fresh combinatorial act that produces effective surprise. There must be as a necessary, if not a sufficient, condition a detachment from the forms as they exist. There are so many ways in which this expresses itself in creative activity that one can scarcely enumerate them. Trilling (1955) most recently, in writing of Freud, speaks of the alienation of the poet from his society. It is in part a condition for exploring one's own individuality, in part a means of examining the possibilities of human connection. The university as an institution, protected within its walls, should and sometimes does provide a basis for detachment insofar as it recognizes the inviolate privacy of those who inhabit it. The proverbial abstractedness of the abstract scientist, screening out all but what seems intuitively relevant—this too is a condition for detachment. The creative writer who takes his journey without maps or a voyage into the interior, whether in the Africa of Graham Greene or Joseph Conrad, or in the interior jungle of Henry James or Marcel Proust: again it is detachment.

But it is a detachment of commitment. For there is about it a caring, a deep need to understand something, to master a technique, to re-render a meaning. So while the poet, the mathematician, the scientist must each achieve detachment, they do it in the interest of commitment. And at one stroke they, the creative ones, are disengaged from that which exists conventionally, and are engaged deeply in what they construct in order to replace it.

Passion and Decorum. By passion I understand a willingness and ability to let one's impulses express themselves in one's life through one's work. I use it in the sense, "He has a passion for painting," or "She has a passion for cooking." I do not wish to raise or explore the Bohemian dilemma—whether the condition for passion in work is its expression in other forms of life. I happen to believe that Freud's fixed-quantity of libido (express it here and it must be withdrawn from there) is a kind of first-

12

order nonsense. Passion, like taste, grows on its expression. You more likely do yourself into feeling rather than feel yourself into doing. In any case, it is true of the creative man that he is not indifferent to what he does; he has a passion for it. For the artist, if not for the scientist, there is a tapping of sources of imagery and symbolism that would otherwise not be available— as in the beautiful refrain line of Rimbaud's *Les Illuminations* (1953): "J'ai seul le clef de cette parade sauvage" (I alone hold the key to this wild parade). As for the scientist and the scholar, it is perhaps the eighteenth century French philosopher, Helvétius, who, in his *Treatise on Man* (1795–1796), has put it best: ". . . a man without passions is incapable of that degree of attention to which a superior judgment is annexed: a superiority that is perhaps less the effect of an extraordinary effort than an habitual attention. . . ."

But again a paradox. It is not all passion and vitality. There is a decorum in creative activity: a love of form, an etiquette toward the object of our efforts, a respect for materials. Rimbaud's wild beasts in the end are caged. For all that *Lord Jim* (Conrad, 1900) is a passionate book, full of the range of human impulse, it succeeds in the decorum that is provided by the dispassionate, gentlemanly narrator, Marlowe. Hercules of the myth was not a hairy ape expressing mastery indiscriminately: his shrewd trickery is the decorum. The wild flood of ideas that mathematicians like Hardy (1941) and Poincaré (1905) have described is eventually expressed in the courtesy of equations.

So both are necessary, and there must surely be a subtle matter of timing—when the impulse, when the taming.

Freedom to Be Dominated by the Object. You begin to write a poem. Before long, it, the poem, begins to develop metrical, stanzaic, symbolical requirements. You, as the writer of the poem, are serving it—it seems. Or you are pursuing the task of building a formal model to represent the known properties of single nerve fibers and their synapses: soon the model takes over. Or we say of an experiment in mid-stream that *it* needs another control group really to clinch the effect. It is at this point that one gets one's creative "second wind," at the point when the object takes over. I have asked about a dozen of my most creative and productive friends whether they knew what I meant as far as their own work was concerned. All of them replied with one or another form of timidity, most of them commenting that one usually did not talk about *this* kind of personal thing. The one psychologist among my informants was reminded of the Zeigarnik completion tendency, suggesting that when the watershed was reached, the task then had a structure that began to require completeness.

There is something odd about the phenomenon. We externalize an object, a product of our thoughts, treat it as "out there." Freud remarked long ago, commenting on projection, that human beings seem better able to deal with stimuli from the outside than from within. Richard Chase, in his graceful and learned little book, *Quest for Myth* (1949), makes much of the manner in which myth externalizes the inner terrors and forbidden aspirations of a people, while at the same time respecting the demands of ordinary experience. So with the externalizing of a creative work, permitting it to develop its own being, its own autonomy, serving *it*. It is as if it were easier to cope with out there, as if it permitted the emergence of more unconscious impulse, more material not readily accessible.

I have used the expression "freedom to be dominated" by the object being created. It is a strange choice of words, and I should like to explain it. To be dominated by an object of one's own creation—and its extreme is Pygmalion dominated by Galatea—is to be free of the defenses that keep us hidden from ourselves. For it is the creator who is the product—and again it is Yeats (1933) who has caught this so clearly in his image of the dance:

> O body swayed to music, O brightening glance,
> How can we know the dancer from the dance? [5]

[5] Reprinted with the permission of The Macmillan Company, Macmillan & Co. Ltd., Bertha Georgie Yeats, and A. P. Watt & Son, from *The Collected Poems of W. B. Yeats* by W. B. Yeats. Copyright 1928 by The Macmillan Company. Copyright 1956 by Bertha Georgie Yeats.

And so as the object takes over and demands to be completed "in its own terms," it is temptation to express a style and an individuality. As one friend put it, "If it doesn't take over and you are foolish enough to go on, what you end up with is contrived and alien."

Deferral and Immediacy. There is an immediacy to creating a thing, a sense of direction, an objective, a general idea, a feel. Yet the immediacy is anything but a quick orgasm of completion. Completion is deferred. Let me quote at some length from the conversation of Christian Zervos (1932) with Picasso.

> With me a picture is a sum of destruction. I make a picture, and proceed to destroy it. But in the end, nothing is lost; the red I have removed from one part shows up in another. It would be very interesting to record photographically not the stages of a painting but its metamorphoses. One would see, perhaps, by what course a mind finds its way toward the crystallization of its dream. But what is very curious is to see that the picture does not change basically, the initial appearance remains almost intact in spite of appearances. I often see a light and a dark when I have put them in my picture; I do everything I can to "break them up" by adding a color that creates a counter-effect. I perceive, when this work has been photographed, that what I have introduced to correct my first vision has disappeared and that, after all, the photographic image corresponds to my first vision, the vision before my will imposed the later transformations.

This is not to say that there is not the occasional good luck, the piece that comes off "lickety-split" and finished, the theory hit upon at first fire. If ever Georges Simenon is acclaimed a great creative writer—and that he is more than competent is certain—then we will say he brings it off in a quantum of pure energy and with such intensity, Carvel Collins tells us, that he has developed the custom of getting clearance from his doctor before he flings himself into a new novel.

I have read a good many journals and diaries by writers and have rather come to the conclusion that the principal guard against precocious completion, in writing at least, is boredom. I have little doubt that the same protection avails the scientist.

15

It is the boredom of conflict, knowing deep down what one wishes to say and knowing that one has not said it. One acts on the impulse to exploit an idea, to begin. One also acts on the impulse of boredom, to defer. Virginia Woolf (1953) says, trying to finish *Orlando* in February, 1928: "Always, always, the last chapter slips out of my hands. One gets bored. One whips oneself up. I still hope for a fresh wind and don't very much bother, except that I miss the fun that was so tremendously lively all October, November, and December."

The Internal Drama. There is within each person a cast of characters, his own cast of characters—an ascetic, and perhaps a glutton, a prig, a frightened child, a little man, even an onlooker, sometimes a Renaissance man. The great works of the theater are decompositions of such a cast, the rendering into external drama of the internal one, the conversion of the internal cast into *dramatis personae*. Freud (1953), in his searching essay on "The Poet and the Daydream," is most discerning about this device of the playwright. There have been times when writers have come too close to their own cast in constructing a play, and even so able a craftsman of the theater as Goethe stumbled in his *Torquato Tasso* (1956), an embarrassingly transparent autobiographical piece about the conflict between Tasso, the poet, and Antonio, the politician. It is, perhaps, Pirandello among modern playwrights who has most convincingly mastered the technique, although a younger Italian dramatist, Ugo Betti, showed promise of carrying it further before his premature death a few years ago. In his brilliant *The Queen and the Rebels* (1956), Betti includes an unforgettable scene at the political frontier of a mythical fascist state, the frontier guards searching a bus party for the fleeing queen. As the scene progresses, it becomes patent that the queen acts the spineless nonentity; it is the prostitute in the party who emerges as the queen.

As in the drama, so too a life can be described as a script, constantly rewritten, guiding the unfolding internal drama. It surely does not do to limit the drama to the stiff characters of the Freudian morality play—the undaunted ego, the brutish id, the censorious and punitive superego. Is the internal cast a reflection of the identifications to which we have been committed? I do not think it is as simple as that. It is a way of grouping our internal demands and there are idealized models over and beyond those with whom we have special identification—figures in myth, in the comics, in history, creations of fantasy.

There are some scripts that are more interesting than others. In some, there is a pre-empting protagonist in the center of the stage, constantly proclaiming, save for those moments when there are screamed intrusions from offstage, at which point the declaimer apologizes by pointing out that the voices are not really in the play. In others there is a richness, an inevitability of relationship, a gripping and constant exchange—or perhaps one should call it "inchange." These are dramatic personalities, surprise producers. I suppose it can be said that the first place where we may look for creativity is in the nature of the internal drama, the moving human being.

I would like to suggest that it is in the working out of conflict and coalition within the set of identities composing the person that one finds the source of many of the richest and most surprising combinations. It is not merely the artist and the writer, but the inventor, too, who is the beneficiary.

The Dilemma of Abilities. In the preceding pages we have looked at some of the paradoxical conditions that one might assume would affect the production of effective surprises—creativity. Nothing has been said about ability, or abilities. What shall we say of energy level, of combinational zest, of intelligence, of alertness, of perseverance? I shall say nothing about them. They are obviousy important, but from a deeper point of view they are also trivial. For at any level of energy or intelligence there can be more or less of creating in our sense. Stupid people create for each other as well as benefiting from what comes from afar. So, too, do slothful and torpid people. I have been speaking of creativity, not of genius.

V

I must say something now about my inventors, the Group. Let us not suppose that what one may find they do or say, or accomplish by doing or saying, has any more generality or worth than what one may find in the journals of Arnold Bennett (1932) or Virginia Woolf (1953), or in the commentaries of Albert Guerard on the writing of Joseph Conrad (1958) or Thomas Hardy (1949) or André Gide (1951). For there is a curious egalitarianism about observations on the creative process. Looking at the process from the inside, except possibly for the person who has led an exquisitely self-examined life, seems no better than looking at it from outside. There is a refreshing Yankee bluntness in Amy Lowell's (1930) remark:

> In answering the question, How are poems made? my instinctive answer is a flat, "I don't know." It makes not the slightest difference that the question as asked me refers solely to my own poem, for I know as little about how they are made as I do of anyone else's. What I do know about them is only a millionth part of what there must be to know. I meet them where they touch consciousness, and that is already a considerable distance along the road of evolution.

She perhaps is too bluntly modest, for already she has told us something: that there emerges a product, partly finished, emerging out of silence. And so too looking from the outside: one sees the product emerge; there is much that went before. But what part of the earlier course of events is relevant? That the theoretical physicist took a coffee break before the idea of the neutrino came upon him? That Poincaré took the trip from Caen to Coutances? The Group with which we are concerned is as unique and full of idiosyncrasy as any other person or entity whose creative efforts we might study. It operates as a group, aloud, even noisily. Its deliberations are recorded and the sketches its members make are on huge sheets of paper rather than on a blackboard. We may go back and hear and look again, unquestionably an advantage. The hope was that in an externalized colloquy one might be able to acquire cues as to the manner in which the process of discovery and invention progressed, what things blocked the progress, what things swelled it. Perhaps because the members had to talk to share their notions with their tightly knit little community we would be able to catch more on the visible or audible wing. I have no illusions about this. In the end, there is still the question of how some members had fruitful things to propose and others were barren. But perhaps even here it was possible to find out something. For there were places and situations where the barren became useful and the fruitful were silent.

It is a Group that belongs to an engineering consulting firm of the kind that designs dams for India, atomic reactors for the government, and the rest. They work apart from the rest of the firm, physically and intellectually. It is the leader of the Group, not the personnel office, that hires the members. The Group that year consisted of six members, including the writer, and a highly skilled shop technician. The offices of the company front on a lake in a midwestern city that boasts a fine university which is situated close by. Behind the main building, chastely modern in design, there is a rather scuffed building that earlier served as a shop and drafting center. It is there that the Group works. Its quarters, a suite of rather ramshackle offices letting on to the beautifully equipped shop, have the air of a boys' club. There are models around, a half-finished sculpture, a large, barn-like room with old bookcases and redone couches, the walls hung with cellulose soundproofing that reminds one of attic space under the rafters on rainy afternoons in childhood. The windows give out upon a parking lot. The dress of the members is studiedly casual, from tweeds to turtlenecks. The two secretaries are part of the culture: clever, somewhat sardonic girls, educated at eastern colleges.

The members of the Group are in no conventional sense engineers. Their backgrounds are various and their job histories somewhat too checkered with changes to leave a conventional personnel office happy. There is a young man, an ex-Navy flier, who as an undergraduate at Brown studied linguistics and acoustics.[6] Another has worked as a designer of furniture with a certain success. He is a new member. One of the older members, approaching fifty, was an architect and works a bit at it still. The man closest to the leader of the Group, a somewhat religious man, was trained in paleontology. The architect and paleontologist

6 The reader will recognize, of course, that appropriate disguises are being introduced to protect the anonymity of the Group and its members. Yet, though details have been changed, I hope that I have retained the spirit.

are men of independent means, of good families, descended from New England gentry. So too is the furniture designer, though from a less established background. The ex-flier, who also paints rather well in oils, comes from humble immigrant origins. The shopman is a taciturn "Minnesota Swede."

The leader of the Group and its founder, the man who sold the idea to the engineering firm nearly ten years ago, is a flamboyant, wittily noisy, easy laughing man-about-town. He is short, rounded square with a rolling gait, crew cut, bushy eye-brows: a more muscular Henry VIII. He is a contrast to his two contemporaries who are tall, handsome, solidly lithesome, conventionally groomed. The ex-flier is slight, with a transparent skin and a somewhat watery aspect. The leader had studied some mathematics and philosophy as an undergraduate at Dartmouth. He too is independently well-off, a fine skier and swimmer, a born clowner, a man with a distinguished but ambiguous war record, a physically timid man in spite of his physical exploits.

The Group is very close in its relations. All of them had either been psychoanalyzed or had had some contact with psychiatry. They are psychoanalytic in outlook, and candid about it. They work hard and they are paid "when actually employed," as the personnel records say. The work is varied: jobs are sent their way from the research and development section of the company—the unconventional jobs that either fall outside the scope of the "main office" or relate to something the Group has worked on before. But mostly the jobs come from outside: from business, the armed services, and civilian agencies of the government. The Group thinks of itself as a court of last resort—the jobs they take on are ones that have already stumped others. Failure, then, is no great sin.

Let me give a picture of the mode of work on a job. The job, let us say, is to design a prototype model or models of solar energy units for small homes, ones that can be used for generating electricity to be stored in accumulator batteries. It has been screened first by the Group leader, determining whether they would take it on, whether it is general enough and interesting enough. The Group meets, it is nine o'clock in the boys' club room, the excellent tape recorder is turned on. This is almost a ritual. Walt (I shall call the Group leader that) leads in some literate and bawdy wisecracking as the equipment is being put in order. Then Walt will begin the presentation, and this is carefully done. It will consist of skirting the specific problem, talking about the general case. In this instance it may be the general question, "How do you catch light or heat?" or even, "What is something that is radiant?" This is the Group's ideology and the members do not feel "left out." Walt will enliven the presentation with his usual style of literate bawdiness: "Let us not begin by making little wee-wee holes in the snow. What gives with radiation and how do you capture as much of it as possible? and for Christ's sake, no zippers please" (referring to the tendency to come up with gadgets before they have the problem in the broad).

Likely as not, the Group will get under way through the impetus of somebody's metaphor, and in this company, the metaphors at the outset are almost sure to be organic. "What does a person radiate?" And somebody will say, "Glances?" And then, "Well, how do you catch a glance?" Or, "A dog's in heat, how do all the mutts in the neighborhood find out?" After a while, Walt will become a bit more specific. "Hey, knuckleheads, how do we get out of this one, if it's radiant energy like the sun? Maybe get some blonde cuties to lie out in the sun to lure it down, huh? Get Minsky to design them." Gradually, the problem emerges until it is all there, and for a while Walt and the others will attempt to keep the touch light with, "Wish we could do this one sitting on the beach in Acapulco," or "I can't think of sun without my bikini."

After an hour or an hour and a half, somebody will ask for the tapes to be played back, and the Group will sit and listen, until somebody picks up a compelling cue, urging that "the voices be turned off." The playback has a striking function in allowing the Group to re-examine its ideas with a sense of distance and detachment, and it is very often the case that one hears things in these playbacks, good ideas, that went unheard in the din and commitment of the original event. At any given point, a member may come forth with, "By god, I have the solution," and the others will stop and listen with some appropriate preliminary remark like, "Duck, here comes the cannon ball express again," for quick solutions are distrusted good-humoredly. The session will come to an end after two and a half or three hours, with breaks in between (in the room) for coffee. People drift in and out in the sagging middle period to make a phone call, but not often. Up to a dozen such meetings will be held before the project is completed, the times between being spent in tracking facts in the literature, going to talk to somebody about an expert matter, mocking up models, consulting the client. Sometimes the subject will be dropped for several weeks on the plea of getting nowhere, or of boredom. Along the way, ideas will come up for the new design of a pressure cooker, or a draft-proof sleeping bag, or a new way to scrimshaw a boat's fixtures—byproducts of the main concern. These are not pursued for more than a few minutes: "They'll keep on the tape," or "OK, Bruner, you won't forget it, you would-be-millionaire."

Very early one notices an interlocking set of identities, the meshing of several casts of characters, each brought by a different member. One, in a flamboyant mood, will parade his wild ideas, addressing them to another who, that day or in general, acts as tamer, counting on the tamer to bring him to earth at the appropriate moment. Another pair will reinforce each other with one being concerned about convenience and comfort in the product, the other with ease of production. And perhaps most important, all the members share in a community where elegance and generality are a standard—a set of Renaissance self-images that all reinforce in each other as a means of keeping the ubiquitous pragmatist at bay until needed. Beneath the surface other identities clash.

As the project moves to a close, as models are constructed and contempt is heaped upon all prior efforts outside the Group to deal "muddily" with the problem, the roles become stabilized. The architect may come to act more exclusively like one, the fringe of fantasy suppressed. By now the models and the emerged idea will have taken over. *It* dominates, and you may see the Group standing around the drawing board or around the model, talking about "it" needing this or that. Reference to "I," such as "I think we need to do so-and-so," begins to drop out. Walt will say to the furniture designer, "Leave the goddamned thing alone;

22

stop hanging things on it, or it will end up like a fisherman's hat."

There is much talk in the Group, in pauses, about the process that they use. The members are self-conscious, they write memoranda about it, eagerly try to sell it to their clients, several of whom have, indeed, set up groups within their own companies to use much the same procedure on recalcitrant or off-beat problems.

This will do for a sketch. What has this to do with what went before?

VI

Let me say, first, that the Group has produced nothing that is likely to revolutionize the life of either consumers or producers. They have obviously succeeded in producing things that are more imaginative than what comes out of the run-of-the-mill research departments of clients. I am constrained in being able to discuss specific products out of a sense of confidence, but I can say that foresting operations through the use of mechanical axes have been considerably altered by one invention of the Group, that missile loading hazards from red-fuming nitric acid have been reduced by an ingenious suit designed by the Group, that, indeed, a draftproof sleeping bag has been designed, that a simple and truly elegant solution for reducing the price of gas per successive gallon delivered has been worked out (the service cost for delivering gas to a car is about the same whether one delivers one or ten gallons; this has made the oil industry eager to increase the bulk of delivery per sale, and it is now a question whether gas station operators can be led to install the device on their taximeters). But be that as it may, for we cannot judge the pragmatic excellence of an effective surprise in any deep sense at its moment of emergence.

The creativity of the Group comes in considerable measure, let me say in the spirit of hypothesis, from the following factors:

Detachment and Commitment. Detachment for this Group comes in a variety of ways, crucial ways. Being "out back," away from the company, operating in a kind of den—this surely helps. The literate and aesthetic quality of the little culture marks it off from the "square-headed engineers" who couldn't solve the problem at hand with their conventional methods. "Experts you want to call in on this one yet! Go see them in the woodwork and pick their termite brains. Then let's see what we can do." It matters greatly that the image the Group has of itself is that of elegant generalists, not wedded to any particular way of proceeding. The members identify more with the university community than with the firm which, they feel, would cheerfully get rid of them were they not doing such a "terrific" job.

Minimizing the cost in self-esteem for error and wildness of hypothesis also increases detachment from the conventional, and in a major way. Both the "last resort" psychology of the Group and the manner in which unfit ideas are rejected reinforce this cost reduction. Rejection of ideas is never conventionally polite, but it is warm and direct. To Walt somebody will say, "How can such an occasionally intelligent character like you come up with such a turkey! Go out and take a pep pill, boy." Or, "Look, the reason that idea is no good, aside from the fact that it doesn't work, is that you got it from a pterodactyl, and they're extinct."

It is also by the use of the general formulation, the worship of the general case, that the members achieve detachment from conventional procedure—"zipper methods." In a sense, their pride is in doing it differently, more simply, in a way that is not trivial and one-shot.

The commitment comes with these men (and I believe this is their weakness) out of the sense that their operation is what marks them as creative men—a status that none of them has achieved on his own. Ernst Kris (1943) wrote of the covenant of the gangsters, the sense of all being in this together and being in danger of hanging separately. So with our men: they have an image of themselves as humdrum without the Group as a mode of expression. It makes for a certain preciousness, a certain overly-long lingering on body imagery and organic metaphor.

Yet, for all this, there is no question that as a product development grows, the Group becomes committed to it, pursues

24

it, takes pride in it. There are few instances of an injured sense of priority about ideas. Walt goes out of his way to give everybody credit—both within the Group and with the clients. And what has become quite interesting recently is that there is a sense of pride in parentage—that others have picked up the idea of this kind of free-wheeling, not-expert group. "Hey, I hear the chowder-heads at ABC Motors are toying around with the idea of setting up like us to get themselves out of the tail-fin dilemma." Or, "That was Jack Wheatland from ABC Molybdenum on the phone to say their gang is coming to visit next weekend. Come over to my place Sunday afternoon and we'll give them some tender loving care with the martinis."

Passion and Decorum. I have never seen a work group in which there was such a wide latitude for the expression of impulse in connection with work. From the point of view of efficiency, it is wasteful, I rather suspect. The exploration of the "wild parade" of which Rimbaud (1953) wrote is almost compulsive and no metaphor is rejected until examined, at least in the early stages. Of only one thing is the Group especially wary, and of this they are not always consciously aware. When a member proposes metaphoric notions over a series of meetings that seem to be expressing an acting-out of personal troubles in his life, there is a growing access of politeness, and the usual camaraderie of idea-rejection freezes into measured protectiveness. Yet there are areas in which metaphors do not occur, where ideas are not exploited. There is a taboo, unwritten, on mention of homosexuality, for the working relationship is too close for that. No reference is made to relations with wives, and it is as well since several of the wives feel the Group to be too dominant in the lives of their husbands, too dependency-making. But in general, almost anything goes, provided it can be transformed into the grammar of the problem.

The principal source of decorum is in the adoration of elegance and generality: let the hypotheses be wild, the solution must be as elegant and generalized as possible. The sense of the Group's identity depends upon this idea, of course, for it is in this respect that they see themselves as intellectuals rather than drones, inventors rather than amateur engineers. But there is something more, too. It is interesting that, to a man, the members have a sense of the goodness and the fitness of materials. It comes partly from the fact that before a problem ever reaches the material stage, likely as not it has been hammered out in terms of what kind of materials are required. "Don't talk hardware yet, for Pete's sake, let's figure out what the splining joint has to do first, and then we can go into the shop and get the stock that does the trick—or invent something that does it." So the material, on the whole, is deduced. And when it fills the requirements, it is treated as an ally. An instance is provided by a project on self-replacing surfaces, elaborately explored until it narrowed itself down to an organic material like a lichen or moss, and these immediately became "darlings" in their own right, to be studied and cultivated.

Autonomy of the Object. The Group is quite self-conscious on this score. "It's on the tape," or "Get Elaine to bring in that bunch of sketches from the time before last," are typical comments in the early stages. At the later stages, models take over, and when they do, there is a notable reduction in strain. The most extreme example is a can opener of a revolutionary design, a closely guarded trade secret, that lives a magical life of its own. There is about some of the members a quality of unquenched adolescence that includes a real passion for externalized models, and it helps.

The Internal and the External Cast. Unfortunately, space does not permit a proper account of the manner in which the Group interacts in a way to bring out the diversity of each member's cast. For to describe the matter in appropriate detail would take more by way of description of personalities and of the situations in which they express their complex identities than can be accomplished here. Let me, instead, give some examples and then, perhaps, propose a conclusion or two. The young ex-Navy flier is a good case in point. He sees himself as an intellectual, and in his cast of thought, in his reading and listening and painting, he is that. At the same time, coming from origins where this identity and way of life were either not known or considered to be idleness for those who could afford it, he has also a sense of doubt about his genuineness as an intellectual. It is this latter character, the doubter, who searches for a criterion of usefulness, the first character for a sense of depth. The two characters do not yet live easily within him. He paints, and at the same time he speaks of wanting to design a new, technically better set of brushes—not on aesthetic grounds, but because "the brushes we have now are technically pretty primitive, you see." In relating himself to Walt, the Group leader, both characters express themselves in a kind of "nothing-is-very-serious, anything-goes" relationship. The relation is a source of unity for him. When the unity dissolves into conflict, there are two members of the Group to whom the components can turn: the idealistic paleontologist for the intellectual, the technique-minded architect for the pragmatist. One has the impression, observing this obviously talented and subtle young man, that the relations he has developed within the Group make possible a blending of his identities and, when this is not possible, there are relations that form a retreat for each aspect of him. He is enormously effective as a participant, lively and rich in his flow of hypotheses and capable of a nicety of self-criticism. Outside the Group—I have observed him not only in casual settings, but also in a conference of designers—there is awkwardness, with only an occasional flash of the talent one had come to expect from sessions in the boys' club room. In that setting, the only things that broke his stride, and that rarely, were competition for the father-figure of Walt—the early and quickly conquered relationship into which he fell with the young furniture designer—and the presence in the Group of a handsome, talented, professional woman as observer—my associate, Dr. Jean MacKenzie Pool. The first was a threat to his sense of protected unity as well as to a deeper attachment; the second was a lack of repertory for relating to a professional woman in an atmosphere where humorous bawdiness was in the air and where the activity was libidinized in some measure, a measure sufficient for Walt to exclaim on one occasion: "Nature is an old whore; she'll do anything."

In general, it seems to me, one can make the following points about this subtle matter. First, the Group provides a matrix of relations that for virtually every member permits expression of a wider range of identities than one normally finds in a work setting. Having provided the condition for more of each member's cast to be onstage, it then provides a focus of work for their expression, a passion for whatever enterprise is on the board. So while the Group may be lacking in expertise, it is not lacking in rich hypotheses for guiding the members to information as they need it.

VII

The chapter in Henry Adams' *Education* (1918), "The Dynamo and the Virgin," is urbane, but beneath the urbanity there is a deep perplexity about what moves men, what moves history, what makes art. He had spent the summer and fall of 1900 haunting the Great Exposition in Paris, particularly the hall of dynamos, until the dynamos "became a symbol of infinity . . . a moral force, much as the early Christians felt the Cross." During this summer, he made excursions to Notre Dame of Amiens and to Chartres, and it was then he came to realize that the Virgin as symbol was also a source of energy. "All the steam in the world could not, like the Virgin, build Chartres." I end with the same perplexity in attempting to find some way of thinking reasonably about the creative process. At the outset I proposed that we define the creative act as effective surprise—the production of novelty. It is reasonable to suppose that one will some day devise a proper theoretical model capable of understanding and predicting such acts. Perhaps one will understand the energies that produce the creative act much as one has come to understand how the dynamo produces its energy. It may be, however, that there is another mode of approach to knowing how the process generates itself, and this will be the way in which we understand how symbols and ideas like the Virgin capture men's thoughts. Often it is the poet who grasps these matters most firmly and communicates them most concisely. Perhaps it is our conceit that there is only one way of understanding a phenomenon. I have urged that just as there is predictive effectiveness, so is there metaphoric effectiveness. Our patience may be tested as scientists before we are through. For the while, at least, we may have to live with a metaphoric understanding of creativity, hoping that in time we may be able to tame our metaphors to a useful predictiveness.

REFERENCES

Adams, H., *The Education of Henry Adams, An Autobiography* (Boston: Houghton, 1918).

Bennett, A., *The Journal of Arnold Bennett, 1896–1910* (New York: Book League of America, 1932).

Betti, U., *Three Plays*, trans. H. Reed (London: Gollancz, 1956).

Chase, R. V., *Quest for Myth* (Baton Rouge: Louisiana State University Press, 1949).

Conrad, J., *Lord Jim, A Romance* (Garden City, N. Y.: Doubleday, Page, 1900).

Culbertson, J. T., "Some Uneconomical Robots," in *Automata Studies*, No. 34, eds. G. E. Shannon and J. McCarthy (Princeton, N. J.: Princeton University Press, 1956).

Eliot, T. S., *The Love Song of J. Alfred Prufrock* (New York: Harcourt, Brace, 1917).

Faulkner, W., *Sanctuary* (New York: Modern Library, 1932).

Freud, S., *The Standard Edition of the Complete Psychological Work of Sigmund Freud* (London: Hogarth, 1953).

Ghiselin, B., ed., *The Creative Process* (Berkeley: University of California Press, 1952).

Goethe, J. W., *Torquato Tasso*, new trans. B. Kimpel and T. C. D. Eaves (Fayetteville: University of Arkansas Editions, 1956).

Guerard, A. J., *Thomas Hardy: The Novels and Stories* (Cambridge, Mass.: Harvard University Press, 1949).

———, *André Gide* (Cambridge, Mass.: Harvard University Press, 1951).

———, *Conrad the Novelist* (Cambridge, Mass.: Harvard University Press, 1958).

Hardy, G. H., *A Mathematician's Apology* (Cambridge, England: Cambridge University Press, 1941).

Helvétius, C. A., *Oeuvres complètes* (Paris: Didot, 1795–1796).

Jung, C. J., *Modern Man in Search of a Soul*, trans. W. S. Dell and C. F. Baynes (New York: Harcourt, Brace, 1933).

Kris, E., "The Covenant of Gangsters," *J. crim. Psychopathol.*, 4 (1943), 445–458.

Lowell, Amy, *Poetry and Poets* (Boston: Houghton Mifflin, 1930).

Lucretius Carus, T., *De Rerum Natura*, new trans. C. E. Bennett (New York: W. J. Black, 1946).

Melville, H., "Hawthorne and His Mosses," *Literary World* (August 17 and 24, 1850).

Morris, C. W., *Foundations of the Theory of Signs* (Chicago: University of Chicago Press, 1938).

Poincaré, H., *Science and Hypothesis* (London: Scott, 1905).

Rimbaud, J. N. A., *Les Illuminations*, new trans. W. Fowlie, with French text (New York: Grove Press, 1953).

Trilling, L., *Freud and the Crisis of Our Culture* (Boston: Beacon Press, 1955).

Woolf, Virginia, *A Writer's Diary* (London: Hogarth, 1953).

Yeats, W. B., "Among School Children," in *The Tower* (1928), in *The Collected Poems of W. B. Yeats* (New York: Macmillan, 1933).

————, Preface to *The King of the Great Clock Tower* (New York: Macmillan, 1935).

————, "Long-legged Fly," in *Last Poems and Plays* (New York: Macmillan, 1940).

Zervos, C., *Pablo Picasso*, trans. Brewster Ghiselin (Paris: Editions Cahiers d'Art, 1932).

2

THE BIRTH AND
DEATH OF IDEAS

MARY HENLE
Graduate Faculty of Political and Social Science
New School for Social Research

Perhaps the most astonishing thing about creative thinking is that creative thinkers can tell us so little about it. How do they get their creative ideas? "Often enough they crept quietly into my thinking . . ." said Helmholtz; "they were simply there and that was all I could say. But in other cases they arrived suddenly, without any effort on my part, like an inspiration. . . . Often they were there in the morning when I awoke . . ." (Woodworth, 1938). Poincaré (1952) describes his work on a number of mathematical problems. "When we arrived at Coutances, we got into a break to go for a drive, and, just as I put my foot on the step, the idea came to me, though nothing in my former thoughts seemed to have prepared me for it. . . ." In connection with another problem, "One day, as I was walking on the cliff,

31

the idea came to me. . . ." Again, "One day, as I was crossing the street, the solution of the difficulty which had brought me to a standstill came to me all at once."

But this is getting ahead of the story. The very fact that these thinkers can say so little about the nature of the creative process is itself an important datum. We will return to it. I should like to consider a number of possible characteristics of the creative production and examine the conditions under which creative thinking occurs. This will be mainly in the framework of problem-solving. Then I should like to extend the investigation to creative thinking in the life of the individual.

THE CHARACTERISTICS OF CREATIVE THINKING

What are the characteristics of a production we call creative? One might consider correctness to be a bare minimum. We need some way of distinguishing between the delusions and inventions of the psychotic and the productions of the scientist. Again, novelty is frequently considered to be the earmark of the creative solution. In addition, I should like to examine two further characteristics which I shall name freedom and harmony.

Correctness

As soon as we consider correctness as a possible characteristic of creative solutions, we have entered the difficulties of our problem. For it is no easy matter to know when a thinking process is correct.

I will take as my example a kind of thinking not usually called creative, syllogistic reasoning. Indeed the syllogism is frequently described as tautological, since nothing may be deduced from the premises which is not already contained in them.[1] I have been studying syllogistic reasoning in connection with the question of whether the deductive reasoning which we encounter in

---

[1] I am not here concerned with Wertheimer's (1938) point that in certain cases solution of a syllogism brings about a true advance in our knowledge.

everyday life might be put into syllogistic form if we knew everything that enters into the reasoning process. Thus if we know not only the stated premises, but those implicit ones slipped in by the thinker, the alterations silently introduced by him in the meanings of propositions or of terms, the omissions, and so forth— can we then recast the thinking in syllogistic form? [2]

As a first step, we have been studying subjects' ability to evaluate conclusions drawn from premises in the context of a simple story. The most striking result of the study to date is the finding that it is extremely difficult for the investigator to recognize a fallacy when he meets one. What appears to be a fallacy often arises from the subject's introduction of extraneous material, his reinterpretation of given premises, and so forth.[3]

It often requires prolonged questioning to determine the material from which a subject is reasoning; only when we know this can we evaluate the process itself. If this is the case with so structured a kind of thinking as solving syllogisms, how much more it must be true of the thinking we call creative. Here the material with which the thinking is concerned is very much richer, the process is not so narrowly limited by the structure of the problem, and testable consequences of the thinking can often not be drawn for years. Whatever the desirability of doing so, it would seem that we are hardly able to characterize creative thinking by its correctness.

Further, even in cases in which the distinction between correct and incorrect solutions is clear, we cannot treat all errors alike. Köhler (1927) distinguishes between "good errors" and stupid ones. In the former, "the animal does not make a stupid,

---

[2] It is, of course, not maintained that people *do* use this form under everyday conditions. The problem under investigation is not the form of thinking, but its validity in certain cases in which it seems to be in error. The strangeness of even a modified syllogistic form when it appears in small talk is well illustrated by this conversation taken from *The Crock of Gold* (Stephens, 1933):

"Your stirabout is on the hob," said the Thin Woman.
. . . I hope there's lumps in it. . . ."
"Finality is death. Perfection is finality. Nothing
is perfect. There are lumps in it," said the Philosopher.

[3] See Henle, "On the Relation Between Logic and Thinking," *Psychol. Rev.*, 69 (1962), 336–378.

but rather an almost favourable impression, if only the observer can get right away from preoccupation with human achievements, and concentrate only on the nature of the behaviour observed." Such solutions "may, in a certain sense, be absolutely appropriate to the situation," although they do not solve the problem. Thus an ape who does not have a stick long enough to draw the objective to him, and who has not yet solved the problem of making a long stick out of two short ones, establishes contact with the prize by means of two sticks laid end to end; or "two animals suddenly lift a box that stands too low, and hold it high against the wall. . . ." In such cases the structure of the problem is clearly understood; only the means are lacking for its solution.

Likewise in the case of correct solutions a similar distinction seems necessary. There is a difference between a correct solution achieved by rote and another which is the result of a genuine grasping of the requirements of a problem. Clearly, only the latter is a creative achievement. Wertheimer (1959) has presented many examples of both kinds.

Thus it seems not only that it is often difficult to know whether a given thinking process is correct, but also that among errors and among correct solutions themselves we must make distinctions. Some errors and some solutions are creative, others are stupid or pedestrian. Again correctness fails us as a criterion of creative thinking. And yet we cannot simply dismiss it. We demand a relation to reality in the creative solution. As mentioned above, we do not ordinarily call the inventions of the psychotic creative. This is, at least in part, because these productions tend to be unrelated to the task at hand. The creative solution is not merely an expression of the individual, but must do justice to the requirements of the problem before him—requirements which the crazy solution ignores. It is of interest to note that this distinction is an old one. Jung (1953) quotes a fifteenth century alchemist as saying that "the work must be performed 'with true and not with fantastic imagination.' "

We may reformulate our first criterion by saying that the creative solution, whether or not it is correct, is one which does justice to the requirements of the problem. This characteristic will be discussed below under harmony.

Novelty

Novelty is frequently considered to be characteristic of the creative solution. For our examples of creative processes we look to the invention, the new idea, the new solution to a practical or theoretical problem.

And yet novelty as such is neither a necessary nor a sufficient condition of creativeness in thinking. The process of truly understanding another's solution to a problem seems to be very similar to that of finding a solution oneself. In both cases there is the grasping of the problem, understanding its demands, seeing the difficulty, noting the relevance of the solution to these requirements, seeing how it grows out of them. The chief difference seems to be that in the one case the solution arises from outside, while in the other case it arises from within oneself.[4] This is the point that Poincaré (1952) seems to miss when he asks with astonishment: "How does it happen that there are people who do not understand mathematics? . . . There is nothing mysterious in the fact that everyone is not capable of discovery. . . . But what does seem most surprising, when we consider it, is that any one should be unable to understand a mathematical argument at the very moment it is stated to him." If, as I am suggesting, understanding is itself creative, the mystery disappears.

Nor is novelty enough for a solution to be creative. An event may be novel without being creative. Writing of mathematical discovery, Pioncaré (1952) points out that it is not a matter of "making new combinations with mathematical entities that are already known. That can be done by any one, and the combinations that could be so formed would be infinite in number, and the greater part of them would be absolutely devoid of interest. Discovery consists precisely in not constructing useless combinations, but in constructing those that are useful, which are an infinitely small minority."

And yet, while a creative process need not be novel, nor a novel one creative, we seem to be unable to ignore novelty in our

4 Actually, following another's thinking process *is* novel for the learner himself. It is only in a historical sense that novelty is absent: the *process* is still new, although achievement of the solution may not be. See below.

35

description of creative thinking. The issue becomes clearer if we ask: novelty with respect to what? This brings us to the next characteristic of the creative process to be examined.

Freedom

If a solution is novel with respect to our own conceptual system, if we free ourselves from our own ideas, our own views of situations in order to solve a problem, the process is a creative one. The ideas from which we must free ourselves may arise from the manner in which the problem situation is set up, the familiar functions of objects, the appearance of things; or they may derive from the theories and assumptions prevalent in our field of knowledge or our culture, or from long-standing prejudices about ourselves and other people. Let us consider some examples.

A simple case is the detour problem in which the direct path to the goal is blocked; it can be reached only by indirect means (cf. Köhler, 1927; Lewin, 1935). The child wants to reach an objective on the other side of a barrier. The situation is so structured that he must turn his back on the goal in order to reach it. He must free himself from the prevailing views of spatial direction, seeing the direction away from the objective as the first part of the path toward it, if he is to achieve a genuine solution, not merely a chance one.

Another problem which, for a productive solution, requires freeing oneself from the operations which seem to be called for by the problem itself is the "Gauss problem" described by Wertheimer (1959). The six-year-old Gauss was able to solve the sum of the series $1 + 2 + 3 + \cdots + 9 + 10$, not by performing the successive additions which appear to be called for, but by looking beyond these to the structure of the problem. The process was a creative one not because it achieved a correct answer, which Gauss's classmates also presumably did, but precisely because it freed itself from the obvious method, which was not only cumbersome but, more important, was unrelated to the structure of the problem itself.

Duncker (1945) and others have performed experiments on the role of functional fixedness in obstructing problem solution. An object which is needed in the solution of a problem, but which has already been used in another function in the same experimental situation, is less readily employed to solve the problem than when it has not been presented with a competing functional meaning. A box, for example, will be less readily employed to solve a problem requiring a candle holder when it is presented as a container filled with experimental material than when it is available empty. In this case a creative solution requires freeing oneself from the common meanings that objects have, not only by virtue of our experience with them, but by virtue of the actual functions which they serve in the experimental situation.

Galileo's discoveries about the acceleration of moving bodies (described by Wertheimer, 1959), as thinking processes, represent a creative achievement not only because of their significance for the development of physics, but also because they required a far-reaching freedom on the part of the scientist. Galileo had to free himself from the prevailing theories about the nature of movement as well as from the evidence of a lifetime of experience with moving objects. As another example, Köhler (1953) describes Faraday's work as "reversing figure and ground all over physics."

Freedom, then, is the essence of creative thinking. Such thinking consists in breaking out of our conceptual system, our system of assumptions and meanings and knowledge when it no longer does justice to the given material.

Since I have been stressing problem-solving, I must now add that the asking of questions is equally a part of creative thinking, and that again the commonplace—not the unknown—is the enemy of such thinking. To see a new problem is a creative achievement, and a difficult one because we know so much. Köhler (1940) has remarked that an important reason for the difficulties in psychological investigation is the "extreme familiarity of psychological experiences as such. . . . People do not tend to ask any questions about facts with which they are thoroughly acquainted; they ask questions about unusual events."

The point is that what we know or think we know we do not think about. Here is the relation between wisdom and knowing what we do not know, so clearly expressed by Socrates in the *Apology*. He relates that he had examined a man who "thought that he was wise, yet he was not wise. . . . So when I went away, I thought to myself, 'I am wiser than this man: neither of us probably knows anything that is really good, but he thinks that he has knowledge, when he has not, while I, having no knowledge, do not think that I have. I seem, at any rate, to be a little wiser than he is on this point: I do not think that I know what I do not know.' " (Guardini, 1948).

Harmony

Another characteristic of the creative production I should like to refer to as harmony. It is unlikely that just any idea or solution or question, even when it represents a break with the individual's previous thinking, can be called creative. Again we must consider the relation of the solution to the problem as well as to the thinker.

In science we may say that an idea is creative if it has grasped some aspect of the harmony of nature. We are less interested in the discovery of isolated facts as such than in discoveries that throw light on the order of nature—those that can be related to other facts. "The facts that interest [scientists]," writes Poincaré (1952), "are those that may lead to the discovery of a law, those that have an analogy with many other facts and do not appear to us as isolated, but as closely grouped with others." He continues: "Facts would be barren if there were not minds capable of selecting between them and distinguishing those which have something hidden behind them and recognizing what is hidden—minds which, behind the bare fact, can detect the soul of the fact." Thus the great ideas which are landmarks in science have tended to be those which give us new orderings of facts previously unrelated, new and more comprehensive organizations of knowledge. A given fact is understood in a new way in its role in a broader structure.

So important is the procedure of going from given knowledge and understanding by analogy to new knowledge and understanding, that someone has defined genius as the ability to see analogies. Of course not all analogies are creative. Again our test is reference to the problem itself, to the processes which, despite their differences, are being related by analogy. When the analogy goes to the heart of the matter, sees "the soul of the fact," the process is creative.

In the more modest problem-solving of classroom and laboratory, the creative solution is again one which goes to the heart of the matter, which arises out of the structure of the problem itself. Wertheimer (1959) has given many examples of such problem-solving, contrasting it with what he calls "ugly" solutions. Although the context in which a given aspect of the solution can be understood is much narrower than in scientific problem-solving, the creative solution is, here too, one which reveals the order of the situation presented, which clarifies this structure and understands each item in its role and function.

The word "elegance" is often used to refer to the harmonious character of a creative solution. The elegant solution has already been illustrated by young Gauss's handling of the problem of the sum of a series. The elegant solution is elegant precisely because it clarifies the structure of the problem.

We may summarize the discussion so far by saying that the creative solution, the creative idea, is one which the individual achieves by freeing himself from his own conceptual system, and by which he sees in a deeper or more comprehensive or clearer way the structure of the situation he is trying to understand.

THE CONDITIONS OF CREATIVE THINKING

What are the conditions of creative thinking? Here we are everywhere confronted by paradoxes. I should like to bring several of them to your attention.

Receptivity

We cannot get creative ideas by searching for them; but if we are not receptive to them they will not come. Creative ideas are not, in other words, under our voluntary control; yet they require a certain attitude on our part.

Examples have already been given of thinkers who were unable to solve a given problem and then the idea came to them "like a foreign guest" (Goethe). Many others have reported the same experience. "The worst of it is," said Goethe, "that thinking doesn't help thought. You must have the right start by nature for bright ideas to spring forth like free children of God, as it were, hailing us with the cry: 'Here we are'" (Weigand, 1949). Nietzsche writes: "One hears—one does not seek; one takes—one does not ask who gives: a thought flashes out like lightning, inevitably without hesitation—I have never had any choice about it. . . . Everything occurs quite without volition. . . ." (Ghiselin, 1952.) Mozart speaks in the same way about his ideas: *"Whence* and *how* they come, I know not; nor can I force them" (Ghiselin, 1952). Again Shaw (1953), in his Postscript to *Back to Methuselah,* comments: "An author is an instrument in the grip of Creative Evolution. . . . When I am writing a play I never invent a plot: I let the play write itself and shape itself, which it always does even when up to the last moment I do not foresee the way out. Sometimes I do not see what the play was driving at until quite a long time after I have finished it; and even then I may be wrong about it just as any critical third party may." A similar idea is expressed by Jung (1945): "One might almost describe [the artwork] as a being that uses man and his personal dispositions merely as a cultural medium or soil, disposing his powers according to its own laws, while shaping itself to the fulfillment of its own creative purpose."

On the other hand, if we are not receptive to our creative ideas, they will not come. Some thinkers have attempted to describe this attitude of receptiveness. It involves detaching oneself from one's ongoing concerns and without particular expectations, heeding the ideas that come. This attitude has perhaps been most vividly described by persons who have reported mystical or near-mystical experiences. John Tettemer (1951), for example, a former monk who, during a prolonged period of enforced inactivity and solitude, came to a complete re-orientation in his thinking, describes his attitude in the following way: "I allowed my mind total freedom to open to the riddle of the mystery of existence. . . . This opening of the mind did not entail an effort to solve the riddle, but rather to let it find its foothold in my soul, to the end that I might the more fully realize it. It is a process similar to the stage of contemplation in prayer, where the faculties of intellect, sense and imagination are quieted, and one contemplates, without mental movement or flexing, the object under consideration." As another example, we may consider Swedenborg's attitude during his mystical experiences: "The mind could in a measure stand away from the senses and thus receive a fuller light from the soul" (Toksvig, 1948).

In a different context, Jung (1958) describes active imagination as a "special training for switching off consciousness, at least to a relative extent, thus giving the unconscious contents a chance to develop."

Likewise in the more ordinary kinds of thinking, a receptiveness to the ideas that come, without expecting them to be other than they are, seems to be an essential condition of their appearance. "It will come if it is there and if you will let it come," said Gertrude Stein (Ghiselin, 1952).

Various explanations have been offered of the typical course of creative thinking (cf. Wallas, 1926): a period of intense preoccupation with a problem, an incubation period, and finally the emergence of the idea as if by itself. Poincaré (1952), for example, views the incubation period as a time of unconscious work. Woodworth and Schlosberg (1954) suggest, among other things, that solution may come after incubation because of the freshness with which one returns to the problem, or because of the dropping out of interferences, and specifically of erroneous sets. In line with their final suggestion, it may be that a period away from the problem that occupies us may often be necessary for us to drop our preconceptions about what the solution should be. A further function of the incubation period will be suggested below.[5]

Receptivity to ideas demands, in addition to this attitude which Nietzsche describes as hearing and taking, a more active welcoming of them. Graham Wallas (1926) relates the story of a man "who had so brilliant an idea that he went into his garden

---

[5] It should not be assumed that a clear-cut incubation period is always necessary for the emergence of new ideas. Solutions do occur to us when we are sitting at our desks searching for them. It is possible that the incubation period has been overemphasized in the reports of creative thinkers because of the surprising nature of the arrival of the idea after an incubation period.

to thank God for it, found on rising from his knees that he had forgotten it, and never recalled it." Hobbes (quoted by Humphrey, 1948) avoided this danger by taking out his notebook "as soon as a thought darted."

Welcoming a new idea is, of course, much more than not forgetting it. It involves first of all formulating it. Words are brought forth to cloak the idea, one and another tried on for fit. Here it is important to avoid giving the newcomer a premature clarity which may distort or even destroy it. The idea needs to be worked out with all the sagacity and critical ability one possesses. What does it mean? It does not always present itself ready to use. The idea needs to be tested; in this testing it must be subjected to the same scrutiny to which we might subject the idea of an opponent. Indeed, a discussion with oneself, presenting arguments pro and con, is sometimes a helpful way of developing an idea, as will be discussed below. At other times the simple following through of implications is the more appropriate method. Not only must the idea itself be examined, but it must find its place in our system of ideas. This often means revising others in the light of it.

We are dealing here in part with Wallas' stage of "verification." This is part of the welcome, it seems to me, that the new idea deserves. Newton is reported to have said that he came to discover the law of gravitation "by always thinking about it" (Humphrey, 1948). Poincaré observes (1952):

> It never happens that unconscious work supplies *ready-made* the result of a lengthy calculation in which we have only to apply fixed rules. . . . All that we can hope from these inspirations, which are the fruits of unconscious work, is to obtain points of departure for such calculations. As for the calculations themselves, they must be made in the second period of conscious work which follows the inspiration, and in which the results of the inspiration are verified and the consequences deduced.

The thinkers who have described their creative work have, naturally enough, described mainly the ideas that turned out to be valid or productive. It would seem that the unsuccessful ones too merit study. The possibility remains open not that the idea is

42

false, but that we have been unable to understand or to receive what has presented itself.

Immersion

A second condition of creative thinking has been widely recognized to be immersion in one's subject matter. We recall that Newton arrived at the law of gravitation by always thinking about it. Poincaré's (1952) reports are similar: "For a fortnight I had been attempting to prove. . . ." "I then began to study arithmetical questions without any great apparent result. . . . Disgusted at my want of success. . . ." "But all my efforts were of no avail at first, except to make me better understand the difficulty, which was already something." Wertheimer (1959) writes that Einstein tried for years to clarify the problem of the relation of mechanical movement to electromagnetic phenomena. Gauss had for four years been trying in vain to prove a theorem, when the solution came suddenly to him (Humphrey, 1948).

In general, the mathematician tends to get his good ideas in mathematics, the musician in music, the psychologist in psychology. Our creative thinking tends to be in fields and in relation to problems that we know a good deal about.

But here too we are confronted by a paradox. It has already been pointed out that knowledge may work against creative thinking, for we do not think about what we know. We cannot become steeped in a field without also becoming steeped in the ideas current in that field. And existing ideas tend to blind us to new ones. It seems that creative ideas do not occur to us unless we spend a great deal of time and energy engaged in just the activity which makes their emergence most difficult.

The paradox is not easy to resolve. In the light of existing knowledge, it can only be suggested that the period of "preparation" (Wallas, 1926), of steeping ourselves in the subject, needs to be examined more closely. We may follow up the hint that Poincaré has given us. It may be that immersion in our subject matter is a condition of creative thinking not only because it gives us the materials with which to think, but also because it acquaints us with the difficulties of the problem.

Seeing Questions

This brings us to a third condition of creative thinking. A question tends to call forth its answer, a problem its solution. Duncker (1945) in particular has dealt with problem-solving in terms of the successive reformulations of the problem until solution is reached. It is a commonplace both of life experience and of laboratory demonstrations that we find what we are looking for more easily than when the search is not so guided (cf. Henle, 1955). We may say, then, that a question, a problem, is often a condition of creative thinking.

But, paradoxically, we must also recognize that a question limits creative thinking. We are unlikely in our thinking to go beyond the problem before us. "The way a question is asked," writes Langer (1942), "limits and disposes the ways in which any answer to it—right or wrong—may be given. . . . A question is really an ambiguous proposition; the answer is its determination."

While the question tends often to limit us to finding an answer, as mentioned earlier, in particular cases the important creative task may be precisely to pose a question rather than to answer one. Or else the task may be to revise the problem that confronts us, to see it in a new way or in a broader context. Wertheimer (1959) writes:

> "Problem solved, task finished," is not the end. The way of solution, its fundamental features, the problem with its solution function as parts of a large expanding realm. Here the function of thinking is not just solving an actual problem, but discovering, envisaging, going into deeper questions. Often in great discoveries the most important thing is that a certain question is found.

Utilization of Errors

If the goal of problem-solving is correct solutions, we must at the same time recognize the role of error in helping us to arrive at better solutions. Even in maze learning, guided trials which eliminate errors do not produce mastery (cf. Carr, 1925). When we come to creative thinking, where the possibilities of error are increased, the importance of mistakes is also enhanced. In science wrong hypotheses, like correct ones, increase our knowledge in the process of testing them; in addition they show us the difficulties of our problem and often strengthen our motivation to find better ones. This is the meaning of Bacon's widely quoted remark that "truth comes out of error much more readily than it comes out of confusion." Or, as another writer put it a century ago: "A hypothesis which goes down under the impact of new facts dies an honorable death; if, in the course of testing it, it itself brought forth these facts which destroyed it, it deserves a monument of gratitude" (Henle, 1846).

Likewise in the individual's own life, where the opportunities for mistakes are again multiplied, growth (if not truth) seems to come out of error. The acceptance of the mistake as our own is the first step in this process. Then the error can present a problem and thus get the thinking process started.

Detached Devotion

The last condition of creative thinking to be discussed concerns the motivation of the thinker. Once more paradoxically, creative work seems to demand both a passionate interest on the part of the thinker and a certain detachment from his work and ideas. It seems safe to say that significant discovery, really creative thinking, does not occur with regard to problems about which the thinker is lukewarm. "I could not live without devoting all my hours to [art]. I love it as the whole end of my life," says Picasso (Ghiselin, 1952).

On the other hand, laboratory findings (cf. Birch, 1945, for example) as well as everyday observation suggest that very intense motivation may impede problem-solving. If the individual is narrowly concentrated on the goal, to the exclusion of other relevant aspects of the problem situation, he is often unable to achieve a solution. The creative thinker must stand sufficiently detached from his work that he is able to examine it, criticize it, destroy or reject it if necessary. "With me," says Picasso, "a picture is a sum of destructions. I make a picture and proceed to destroy it" (Ghiselin, 1952).

It may be that one function of the incubation period, so often reported in creative thinking, is that of enabling one to achieve sufficient detachment from a particular problem within an area of intense interest. Perhaps a more important clue to the simultaneous operation of passionate interest and detachment as conditions of creative thinking lies in the nature of the motivation itself. "In a sense a subject may become virtually blind if he looks only at that goal, and is entirely governed by the urge toward *it*," writes Wertheimer (1959). "Often he must first forget what he happens to wish before he can become susceptible to what the situation itself requires. . . . Real thinkers forget about themselves in thinking. The main vectors in genuine thought often do not refer to the I with its personal interests; rather, they represent the structural requirements of the given situation."

The condition of intense interest together with detachment can be achieved, in other words, if the ego lends itself to the work rather than dominating the task. The forces responsible for carrying on the work derive to a large extent from the perceived demands of the task itself rather than from the personal needs of the individual (cf. Asch, 1952; Henle, 1957). Thus van Gogh is able to say in a single letter: ". . . when I once got started, I became so eager that many a morning I got up at four o'clock," and, "I . . . can keep my personal feeling out of it much better than I could at first" (Ghiselin, 1952, p. 54). Shaw's description of the author as an "instrument in the grip of Creative Evolution" has been cited above.

The requirement of work with devotion but at the same time with detachment is more difficult to meet, but no less necessary, when the problem-solving concerns the individual's own life.

CREATIVE THINKING IN THE LIFE OF THE INDIVIDUAL

I should like to proceed to creative thinking in the life of the individual. An attempt will be made to understand this thinking without making any new assumptions about the nature of the creative process or about its conditions.

It might be thought that in reflecting about our own lives the processes are markedly different from those involved in ordinary problem-solving: that the obstacles to creative thinking are emotional in the first case, cognitive in the other. I think that no such sharp distinction can be made. It is not purely a cognitive matter, for example, if we find ourselves forced to give up ideas of long standing. On the other hand, our thinking about our lives, as we will see in the examples to follow, is by no means lacking in cognitive content. Often this is its main content. Here we are dealing with a meeting ground of cognitive and affective aspects of experience; and here we will have to face the problem of their relation.

Scientific psychology, while it has given some attention to certain aspects of the creative process, has had nothing to say about the particular problem now before us. Thus we are forced by the urgency of the problem, it seems to me, to take our material where we can find it.

When we come to creative thinking in the life of the individual, we are confronted with the most astonishing paradox of all: here, it usually seems, we do the least creative thinking, yet this is precisely the area in which we are best equipped for it and where the rewards of such thinking are greatest. Although it would be hard to establish quantitatively, experience suggests that we fall into an occupation, fall into marriage and other relations, fall into a way of living with alarming frequency, not stopping to ask ourselves: Is this the way of living for me? When we do think creatively in relation to our own lives, it seems most frequently to be in the sense of overcoming obstacles which stand between us and these so often unexamined goals. Even the creativeness of such thinking is limited by being in the service of an end which has not been thought out. We limit ourselves to the solution of a problem which has much of the arbitrariness of the laboratory situation; we neglect to ask the creative question, to set the problem itself in its wider context.

As a single example, we tend to ask ourselves: Why is the thing I am doing right? We neglect the more significant question: Is the thing I am doing right? Or: What is the right thing to do in this situation? Since the problem of rationalization has been so much discussed, I will only add that qua thinking there is nothing much wrong with rationalization; it may even be creative. The only trouble is that the thinking proceeds in a too narrow or otherwise inappropriate context, all too often a context determined by our own ego rather than by the problem at hand.

And yet, I repeat, it is in relation to his own life that the individual has the greatest scope for creative thinking. If we consider again the conditions of such thinking, we recognize several important ones here. Our own life is a subject in which each of us is steeped, one in which we have access to information which is available to no one else. Here questions or problems arise at every point, and there is no shortage of errors to help us arrive at better solutions. The passionate interest which seems to be an indispensable condition of the creative solution seems nowhere more in evidence than in our own concerns. We see again the importance of detachment, which is perhaps the one crucial condition that is missing when we think about our own lives.

In the life of the individual, the problem which is the condition of creative thinking usually takes the form of an inner conflict of some kind. Yet creative thinking in our own lives, as has been pointed out, is not properly confined to problem-solving since, to a large extent, its role is the re-examination of the very problems that present themselves.

What form does such thinking take? Plato, in the *Sophist*, gives us a hint (trans. 1871–1908, Vol. 3):

Stranger: Is not thought the same as speech, with this exception: thought is the unuttered conversation of the soul with herself?

Theaetetus: Quite true.

Stranger: But the stream of thought which flows through the lips and is audible is called speech?

Theaetetus: True.

Stranger: And we know that in speech there is affirmation and denial?

Theaetetus: Yes, that we know.

I have said that creative thinking is infrequent in relation to our own lives, but it does occur. I should like to give some examples of the "unuttered conversation of the soul with herself" —of the inner discussion.[6] This is an important form of such

[6] I am indebted to Leonore L. Fabisch for referring me to the inner dialogue and to some of the material used in this paper.

thinking, the most graphic perhaps, though of course not the only one.

The personal use of the silent dialogue of the soul with herself has been described by Montaigne in his essay "Of Solitude" (ed. 1946):

> We must reserve a little back-shop, all our own, entirely free, wherein to establish our true liberty and principal retreat and solitude. In this retreat we should keep up our ordinary converse with ourselves, and so private, that no acquaintance or outside communication may find a place there; there to talk and laugh, as if we had neither wife, nor children, nor worldly goods, retinue or servants: to the end that, should we happen to lose them, it may be no new thing to do without them. We have a soul that can turn upon itself, that can keep company with itself; it has the wherewithal to attack and defend, to receive and give. . . .

This retreat Montaigne considers most appropriate for the latter part of life. "We have lived enough for others; let us live for ourselves, at least this remaining bit of life." And he adds a wise warning:

> What you should concern yourself about is not that the world should talk about you, but how you should talk to yourself. Retire within yourself; but first prepare to receive yourself there: it would be madness to trust to yourself if you cannot govern yourself. There are ways of going wrong in solitude as well as in company.

An eighteenth century advocate of the inner dialogue is Shaftesbury. In his "Advice to an Author" he writes (1900):

> One would think there was nothing easier for us than to know our own minds, and understand what our main scope was; what we plainly drove at, and what we proposed to ourselves, as our end, in every occurrence of our lives. But our thoughts have generally such an obscure implicit language, that 'tis the hardest thing in the world to make them speak out distinctly. For this reason the right method is to give them voice and accent.

C. G. Jung has reintroduced the inner dialogue into contemporary psychology. He and his followers use it as a means of "coming to terms with the unconscious." It is of real interest, it seems to me, in connection with a psychology of thinking. Jung (1953) describes the inner discussion as a "living relationship to the answering voice of the 'other' in ourselves, i.e., of the unconscious." It is the confrontation of opposing points of view, of "affirmation and denial," of question and answer within the self. As in the case of the "outer" dialogue, it makes no progress if the two parties are truly of one mind. Then there is nothing to discuss.

Since the problems with which the inner dialogue deals are timeless, I will not confine myself to contemporary material. My first example is a dialogue of an Egyptian man with his Ba or soul. It was written roughly 4,000 years ago, in Middle Kingdom Egypt. I follow the translation into German and the interpretation of Jacobsohn (1952).

Although the first part of the papyrus has been lost, it is clear at the outset that there is tension between the man and his Ba. The man, who is tired of life and who is preparing suicide, is shocked at the resistance of his Ba: "It is too much for me today that my Ba speaks not in common with me; it is even beyond what exaggeration can express. It is as if he has become indifferent to me. . . ." If even here on earth the Ba opposes the man, things will go hard with him in the Beyond; and he expresses anxiety over his sins: this must be what is bothering the Ba. He pleads with his Ba: "Overlook my sins so long as I, miserable creature, still live! "

The Ba's answer is short and unexpected. He does not try to dissuade the man from suicide, but indeed seems to reproach him for his wavering. He asks: "What, then, is your goal, that you are concerned with the good like a lord who is concerned with his possessions?" As we shall see directly, it is the formal "good" which the man has in mind and which the Ba thus dismisses, the good as defined by the collective norm. Instead he asks: What is it that you yourself really want? The man replies that he is indeed concerned with the good. It now appears that he is specifically concerned with carrying out the funeral rites correctly, so that all will go well with him and his Ba in the Beyond. He repeats his plea: "So be kind, my Ba, my brother" for the short time until this has been accomplished.

The Ba brushes aside the arguments of the man. The funeral rites are of no concern to him. He adds: "Now listen to me! Behold, it is good when men listen. Follow the beautiful day and forget your sorrow!" Then he tells a parable: A man has loaded his crops into a ship and starts his voyage. As he approaches home, a storm comes up. The man escapes with his wife, but his daughter perishes. "Then, at the end of this experience he sat there, recovered his speech, and he said: I have not wept on account of the girl. She cannot return from the West to the earth. But I mourn for her children who are already destroyed in the egg and who have seen the face of the crocodile god before they have lived." Jacobsohn points out the real cause of the mourning as the Ba sees it is not the child, that is, the life the man and his Ba have lived together. "But that something not yet visible, something unknown, something still unborn, which might have issued from the life of the man and his Ba, cannot come into existence and is nipped in the bud, this is the real reason for grief and sorrow."

A second parable relates that a man asks his wife for something; she does not immediately comply with his request. He goes out and sulks, while his wife has learned that he is unable to listen to her.

Now the man understands. What really stands between him and his Ba is not any failure on his part to observe the funeral rites correctly, but rather the man's inability to listen, his obstinate refusal to consider and accept a different point of view within himself, the Ba's point of view.

With this new realization, the man is filled with emotion: "Behold, my name is abhorred" because I have sinned against you. He has a new respect for his Ba and now feels obliged to account to him for what he does. This is a long step from his earlier preoccupation with ritual. Now the man unburdens himself and tells why he is driven to the point of suicide: "To whom, then, shall I speak today? The brethren are evil; the friends of today are without love." He continues that greed, violence, plunder, and evil are the rule; honest, friendly human relations no longer exist. Under these conditions, "Death is standing before my eyes today as when a sick man returns to health, as when a

51

person goes forth in freedom after falling victim to an illness. Death is standing before my eyes today like the fragrance of myrrh, . . . like the end of stormy weather, . . . as when the sky is cleared of clouds. . . ."

The Ba replies: "Now give up your complaint, you who belong to me, my brother! You may die of your sorrow or you may again cling to life, whichever you now say. . . . In either case we shall have a home together!"

Thus the harmony is restored. The man has come to a new understanding of himself, of the obstinacy which separated him from his Ba. He is thereby enabled to accept a different point of view in himself and thus to achieve the wholeness he lacked, whose absence made him so desperately lonely. Jacobsohn sums up: "The Ba no longer appears as a hostile opposing power, but as one who belongs, as brother. . . . The 'homeland,' the release that he longed for, and that he sought in the 'Beyond,' in death . . . is granted to him here and now through his Ba. The still unborn potentiality at which the first parable of the Ba hinted has here become a reality; the man who is tired of life has now found that treasure which even death can no longer take from him."

We do not know what became of this man who, 4,000 years ago, was tired of life. Jacobsohn ventures the guess that writing his experience may have been a help to him in turning again to life. But whatever his fate, we know that here is a man who was able to use the inner discussion to become acquainted with an aspect of himself hitherto unknown—or better, taken for granted. By coming to terms with this part of himself, he achieves a wholeness that was so painfully lacking before, becomes more of a human being, more himself.

If we consider the thinking process as such, we find that in the course of it the man has achieved a deeper insight into his own nature by freeing himself from his own preconceptions. Thus it meets our criteria of creative thinking.[7]

Benjamin Franklin, too, "conceiv'd the bold and arduous Project of arriving at moral Perfection" (ed. 1949). He concluded

[7] See Hugh of St. Victor (trans. 1945) for a 12th century example of a dialogue of a man with his soul.

"that the mere speculative Conviction that it was our Interest to be compleatly virtuous was not sufficient to prevent our Slipping, and that the contrary Habits must be broken and good ones acquired and established, before we can have any Dependance on a steady uniform Rectitude of Conduct." He therefore devised his own method, "conceiving then that agreable to the Advice of Pythagoras in his Golden Verses daily Examination would be necessary." Although Franklin describes only his manner of recording his daily examinations, not the examinations themselves, it seems that at least some of them involved inner discussions. He hints that such discussions were more complex than he had counted on: ". . . something that pretended to be Reason was every now and then suggesting to me, that such extream Nicety as I exacted of my self might be a kind of Foppery in Morals, which if it were known would make me ridiculous; that a perfect Character might be attended with the Inconvenience of being envied and hated; and that a benevolent Man should allow a few Faults in himself, to keep his Friends in Countenance."

Franklin's inner examinations had the same consequence as the ancient Egyptian's: self-knowledge and help in coming to terms with himself. He writes: "I was supriz'd to find myself so much fuller of Faults than I had imagined, but I had the Satisfaction of seeing them diminish." Further: "In Truth I found myself incorrigible with respect to *Order*. . . . But on the whole, tho' I never arrived at the Perfection I had been so ambitious of obtaining, but fell far short of it, yet I was by the Endeavour a better and a happier Man than I otherwise should have been, if I had not attempted it."

Some of Montaigne's rambling essays take the form of the inner discussion. In the essay "That to philosophize is to learn to die" (ed. 1946), he remarks that he is just past thirty-nine years of age and expects to live at least that much longer. "Meantime it were folly to encumber myself with thoughts of a thing so far off." But an answering voice in him exclaims: "But what! young and old leave their lives on the same terms. . . . Moreover, poor fool that thou art, who has set a term to thy life? Thou reliest on physicians' tales; look rather at experience and facts." He relates to himself enough anecdotes to convince his doubting side that it is never premature to think of death.

He tries another escape: "What matter, you will say, how it comes about, as long as one does not torment oneself. I am of this mind. . . ." But again the other side brings him back to the problem: "But it is folly to think by that way to come to it." He refers to the distress of meeting death unprepared and concludes, "Were it an enemy that could be avoided, I should advise borrowing the weapons of cowardice. But since that cannot be . . . let us learn with firm foot to resist and fight him. . . . Let us disarm him of his strangeness. . . ."

After a time the doubter again appears: "I may be told that the reality so far exceeds our imagination that the best fencing is of no avail when it comes to the point." The answer is immediate: "Let them say; premeditation without doubt gives one a great advantage. . ." and the meditation continues. In conversation with himself Montaigne achieves clarity on a problem he might have avoided had he left himself to himself.

In the course of a very lively inner discussion, Shaftesbury (1900) finds himself reflecting on the value of such "self-converse." "What! am I to be thus fantastical? Must I busy myself with phantoms? fight with apparitions and chimeras?" The answering voice has no doubts: "For certain, or the chimeras will be beforehand with me, and busy themselves so as to get the better of my understanding." The ego is not yet convinced: "What! talk to myself like some madman, in different persons, and under different characters!" Again the other side finds an answer: "Undoubtedly, or 'twill be soon seen who is a real madman, and changes character in earnest without knowing how to help it."

It should not be assumed that insight and clarity are always achieved in the inner conversation, any more than in the case of problem-solving. A fictional example of an inner dialogue which fails to make progress is Ivan's conversation with the devil in Dostoyevsky's *The Brothers Karamazov* (ed. 1950). Ivan, in his delirium, is visited by the devil who takes the form of a poor relation, and whose inner character is clearly recognized: ". . . it's I, I myself speaking, not you," says Ivan. Again: "You are my hallucination. You are the incarnation of myself, but only of one side of me . . . of my thoughts and feelings, but only the nastiest and stupidest of them. . . ." "Scolding you, I scold myself," Ivan declares; "you are myself, myself, only with a different face. You just say what I am thinking . . . and are incapable of saying anything new!" The devil reveals more of his nature when he does say something which Ivan is forced to recognize as new; and again when he summarizes his role: "Before time was, by some decree which I could never make out, I was predestined 'to deny' and yet I am genuinely good-hearted and not at all inclined to negation. 'No, you must go and deny, without denial there's no criticism and what would a journal be without a column of criticism?' . . . They've made me write the column of criticism and so life was made possible."

The conversation ends with Ivan throwing a glass of tea at his visitor. He has been tormented by him, but has learned nothing from him. The reason seems to be his failure to accept what he recognizes as his own inferior side. Thus: "I am bored with you, agonisingly and insufferably. I would give anything to be able to shake you off!"

My final example of an inner dialogue is a contemporary one. It is selected because it was written without thought of publication; it simply represents the effort of an individual to achieve greater understanding. The conversation is with a part of the self who is more withdrawn from the pressures of everyday living and thus in closer touch with inner realities. I shall simply refer to the two characters as "the Ego" and "the Other."

Ego: I came across those famous lines of Donne:
      ". . . any man's death diminishes me, because I am involved in Mankind; and therefore never send to know for whom the bell tolls; it tolls for thee."
    Can it be true? Of course it's true with friends. But does any man's death diminish me?

Other: There may be something to it. Let's look at it.

Ego: I heard the other day about a man who committed suicide in a particularly nasty way. I had known he existed. But I had never met him and never thought about him until I heard this story. Am I diminished by his death?

Other: Mankind is, so you must be.

Ego: I've never heard anything about him that wasn't opportunistic or irresponsible or nasty.

Other: Let's assume what can't be true, that he was only a nasty, irresponsible opportunist. Have you never been nasty or irresponsible or opportunistic?

Ego: Of course I have.

Other: Then you and he have something in common. You need people like that. They live obviously and consistently an aspect of human nature that you don't live in an obvious or consistent way. So it's harder for you to see in yourself. If you see it in him, you have to recognize it as part of human nature, that is, as your own potentiality. To accept this aspect in you, you need first to recognize it. That's where this man helps you. If you can accept him in yourself, you don't have to be his victim, and you won't be compelled to live him. Certainly you have been diminished by his death.

Ego: I didn't know him during his life.

Other: But you did get to know him through his death. Now you know your loss. You'd better try to find yourself someone like him to replace him.

Ego: A man died yesterday; let's call him John Doe. I had never heard of him until I looked him up in the obituary column. Am I diminished by his death?

Other: Undoubtedly. Unfortunately we don't know in what way. But whoever he was, he was a unique individual, a part of mankind that will never be repeated. If you had known him, he would have been able to show you something about human nature that no one else could show you as he could. For all I know it was mediocrity. Or simple goodness, or loneliness, or laziness, or stupidity. If he had any of these traits, you do too in some way because both of you are involved in Mankind.

Ego: But do I need this particular man to show them to me?

Other: Only he could have shown them to you in his particular way. It's a pity we didn't know him. Surely the bell tolls for you. Fortunately, whatever he was, there are others who can in some measure replace him for you, since he was involved in Mankind.

Ego: I can see too that the bell tolls for me whenever an animal dies. Krutch (1956) put it very well. "Something which wanted to live is dead. There is that much less vitality, consciousness, and perhaps, joy in the universe."

Other: And that much less animal. That much less brutishness
and impulsiveness and inability to reflect. Don't forget
that the bell tolls for these things too.

The inner discussion has been illustrated as one way to
creative thinking in relation to our own life. It is, of course, by
no means suggested as the only one. If we look back over the
successful examples that have been presented, we can see in them
the same characteristics previously found for creative problem-
solving. There is the same freeing oneself from one's own conceptual system—here the concepts about oneself and other people
are the relevant ones—and the same seeing more deeply or more
broadly into the nature of the phenomenon under discussion.[8]

While the effects of creative problem-solving are clear—
better, more relevant answers and questions—we need briefly to
examine the possible consequences of creative thinking in the life
of the individual (in whatever manner it proceeds).

1. Creative thinking in relation to one's own life brings us
self-knowledge. This has been true in even the most superficial
of our examples. Benjamin Franklin, who was largely concerned
with examining his acts, not his motives, was surprised to find
himself so full of faults. Even the delirious Ivan, whose inner
conversation ends in a burst of temper, discovers a new aspect of
his other side. "Wisdom," Shaftesbury reminds us (ed. 1900), "as
well as Charity may be honestly said to begin at home."

2. Similarly such meditation about one's own life carries
the reward of increased understanding of common human problems. Thus Montaigne is led in his inner dialogue to his medita-
tions on death. Again, in our final example, the discussion within

8 The difficulties of knowing when a thinking process is correct, pointed to
above in connection with a much simpler kind of reasoning, are of course
increased when we consider creative thinking in one's own life.

A prior question which arises in this connection is: how are we able to
know ourselves at all when the condition of objectivity of other observation
—the separation of subject and object, of knower and known—is absent?
While this difficult problem cannot be treated here, one aspect of a solution
suggests itself. The duality implicit in the inner dialogue suggests that the
self is not only single, but may also be dual at any given time, so that the
possibility of standing apart and observing ourselves is indeed present to
some extent.

the self gives the thinker a new view of the manner in which the individual is "involved in Mankind." It is evident that increased clarity with regard to general human problems is an important avenue to self-knowledge.

3. It has been mentioned earlier that the creative thinking we ordinarily do in relation to our own lives is aimed at thinking up ways of overcoming obstacles that keep us from reaching our goals. Much more important is the examination of these goals themselves. The point has been made very clearly by Wertheimer (ed. 1959):

> Thinking is not merely to solve set problems. The goal itself, as a part of the situation, may be structurally sensible or foolish. . . . Often the thinker, in the course of trying to solve a set problem, stops, realizing that the situation requires quite different things, requires changing the very goal. . . .
>
> In life such cases are often of a serious character. Sometimes men . . . after trying hard to reach a certain goal and working at it a long time, suddenly realize that the goal itself, as set, was out of place, unrelated to the real requirements, to more essential goals. This in itself may be a discovery of something that was not at all realized before—namely, that the means for a sought goal would endanger, would kill a much more important goal. Thinking is not merely concerned with means; it concerns the ends themselves in their structural significance.

In life, the context within which the sense of a goal must be evaluated consists of the real requirements of the situation, but no less of the deeper needs of the person—not just those needs which are momentarily insistent or of which he is most clearly aware. It goes without saying that this task of rethinking one's goals is a continuing one, at best only imperfectly achieved.

4. Meditation on life, one's own life, is an avenue to the development of inner resources. "He who can transmute and turn upon himself the offices of friendship and fellowship, let him do so," writes Montaigne (ed. 1946). He suggests this as a help in withstanding losses: he recommends developing the inner relation as if we had neither family nor friends nor possessions "to the end that, should we happen to lose them, it may be no new thing to do without them."

5. Perhaps a more general statement of the same point is Jung's (1953): "The psychologist is familiar with this 'inner dialogue'; it is an essential part of the technique for coming to terms with the unconscious." As illustrated most impressively by the example of the ancient Egyptian, the "creative dialogue" (Jung) may enable the individual to understand, accept, and live more richly with aspects of himself hitherto unknown. As Montaigne (ed. 1946) expresses it, "The greatest thing in the world is to know how to belong to ourselves."

It should not be assumed, of course, that such wholeness and acceptance are ever achieved completely or permanently. Creative thinking in relation to the self needs to be a continuing activity. It shows the same spiral process of "question—solution—new question" that characterizes other kinds of productive thinking.

It may be added that, since it is the unknown in us which seems to be the source of our creative ideas, by better coming to terms with this unknown, we may come into better contact with our own creativeness.[9]

6. It follows from all the above that creative thinking in relation to our own life gives us increased freedom of choice, and thus greater freedom of action. Where we do not see alternatives we cannot choose. We have no real possibility of choosing among goals until we have examined them. The more we know, the less we are blinded or impelled by the unknown. Every extension or deepening of awareness, in sum, adds to our personal freedom.

It was pointed out earlier that creative thinking is characterized by freedom, that it is a product of freedom. It can now be seen in its other aspect, that of adding to our very freedom.

THE DEATH OF IDEAS

We have been concerned up to now with the birth of ideas. I should like to add a few words about an equally important phase of the creative process, namely, the death of ideas.

[9] Cf. Jung (1954): "The unconscious is seen as a creative factor, even as a bold innovator, and yet it is at the same time the stronghold of ancestral conservatism."

The developing individual—and I am referring to development at any age—outgrows his ideas. New ideas displace old ones. Montaigne's (ed. 1946) advice is as applicable to ideas as it is to human beings: "Give place to others, as others have given place to you." It is not that the old ideas are necessarily wrong; it may only be, for example, that later examination shows them to be too narrow or unclear; or they may have to change their place in our structure of beliefs or alter their character in the light of others that have joined our company of ideas. As for wrong ideas, the role of error in the creative process has already been discussed. Sometimes research or experience shows a hypothesis to be wrong before we have a substitute for it. To discard it may leave just the question, the gap which is necessary for further creative work.

It is not, of course, maintained that the creative individual is one who changes his ideas, like clothes, with the fashions. A better analogy is that of the human body which maintains, or only gradually changes, its form despite the birth and death of individual cells. It is precisely because the ideas change in the light of new experience that the thinking of a person is able to maintain its individuality.

I should like to conclude with a parable which was written for those physicians who, in the middle of the last century, preferred to hold on to the existing theory, although it was recognized as being full of holes, until a solid structure of new theory would be available (Henle, 1846):

A pedant for a long time had a nightingale and he was gladdened by its song. Then the bird died. The pedant, finding the silence and loneliness uncomfortable, went out to buy another bird. But only a few nests had been brought to market; the dealer did not know whether the eggs had been fertilized, and in any case would not guarantee that males would be hatched from the fertilized eggs; besides the young, when hatched, would still require attention and care before they would grow into singers. This seemed too hazardous to the pedant, and he went away saying that he would rather keep his dead nightingale. This was acting conservatively; but for what use? It was possible that the trouble of raising the young would go for nothing, but it was certain that the dead bird would never sing.

REFERENCES

Asch, S. E., *Social Psychology* (Englewood Cliffs, N. J.: Prentice-Hall, 1952).

Birch, H. G., "The Role of Motivational Factors in Insightful Problem-Solving," *J. comp. Psychol.*, 38 (1945), 295–317.

Carr, H. A., *Psychology* (New York: Longmans, Green, 1925).

Dostoyevsky, F., *The Brothers Karamazov*, Modern Library Edition, trans. Constance Garnett (New York: Random House, 1950).

Duncker, K., "On Problem-Solving," trans. Lynne S. Lees, *Psychol. Monogr.*, 58, 5 (Whole No. 270) (1945).

Franklin, B., *Memoirs*, ed. M. Farrand (Berkeley: University of California Press, 1949).

Ghiselin, B., ed., *The Creative Process* (Berkeley: University of California Press, 1952).

Guardini, R., *The Death of Socrates*, trans. B. Wrighton (New York: Sheed & Ward, 1948).

Henle, J., *Handbuch der rationellen Pathologie*, 2nd ed. (Braunschweig: F. Vieweg u. Sohn, 1846).

Henle, Mary, "Some Effects of Motivational Processes on Cognition," *Psychol. Rev.*, 62 (1955), 423–432.

————, "On Field Forces," *J. Psychol.*, 43 (1957), 239–249.

————, "On the Relation Between Logic and Thinking," *Psychol. Rev.*, in press.

Hugh of St. Victor, *The Soul's Betrothal-Gift*, trans. F. S. Taylor (London: Dacre Press, 1945).

Humphrey, G., *Directed Thinking* (New York: Dodd, Mead, 1948).

Jacobsohn, H., "Das Gespräch eines Lebensmüden mit seinem Ba," in *Zeitlose Dokumente der Seele*, Studien aus dem C. G. Jung-Institut Zürich, ed. C. A. Meier (Zürich: Rascher Verlag, 1952).

Jung, C. G., *Contributions to Analytical Psychology*, trans. H. G. and C. F. Baynes (London: Kegan Paul, Trench, Trubner, 1945).

————, *Psychology and Alchemy*, trans. R. F. C. Hull, Bollingen Series XX (New York: Pantheon, 1953).

————, *The Practice of Psychotherapy*, trans. R. F. C. Hull, Bollingen Series XX (New York: Pantheon, 1954).

————, *Psychology and Religion: West and East*, trans. R. F. C. Hull, Bollingen Series XX (New York: Pantheon, 1958).

Köhler, W., *The Mentality of Apes*, 2nd ed., trans. Ella Winter (New York: Harcourt, Brace, 1927).

————, *Dynamics in Psychology* (New York: Liveright, 1940).

————, "The Scientists and Their New Environment," in W. R. Crawford, ed., *The Cultural Migration* (Philadelphia: University of Pennsylvania Press, 1953).

Krutch, J. W., *The Great Chain of Life* (Boston: Houghton Mifflin, 1956).

Langer, Susanne K., *Philosophy in a New Key* (Cambridge, Mass.: Harvard University Press, 1942).

Lewin, K., *A Dynamic Theory of Personality*, trans. D. K. Adams and K. E. Zener (New York: McGraw-Hill, 1935).

Montaigne, M. de, *Essays*, trans. E. J. Trechmann (New York: Oxford University Press, 1946).

Plato, *Dialogues*, trans. B. Jowett (New York: Scribner, 1871–1908).

Poincaré, H., *Science and Method*, trans. F. Maitland (New York: Dover Publications, 1952).

Shaftesbury, Anthony, Earl of, *Characteristics of Men, Manners, Opinions, Times, etc.*, ed. J. M. Robertson (London: Grant Richards, 1900).

Shaw, G. B., *The Complete Plays of George Bernard Shaw* (London: Odhams Press, 1953).

Stephens, J., *The Crock of Gold* (New York: Macmillan, 1933).

Tettemer, J., *I Was a Monk* (New York: Knopf, 1951).

Toksvig, Signe, *Emanuel Swedenborg, Scientist and Mystic* (New Haven, Conn.: Yale University Press, 1948).

Wallas, G., *The Art of Thought* (New York: Harcourt Brace, 1926).

Weigand, H. J., ed. and trans., *Goethe. Wisdom and Experience*, selections by L. Curtius (New York: Pantheon, 1949).

Wertheimer, M., "The Syllogism and Productive Thinking," in W. D. Ellis, ed., *A Source Book of Gestalt Psychology* (London: Kegan Paul, Trench, Trubner, 1938).

————, *Productive Thinking*, enlarged ed. (New York: Harper, 1959).

Woodworth, R. S., *Experimental Psychology* (New York: Holt, 1938).

————, and H. Schlosberg, *Experimental Psychology*, rev. ed. (New York: Holt, 1954).

3

THE PROCESSES OF
CREATIVE THINKING

ALLEN NEWELL and J. C. SHAW
The RAND Corporation

HERBERT A. SIMON
Carnegie Institute of Technology

What is meant by an "explanation" of the creative process? In the published literature on the subject, the stages of thought in the solution of difficult problems have been described, and the processes that go on at each stage discussed. Interest has focused particularly on the more dramatic and mysterious aspects of creativity—the unconscious processes that are supposed to occur during "incubation," the imagery employed in creative thinking and its significance for the effectiveness of the thinking, and, above all, the phenomenon of "illumination," the sudden flash of insight that reveals the solution of a problem long pursued. Experimental work—to the limited extent that it has been done—has been most concerned with directional set, including the motivational and cognitive conditions that produce set and that alter set, and interpersonal differences in "inappropriate" persistence of set (stereotypy).

All the topics we have mentioned are interesting enough, and are appropriate parts of a theory of creative thinking. In our own orientation to creativity, however, we have felt the need for a clearer idea of the over-all requirements and aims of such a theory. We propose that a theory of creative thinking should consist of:

1. completely operational specifications[1] for the behavior of mechanisms (or organisms) that, with appropriate initial conditions, would in fact think creatively;

2. a demonstration that mechanisms behaving as specified (by these programs) would exhibit the phenomena that commonly accompany creative thinking (e.g., incubation, illumination, formation and change in set, and so forth);

3. a set of statements—verbal or mathematical—about the characteristics of the class of specifications (programs) that includes the particular examples specified.

Stated otherwise, we would have a satisfactory theory of creative thought if we could design and build some mechanisms that could think creatively (exhibit behavior just like that of a human carrying on creative activity), and if we could state the general principles on which the mechanisms were built and operated.

Put in this bald way, these aims sound utopian. How utopian they are—or rather, how imminent their realization—depends on how broadly or narrowly we interpret the term "creative." If we are willing to regard all human complex problem-solving as creative, then—as we shall point out—successful programs for problem-solving mechanisms that simulate human problem-solvers already exist, and a number of their general

[1] As we shall explain later, we propose that such a set of specifications take the form of *a program,* as that term is used in the digital computer field. We will henceforth refer to them as "programs."

characteristics are known. If we reserve the term "creative" for activities like discovery of the special theory of relativity or the composition of Beethoven's Seventh Symphony, then no example of a creative mechanism exists at the present time.

But the success already achieved in synthesizing mechanisms that solve difficult problems in the same manner as humans is beginning to provide a theory of problem-solving that is highly specific and operational. The purpose of this paper is to draw out some of the implications of this theory for creative thinking. To do so is to assume that creative thinking is simply a special kind of problem-solving behavior. This seems to us a useful working hypothesis.

We start by discussing the relation of creative thinking to problem-solving in general, and by inquiring to what extent existing problem-solving programs may be considered creative. Next we sketch the theory of problem-solving that underlies these programs, and then use the theory to analyze the programs, and to compare them with some human problem-solving behavior exhibited in thinking-aloud protocols of subjects in the laboratory. Finally, we consider some topics that have been prominent in discussions of creativity to see what this analysis of problem-solving has to say about them.

PROBLEM-SOLVING AND CREATIVITY

In the psychological literature, "creative thinking" designates a special class of activities, with somewhat vague and indefinite boundaries (see, e.g., Johnson, 1955). Problem-solving is called creative to the extent that one or more of the following conditions are satisfied:

1. The product of the thinking has novelty and value (either for the thinker or for his culture).

2. The thinking is unconventional, in the sense that it requires modification or rejection of previously accepted ideas.

3. The thinking requires high motivation and persistence, taking place either over a considerable span of time (continuously or intermittently) or at high intensity.

4. The problem as initially posed was vague and ill-defined, so that part of the task was to formulate the problem itself.

Vagueness of the Distinction

A problem-solving process can exhibit all of these characteristics to a greater or lesser degree, but we are unable to find any more specific criteria separating creative from noncreative thought processes. Moreover, the data currently available about the processes involved in creative and noncreative thinking show no particular differences between the two. We may cite, as examples, the data of Patrick (1935, 1937) on the processes involved (for both professionals and amateurs) in drawing a picture or writing a poem, or the data of de Groot (1946) on the thought processes of chess players. Not only do the processes appear to be remarkably similar from one task to another—agreeing well with Wallas's (1926) account of the stages in problem-solving—but it is impossible, by looking solely at the statistics describing the processes, to distinguish the highly skilled practitioner from the rank amateur.

Similarly, there is a high correlation between creativity (at least in the sciences) and proficiency in the more routine intellective tasks that are commonly used to measure intelligence. There is little doubt that virtually all the persons who have made major creative advances in science and technology in historic times have possessed very great general problem-solving powers (Johnson, 1955).

Thus, creative activity appears simply to be a special class of problem-solving activity characterized by novelty, unconventionality, persistence, and difficulty in problem formulation.

Simulation of Problem-Solving

As we indicated earlier, the theory of problem-solving we are putting forth derives from mechanisms that solve problems in the same manner as humans—mechanisms whose behavior can be observed, modified, and analyzed. The only available technique for constructing problem solvers is to write programs for digital computers; no other physical mechanisms are complex enough.

The material in the present paper rests mostly on several programs that we have constructed.[2] These are:

1. *The Logic Theorist.* The Logic Theorist is a computer program that is capable of discovering proofs for theorems in elementary symbolic logic, using heuristic techniques similar to those used by humans. Several versions of the Logic Theorist have been coded for a computer, and a substantial amount of experience has been accumulated with one of these versions and some of its variants (Newell & Shaw, 1957; Newell, Shaw, & Simon, 1957, 1958a; Newell & Simon, 1956).

2. *The Chess Player.* We have written a program that plays chess. It is just now being checked out on the computer, but we have done a good deal of hand simulation with the program so that we know some of its more immediate characteristics (Newell, Shaw, & Simon, 1958b).

When we say that these programs are simulations of human problem-solving, we do not mean merely that they solve problems that had previously been solved only by humans—although they do that also. We mean that they solve these problems by using techniques and processes that resemble more or less closely the techniques and processes used by humans. The most recent version of the Logic Theorist was designed explicitly as a simulation of a (particular) human problem-solver whose behavior had been recorded under laboratory conditions.

Although the Carnegie-RAND group is the only one to our knowledge that has been trying explicity to construct programs that simulate human higher mental processes, a number of workers have been exploring the capabilities of computer programs to solve complex and difficult problems. Many of these programs provide additional information about the nature of the problem-solving process. Some of the more relevant are:

3. *Musical Composition.* A computer program has been written and run on the ILLIAC that composes music employing Palestrina's rules of counterpoint. Some of its music has been performed by a string quartet and tape-recorded, but as far as we are aware, no description of the program has been published.

2 This brief survey reflects the state of affairs at the time this paper was read, in the Spring of 1958.

Other experiments in musical composition have also been made.

4. *Chess Playing.* Two programs besides ours have been written that play chess. Although both of these proceed in a way that is fundamentally different from the ways humans play chess, some of their features provide illuminating comparisons (Newell, Shaw, & Simon, 1958b).

5. *Design of Electric Motors.* At least two, and probably more, computer programs have been written, and are now being used by industrial concerns, that design electric motors. These programs take as their inputs the customers' design specifications and produce as their outputs the manufacturing specifications that are sent to the factory floor. The programs do not simply make calculations needed in the design process, but actually carry out the analysis itself and make the decisions that were formerly the province of the design engineers.

The main objective of these motor design programs, of course, is to provide effective problem-solving routines that are economical substitutes for engineers. Thus these programs simulate human processes only to the extent that such processes are believed to enhance the problem-solving capabilities and efficiency of the programs.

6. *Visual Pattern Recognition.* A program has been written that attempts to learn a two-dimensional pattern—like an "A"—from examples. The program was developed by Selfridge (1955) and Dineen (1955). Although only partly successful, it was a pioneering attempt to use computer simulation as a technique for investigating an area of human mental functioning.

Is the Logic Theorist Creative?

The activities carried on by these problem-solving computer programs lie in areas not far from what is usually regarded as "creative." Discovering proofs for mathematical theorems, composing music, designing engineering structures, and playing chess would ordinarily be thought creative if the product were original and of high quality. Hence, the relevance of these programs to the theory of creativity is clear—even if the present programs fall short of exact simulation of human processes and produce a fairly mundane product.

Let us consider more specifically whether we should regard the Logic Theorist as creative. When the Logic Theorist is presented with a purported theorem in elementary symbolic logic, it attempts to find a proof. In the problems we have actually posed it, which were theorems drawn from Chapter 2 of Whitehead and Russell's *Principia Mathematica* (1925–1927), it has found the proof about three times out of four. The Logic Theorist does not pose its own problems—it must be given these—although in the course of seeking a proof for a theorem it will derive the theorem from other expressions and then attempt to prove the latter. Hence, in proving one theorem, the Theorist is capable of conjecturing other theorems and then trying to prove these.

Now no one would deny that Whitehead and Russell were creative when they wrote *Principia Mathematica*. Their book is one of the most significant intellectual products of the twentieth century. If it was creative for Whitehead and Russell to write these volumes, it is possibly creative for the Logic Theorist to reinvent large portions of Chapter 2—rediscovering in many cases the very same proofs that Whitehead and Russell discovered originally. Of course the Logic Theorist will not receive much acclaim for its discoveries, since these have been anticipated, but, subjectively if not culturally, its product is novel and original. In at least one case, moreover, the Logic Theorist has discovered a proof for a theorem in Chapter 2 that is far shorter and more elegant than the one published by Whitehead and Russell.[3]

If we wish to object seriously to calling the Logic Theorist creative, we must rest our case on the way it gets the problems it tackles, and not on its activity in tackling them. Perhaps the program is a mathematical hack, since it relies on Whitehead and Russell to provide it with significant problems, and then merely finds the answers to these; perhaps the real creativity lies in the problem selection. This certainly is the point of the fourth characteristic we listed for creativity. But we have already indicated

---

[3] Perhaps even this is not creative. *The Journal of Symbolic Logic* has declined to publish an article, co-authored by the Logic Theorist, describing this proof. The principal objection offered by the editor is that the same theorem could today be proved (using certain meta-theorems that were available neither to Whitehead and Russell nor the Logic Theorist) in a simpler way.

that the Theorist has some powers of problem selection. In working backwards from the goal of proving one theorem, it can conjecture new theorems—or supposed theorems—and set up the subgoal of proving these. Historically, albeit on a much broader scale, this is exactly the process whereby Whitehead and Russell generated the theorems that they then undertook to prove. For the task they originally set themselves was to take the basic postulates of arithmetic (as set forth by Peano and his students), and to derive these *as theorems* from the axioms of logic. The theorems of Chapter 2 of *Principia* were generated, as nearly as we can determine the history of the matter, in the same way that subproblems are generated by the Logic Theorist—as subproblems whose solution would lead to the solution of the problem originally posed.

We do not wish to exaggerate the extent to which the Logic Theorist is capable of matching the higher flights of the human mind. We wish only to indicate that the boundary between its problem-solving activities and activities that are important examples of human creativity is not simple or obvious.

AN ABSTRACT MODEL OF
PROBLEM-SOLVING BEHAVIOR

We turn next to the general theory of problem-solving, only returning later to issues that are specific to the "creative" end of the problem-solving spectrum.

Definition of "Problem"

The maze provides a suitable abstract model for most kinds of problem-solving activity. A maze is a set of paths (possibly partly overlapping), some subset of which are distinguished from the others by having rewards at their termini (see Figure 1). These latter are the "correct" paths; to discover one of them is to solve the problem of running the maze.

We can abstract one stage further, and characterize problem-solving by the following rubric: Given a set, P, of elements, to find a member of a subset, S, of P having specified properties. Here are some examples:

1. Solving a crossword puzzle. Take as P all possible combinations of letters of the English alphabet that will fill the white squares of the puzzle. The subset S comprises those combinations in which all consecutive linear horizontal and vertical sequences are words that satisfy specified definitions.

2. Finding the combination of a safe. Take as P all possible settings of the dials of the safe; and as S those particular settings that open the safe. As safes are usually constructed, S consists of a single element.

3. Making a move in chess. Take as P the set of all possible (legal) moves; as S, the set of "good" moves, where the term "good" reflects some set of criteria.

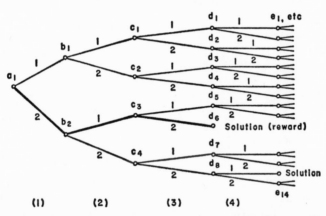

FIGURE 1. A problem maze. Alternatives at choice points, $m = 2$; minimum length of path to solution, $k = 3$. The shortest path to a solution is given by the choices 2–1–2; it runs from choice point a_1, through b_2 and c_3 to d_6, the solution.

4. Proving a theorem in logic or geometry. Take as P the set of all possible sequences of expressions in a formal language for logic (or geometry, respectively); and as S the subset of sequences that: (a) are valid proofs, and (b) terminate in the specified theorem.

71

5. Programming a computer to invert a matrix. Take as *P* the set of all possible sequences of computer instructions; and as *S* a particular sequence that will perform the specified matrix inversion.

6. Translating a German article into English. Take as *P* the set of all possible sequences of English words (of length, say, less than *L*); take as *S* the subset of sequences that: (a) satisfy certain criteria of English syntax and style, and (b) have the same meaning as the German original.

7. Designing a machine. Take as *P* the set of all possible parameter values for a machine design; take as *S* the subset of parameter values that: (a) satisfy the design specifications, (b) meet certain criteria of cost minimization.

In examples 4, 5, and 6 the interpretation in terms of the maze model can be carried a step further by identifying the elements of the sequences mentioned there with the succssive segments of the maze that constitute a path.

A Preliminary View of Problem-Solving Processes

There are any number of ways of classifying the processes that are used by humans to solve problems. One useful distinction differentiates processes for finding possible solutions (generating members of *P* that may belong to *S*), from processes for determining whether a solution proposal is in fact a solution (verifying that an element of *P* that has been generated does belong to *S*). This is a distinction that is often made in the literature, in one set of terms or another. Johnson (1955), for example, distinguishes "production" processes from "judgment" processes in a way that corresponds closely to the distinction we have just made. We prefer to call the first class of processes *solution-generating* processes, and the second class *verifying processes*.

Solution generators range all the way from exceedingly "primitive" trial-and-error searches that take up the elements of *P* in a fairly arbitrary order to extensive calculations that select an appropriate solution at the first try or to elaborate analytic processes that construct a solution by some kind of "working backward" from the known properties of solutions. In spite of the primitive character of trial-and-error processes, they bulk very large in highly creative problem-solving; in fact, at the upper end of the range of problem difficulty there is likely to be a positive correlation between creativity and the use of trial-and-error generators.

How Large is the Maze?

In a sufficiently small maze where a member of S, once discovered, can be identified easily as a solution, the task of discovering solutions is trivial (e.g., a T-maze for a rat with food in one branch). The difficulties in complex problem-solving arise from some combination of two factors: the size of the set of possible solutions that must be searched, and the task of identifying whether a proposed solution actually satisfies the conditions of the problem. In any particular case, either or both of these may be the sources of problem difficulty. By using our formal model of problem-solving we can often obtain meaningful measures of the size and difficulty of particular problems, and measures of the effectiveness of particular problem-solving processes and devices. Let us consider some examples.

The Logic Theorist. We have made some estimates of the size of the space of possible solutions (proofs) for the problems handled by the Logic Theorist. By a possible proof—which we shall take as the element of the set P in this case—we mean a sequence of symbolic logic expressions. If we impose no limits on the length or other characteristics of such sequences, their number, obviously, is infinite. Hence, we must suppose at the outset that we are not concerned with the whole set of possible proofs, but with some subset comprising, say, the "simpler" elements of that set. We might restrict P, for example, to proofs consisting of sequences of not more than twenty logic expressions, with each expression not more than twenty-three symbols in length and involving only the variables $p, q, r, s,$ and t and the connectives "or" and "implies." The number of possible proofs meeting these restrictions is about 10^{235}—one followed by 235 zeros! The task is also not trivial of verifying that a particular element of the set P, as we have just defined it, is a proof of a particular problem in logic; for it is necessary to determine whether each expression in the sequence is an axiom or whether it follows from some of the expressions preceding it by the rules of deductive inference. In addition, of course, the expression to be proved has to be contained in the sequence.

Clearly, selecting possible proofs by sheer trial and error and testing whether each element selected is actually the desired proof is not a feasible method for proving logic theorems—for either humans or machines. The set to be searched is too large and the testing of the elements selected is too difficult. How can we bring this task down to manageable proportions?

First of all, the number we have just computed, 10^{235}, is not only exceedingly large but also arbitrary, for it depends entirely on the restrictions of simplicity we impose on P. By strengthening these conditions we reduce the size of P; by weakening them we increase its size. We must look for a more meaningful way to describe the size of the set P. This we do by considering a simple solution generator that produces members of the set in a certain order, and asking how many members the generator would have to produce, on the average, to obtain solutions to problems of a specified class. Let us generate elements of P according to the following simple scheme, which we call the British Museum algorithm in honor of the primates who are credited with employing it (Newell, Shaw, & Simon, 1957):

1. We consider only sequences of logic expressions that are valid proofs—that is, whose initial expressions are axioms—and each of whose expressions is derived from prior ones by valid rules of inference. By generating only sequences that are proofs (of something), we eliminate the major part of the task of verification.

2. We generate first those proofs that consist of a single expression (the axioms themselves), then proofs two expressions long, and so on, limiting the alphabet of symbols as before. Given all the proofs of length k, we generate those of length (k + 1) by applying the rules of inference in all permissible ways to the former to generate new derived expressions that can be added to the sequences. That is, we generate a maze (see again, Figure 1), each choice point (a_1, b_1, b_2, etc.) representing the legitimate ways of deriving new expressions as immediate conse-

quences of the expressions contained in the proof. Thus, in the figure, d_4 is a proof that can be derived as an immediate consequence of c_2, using path 2.

We estimate that of the sixty-odd theorems that appear in Chapter 2 of *Principia Mathematica* about six (all of which are among the first ten in the chapter) would be included in the first 1,000 proofs generated by the algorithm, but that about a hundred million more proofs would have to be generated to obtain all the theorems in the chapter. (The actual number may be much greater; it is difficult to estimate with any accuracy.) That is to say, if we used this scheme to find the proof of a theorem selected at random from the theorems of Chapter 2, we would, on the average, have to generate some fifty million possible solutions before finding the one we wanted; and the chances of finding the proof among the first thousand generated would be only one in ten. One hundred million (10^8) is a large number, but a very small number compared with 10^{235}. Thus a proof has a very much higher probability of turning up in Chapter 2 of *Principia* if it is relatively simple than if it is complicated. On the other hand, something more effective is needed than the British Museum algorithm in order for a man or a machine to solve problems in symbolic logic in a reasonable time.

Before leaving the Logic Theorist, we wish to mention a variant of the Whitehead and Russell problems which we have also studied, and which will be the subject of some analysis later. At Yale, O. K. Moore and Scarvia Anderson (1954) have studied the problem-solving behavior of subjects who were given a small set (from one to four) of logic expressions as premises and asked to derive another expression from these, using twelve specified rules of transformation. (For details see the discussion in the next section and in the Appendix.) If we again suppose derivations to be generated by working forward from the premises, we can, in the case where there is a single premise, make simple estimates of the number of possible derivations of given length—and hence characterize this particular problem maze.

Assuming (and this is an oversimplification) that each rule of transformation operates on one premise, and that each such rule is applicable to any premise, this particular maze branches in twelve directions (one for each rule of transformation) at each choice point. That is, we start out with a single premise; depending on which rule of transformation we apply, we obtain one of twelve possible new expressions from each of these, and so on. Thus, the number of possible sequences of length k is 12^k. If the problem expression can be derived from the premise in a minimum of seven steps, then a trial-and-error search for the derivation would require, on the average, the construction of $\frac{1}{2} \times 12^7 = 1.8 \times 10^7 = 18,000,000$ sequences.

If only four rules of transformation, on the average, were actually applicable at each stage (a more realistic assumption, since expressions must be of particular forms for particular rules to be applicable to them), the number of sequences of length 7 would still be $4^7 = 16,384$.

Chess Playing. Let us turn now to a second example—choosing a move in chess. On the average, a chess player whose turn it is to move has his choice among twenty to thirty alternatives. There is no difficulty, therefore, in "finding" possible moves, but great difficulty in determining whether a particular legal move is a good move. The problem lies in the verifier and not in the generator. However, a principal technique for evaluating a move is to consider some of the opponent's possible replies to it, one's own replies to his, and so on, only attempting to evaluate the resulting positions after this maze of possible move sequences has been explored to some depth. The maze of move sequences is tremendously large. If we consider the number of continuations five moves deep for each player, assuming an average of twenty-five legal continuations at each stage, we find that P, the set of such move sequences, has about 10^{14} (one hundred million million) members.

Opening a Safe. We can make similar estimates of the sizes of the set P for the other examples of problem-solving tasks we have listed. In all cases the set is so large as to foreclose a solution-generating process that makes a completely random search through the set for possible solutions.

Before we leave our estimates, it will be useful to consider one additional "synthetic" example that has a simpler structure than any we have discussed so far, and that will be helpful later in understanding how various heuristic devices cut down the amount of search required to find problem solutions. Consider a safe whose lock has ten independent dials, each with numbers running from 00 to 99 on its face. The safe will have $100^{10} = 10^{20}$, or one hundred billion billion possible settings, only one of which will unlock it. A would-be safecracker, twirling the dials at random, would take on the average fifty billion billion trials to open it.

However, if the safe were defective, so that there was a faint click each time any dial was turned to its correct setting, it would take an average of only fifty trials to find the correct setting of any one dial, or five hundred trials to open the safe. The ten successive clicks that told him when he was getting "warmer" would make all the difference to the person opening the safe between an impossible task and a trivial one.

Thus, if we can obtain information that tells us which solutions to try, and in particular, if we can obtain information that allows us to factor one large problem into several small ones— *and to know when we have successfully solved each of the small ones*—the search task can be tremendously reduced. This guidance of the solution generator by information about the problem and its solution, and this factorization of problems into more or less independent subproblems, lie at the heart of effective problem-solving processes.

HEURISTICS FOR PROBLEM-SOLVING

We have seen that we can describe most problems abstractly in terms of a maze whose paths are possible solutions, with some small proportion of these being actual solutions. Then we can analyze the problem-solving processes into those that determine the order in which the paths shall be explored (solution generators) and those that determine whether a proposed solution is in fact a solution (solution verifiers).

Our examples show that solution generation and verification need not operate in an inflexible sequence. In the Logic

Theorist, as we saw, certain of the verifying conditions are built into the generator, so that only valid proofs are generated and other sequences of logic expressions are never considered. On the other hand, in chess playing, to verify that a proposed move is satisfactory, it is necessary to consider a large maze of possible continuations, and to search some part of this maze.

In the present section we shall examine some actual examples of successful problem-solving programs to see just what is involved in solution generation and verification, and how the programs reduce the problems to manageable size. We use the term *heuristic* to denote any principle or device that contributes to the reduction in the average search to solution. Although no general theory of heuristics exists yet,[4] we can say a good deal about some of the heuristics employed in human complex problem-solving. Our data derive largely from symbolic logic and chess problems that are formal and symbolic. This characteristic of the tasks undoubtedly limits the range of heuristics that we have observed. However, the kinds of heuristics we have found and can describe (e.g., planning and functional analysis) seem to have rather general applicability.

Efficient Generators

Even when the set P is large, as it usually is in complex problem-solving, it is possible for the solution generator to consider at an early stage those parts of P that are likely to contain a solution, and to avoid the parts that are most likely to be barren. For example, many problems have the following form: S, the set of solutions, consists of all elements of P with property A, property B, and property C. No generator is available that will generate elements having all three properties. However, generators may exist that generate elements satisfying any two of the properties. Thus there are three possible schemes: (1) to generate elements with properties A and B until one is found that also has C; (2) to generate elements A and C until one is found with property B; (3) to generate elements with B and C until one is found with property A. Which generator should be chosen de-

---

[4] See, however, the work of G. Polya (1954, 1957) who has analyzed the use of heuristics in mathematics.

pends on which constraints are the most difficult to satisfy, and on the relative costs of generation. If there are lots of elements satisfying *A*, then generating elements with *B* and *C* is reasonable, since an "*A*" can be expected to show up soon. If "*A*'s" are rare, it is better to generate elements that already have property *A*.

The Logic Theorist provides a clear example of this type of heuristic. Recall that the problem of the Logic Theorist is to find proofs. A proof is a list of logic expressions satisfying the following properties:

A. The beginning of the list consists of known theorems (any number of them);

B. All other expressions on the list are direct and valid consequences of expressions higher on the list;

C. The last expression on the list is the expression to be proved.

Now, although there is no generator that will turn out sequences satisfying all three of these conditions, there are generators that satisfy any two of them. It is easy to write down lists that start with theorems and end with the known expression. The difficult condition, however is *B:* that the list must consist of valid inference steps. Hence, it would be obviously foolish to choose a generator that automatically satisfied *A* and *C*, and simply wait until it generated a list that also satisfied *B*.

It is also possible to construct a generator satisfying *A* and *B*—one that produces lists that are proofs of something. This generator could find a proof by producing such lists until one appeared containing the desired expression—condition *C*. The British Museum algorithm discussed earlier is a generator of this kind. Finally, one can build a generator that satisfies conditions *B* and *C*. Fixing the last expression to be the desired one, lists are produced that consist only of valid inference steps leading to the last expression. Then the problem is solved when a list is generated that satisfies condition *A*, so that the expressions on the front of the list are all theorems. With this kind of generator, the list is constructed "backward" from the desired result toward the given theorems. This is the way the Logic Theorist actually goes about discovering proofs.

How do we choose between these two generators—the one

that requires a search to satisfy C, or the one that requires a search to satisfy A? In the case of logic the answer is reasonably clear. There is only one terminal expression (the theorem to be proved), but there are usually many known theorems.

It should be clear that there is nothing inherently superior in working backward as opposed to working forward. The choice between them resolves itself into a question of which constraints are the most binding. It may well be, of course, that the particular situation found here (many possible starting points versus a single end), which predisposes toward working backward, is relatively common.[5]

Simple Selection Heuristics

When a problem-solver faces a set of alternatives, such as the branches from a choice point in the maze in Figure 1, a common heuristic procedure is to screen out possible paths initially, using a relatively inexpensive test. To see the worth of this procedure, consider a maze having m alternatives at each branch point and length k. If there were a single correct path to the goal, finding that path by random search would require, on the average, $\frac{1}{2}m^k$ trials. If a heuristic test were available that could immediately weed out half of the alternatives at each branch point as unprofitable, then a random search with this heuristic would require only $\frac{1}{2}(\frac{1}{2}m)^k$ trials on the average. This is a reduction in search by a ratio of 2^k, which, if the maze were only seven steps in length, would amount to a factor of 128, and if the maze were ten steps in length, a factor of just over a thousand.

The Logic Theorist uses a number of such selection heuristics. For example, in working backward as described above, it can proceed in several directions from the list of logic expressions it has already obtained. Different theorems can be used with the various expressions already generated to make new valid inferences. Thus, the Logic Theorist generates a maze of subproblems, which corresponds exactly to the abstract pictures we have been giving (Newell & Simon, 1956).

---

[5] Duncker (1945) calls working backward an "organic" procedure, and distinguishes it from the "mechanical" procedures of working forward. Our analysis shows both why the former might be generally more efficient than the latter, and why there is nothing qualitatively different between them.

In Figure 2, two mazes are shown, derived from two attempts, under slightly different conditions, to prove a particular theorem from the same set of known theorems. In each maze, the desired theorem (*2.45) is represented by the top node; and each node below corresponds to a new expression generated (as a sub-problem) from the node immediately above it. In both cases the Logic Theorist found the same proof, which is designated in each maze by a heavy line. When it was generating the lower maze, the Logic Theorist had available two selective heuristics it did not have during the run that generated the upper maze. One of these

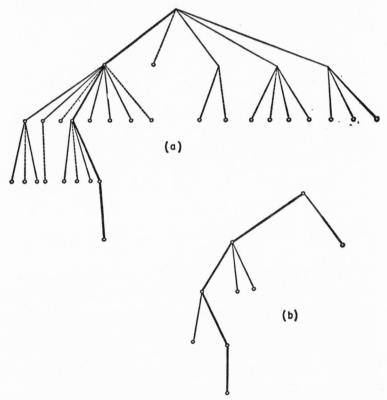

(a)

(b)

FIGURE 2. Mazes of two proofs of Theorem 2.45 from the same initial theorems. Identical programs generated the two mazes, except that the program of maze (b) had two additional selective heuristics. The heavy line is the proof. Dotted lines show additional branches eliminated by selective heuristics already in the first program.

heuristics weeded out new expressions that appeared "unprovable" on the basis of certain plausible criteria; the other heuristic weeded out expressions that seemed too complicated, in the sense of having too many negation signs. These two heuristics reduced the amount of search required to find the solution by a factor of 24/9 or 2.7. However, when the cost of the additional testing is taken into account the net saving in total problem-solving effort after allowing for this testing was 2.3. On the other hand we have experimented with heuristics that were excellent in their performance characteristics (reducing search by factors of 10) but that required so much effort to carry out as to cancel out the gain.

A heuristic need not be foolproof—indeed, most are not. Both heuristics mentioned above eliminate paths that lead to solutions. In rare cases they can even eliminate all paths to solutions. To take another example, a chess heuristic that would instantly remove from consideration any move that left the queen under attack would be an excellent rule of thumb for a novice player, but would occasionally lead him to miss a winning queen sacrifice. Occasionally, heuristics are found that are foolproof. These are usually called algorithms. The British Museum algorithm is an example, for it will always generate a proof, given enough time. ("Enough time" may, as we have seen, sometimes be centuries or millenia.)

Strategies in Solution Generation

Usually the information needed to select promising paths becomes available only as the search proceeds. Examination of paths produces clues of the "warmer-cooler" variety that guide the further conduct of the search. We have already given a simple, but striking, example of this in the clicking safe. As any particular dial is turned to the correct setting, the person opening the safe is informed by the click that he should stop manipulating that dial and go to the next. As a result he need attempt, on the average, only five hundred of the enormous total number of possible settings of the dials.

The sequential availability of cues derives from a deep property of problem-solving tasks that we must examine closely. There are, in general, two distinct ways to describe any particular choice point in a problem-solving maze. In chess, for example, a particular position can be specified by stating (verbally or with a diagram) what piece occupies each square on the board. Alternatively, the position can be specified by giving a sequence of moves that leads to it from the opening position.

Similarly, in logic an expression can be specified by writing it explicitly in the usual way, or equally well by giving a sequence of operations on the axioms (a proof) that will produce it. (In Figure 1, the solution may be described as d_6 or as 2–1–2.) Or, in arithmetic, if we use the symbol x' to mean the integer that follows x, we can write the number five as 5 or as $0''''''$. Or, as a more familiar example, we can designate a house by an address—5936 Phillips Avenue—or by the sequence of turns (go two blocks, turn right, go nine blocks, turn right, go one block) necessary to get there from a given starting point.

In all these cases, we will call the first method of specifying an element of *P specification by state description;* the second method, *specification by process description.* Often problems are set by providing the problem-solver with a partial or complete state description of the solution, the state descriptions of one or more starting points, and a list of allowable processes. The task, in these terms, is to find a sequence of processes that, operating on the initial state, will produce the final state.

We can now see how cues become available sequentially, and why, consequently, strategies of search that use the cues are possible. Each time a process is applied to an initial state, a new state with a new description is produced. If there are relations (known to or learnable by the problem-solver) between characteristics of the state description and distance from the goal (i.e., the final description that represents the solution), these relations can be used to tell when the problem-solver is getting "warmer" or "colder," hence, whether or not he should continue along a path defined by some sequence of processes. If, for example, in Figure 1, the state description corresponding to b_2 indicates that it is closer to the solution than the description corresponding to b_1, then the problem-solver at a_1 will take path 2 instead of path 1, and will be relieved of the necessity of exploring the entire upper half of the maze.

83

Let us examine a concrete example, for which we have data. Consider the following sequence of logic expressions that was written down by a subject solving one of O. K. Moore's problems in our laboratory. (The reader does not need to know what the symbols mean to understand the example. The task involved in these problems is described briefly in the Appendix.)

Step	Expression	Justification for Step
(1)	$R \cdot (-P \supset Q)$	Given
(2)	$R \cdot (\ P \vee Q)$	Rule 6
(3)	$R \cdot (\ Q \vee P)$	Rule 1 (inside parenthesis)
(4)	$(Q \vee P) \cdot R$	Rule 1 (outside parenthesis)

The first line is the expression given to the subject as the starting point of the "maze." The last line is the expression he was instructed to produce by applying the allowable operations. The number at the right of each line is the number of the rule he applied to obtain that line from the previous one. In this example, the state description of the solution is the expression: "$(Q \vee P) \cdot R$." The process description is: "The expression obtained by applying rules 6, 1, 1 to expression '$R \cdot (-P \supset Q)$.' " It is, of course, not at all obvious, except by hindsight, that these two descriptions refer to the same logic expression—if it were obvious, the problem would be no problem.

How can the problem-solver in this instance obtain new information as he proceeds each step down the maze? If we compare the final expression with the intermediate ones, we note that at each stage the newly derived expression resembles the final expression more closely than did the previous ones. For example, expression (1) contains two symbols that do not appear in the final expression; these have disappeared from expression (2). The next step rectifies the order of the symbols within parentheses, while the final step rectifies the order of the symbols in the expression as a whole.

A simple heuristic to follow in such cases is to apply an operator if the result of its application is to produce a new expression that resembles the final expression more nearly than did the previous one. To apply the heuristic, the problem-solver needs some criteria of similarity, but it is easy to see what they might be in the present case. These criteria provide the "clicks" that reduce the amount of search required.

We can test this explanation further by comparing it with the thinking-aloud protocol that the subject produced as he performed the task. We produce here an excerpt from his protocol, slightly edited to make it more comprehensible to the reader:

E. What are you looking at?

S. I'm looking at the idea of reversing the R's.
Then I'd have a similar group at the beginning.
But I can easily leave something like that until the end. . . .
Now I'm trying to see what operation I might apply to expression (1). . . . (He goes down the list of operations.) Rule 4 looks interesting . . . but there's no switching of order. I need that P and Q changed. . . . That doesn't seem practical with any of these rules. . . . I'm looking for a way, now, to get rid of that horseshoe ($\supset$). Ah . . . here it is, Rule 6. So I'd apply Rule 6 to the second part of what we have up there.

E. That gives you (writing)   (2) $R \cdot (P \vee Q)$.

S. Okay. And now I'd use Rule 1 on P and Q, and then with the entire expression.

E. We'll do them one at a time (writing)   (3) $R \cdot (Q \vee P)$. Now the total expression?

S. Yeah.

E. You get (writing)   (4) $(Q \vee P) \cdot R$, and . . . that's it.

S. That's it all right. Okay . . . that wasn't too hard.

It will be observed that the subject thought through the successive changes (bringing the R to the left side, interchanging P and Q, eliminating the horseshoe) in the order opposite to that in which he actually carried them out, but that his process—that of making the expression at hand more and more like the final expression—is precisely the one we have described.

To give a picture of the selectivity involved in this particular piece of problem-solving, we show in Figure 3 a somewhat simplified picture of a portion of the problem maze, including only those branches that would actually be explored if the problem were solved by a systematic search without selectivity. Note that the path to the goal (1–2–6) discovered through systematic search is different from the one (6–1–1) discovered by the subject's selective processes, and that the systematic search generated many expressions that—from the protocol evidence—did not even enter the subject's awareness.

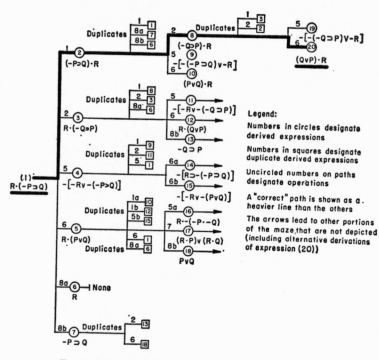

FIGURE 3. Partial diagram of problem maze for deriving
$(QvP) \cdot R$ from $R \cdot (- P \supset Q)$

The same kind of alternation between state description and process description is involved in choosing a move in chess. Because of the tremendous size of the maze of continuations, only a few of all the possible lines of play can be examined. When the player considers a particular move, he can construct in his imagination a picture of the board after the move has been made. He can then examine this new state description to see what features of it are favorable, what features unfavorable, and what likely continuations it suggests. In this way he is guided to examine a few paths through the maze (if he is a good player, his heuristic will usually lead him to examine the important ones), and he can explore these to some depth—deeply enough to be able to evaluate directly the final positions he reaches. The best evidence we possess indicates that the strongest chess players do not examine more than (at the very most) a few dozen continuations, and these to depths ranging from several moves to ten or even more (see Figure 4). The ability of the chess master, so amazing to the novice, to explore in depth derives from his ability to explore very selectively without missing important alternatives. The "clicks" he notices, inaudible to the novice, are loud and obvious to him.

Functional Analysis

Underlying the heuristic of "reducing differences" is the general concept of functional analysis. Functional or means-end analysis provides a generalized heuristic that can be applied to a wide range of problems. We will describe a program for functional

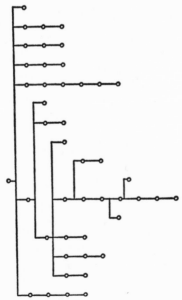

FIGURE 4. Portion of maze of continuations examined by chessmaster in middle-game position. (From de Groot [1946], p. 207.)

ALLEN NEWELL, J. C. SHAW, HERBERT A. SIMON

analysis that we have now incorporated in a revised version of the
Logic Theorist, and which, while not completely general, can
almost certainly transfer without modification to problem-solving
in trigonometry, algebra, and probably other subjects like geometry and chess.

The entities that the program recognizes are *expressions,
differences* between expressions, *operators, goals* and *subgoals,*
and *methods.* The program can be used as a problem-solving
heuristic for problems of the form: "given expression *a* and a
set of admissible operators, to derive expression *b.*" We have
already observed that logic problems can be put in this form—
and so can most other problems formulated in terms of the maze
model.

Associated with each goal in the heuristic is a set of
methods—procedures that may help attain the goal in question.
A method may, in turn, involve establishing subgoals and applying the methods associated with these. At some point, if the
heuristic is successful, a subgoal is attained by one of its methods;
this success reactivates the goal at the next higher level in the
hierarchy, and so on.

Let us be more concrete. There are three types of goals in
the functional problem-solver:

Type 0 Goal: Find a way to transform expression *a* into
expression *b.*

Type 1 Goal: Reduce the difference *d* between expressions *a* and *b.*

Type 2 Goal: Apply operator *q* to expression *a.*

At present, one method is associated with each of these
goals. Briefly, the method associated with the type 0 goal consists
of (Figure 5a): (a) matching the two expressions to find a difference, *d,* between them; (b) setting up the type 1 subgoal of reducing *d*—if this is successful, a new transformed expression, *a'* is
obtained; (c) setting up the type 0 subgoal of transforming *a'* into
b. If the last step is successfully carried out, the original problem
has been solved.

The method associated with the type 1 goal consists of
(Figure 5b): (a) searching for an operator that is relevant to the

88

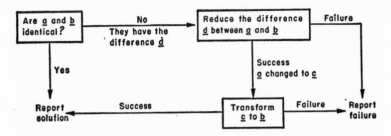

(a)— Type O goal: Transform $\underline{a}$ to $\underline{b}$

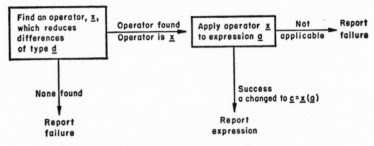

(b)— Type I goal: Reduce the difference $\underline{d}$ between $\underline{a}$ and $\underline{b}$

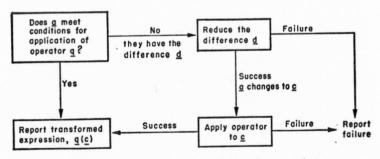

(c) — Type 2 goal: Apply operator $\underline{q}$ to expression $\underline{a}$

FIGURE 5. Goals in Functional Heuristic.

89

ALLEN NEWELL, J. C. SHAW, HERBERT A. SIMON

reduction of the difference, d; and (b) setting up the type 2 goal of applying the operator.

The method associated with the type 2 goal consists in (Figure 5c): (a) determining if the conditions are met for applying q to a; (b) if so, applying the operator; or, if not, setting up the type 1 subgoal of reducing the difference between a and the conditions for applying q.

Let us see how this functional problem-solver would approach the particular logic problem we examined in the last section. The problem-solver is given type 0 goal of transforming expression (1) into expression (4). In trying to reach this goal (Figure 5a), it first matches (1) with (4) to see what differences there are, and notes that the symbols P and Q occur in reverse order in (1) from the order in (4). This generates the type 1 subgoal (Figure 5b) of eliminating this difference. The problem-solver remembers (from instruction or previous description) that operator 1 is relevant to reducing differences of this kind, and sets up the type 2 subgoal (Figure 5c) of applying rule 1 to (1). The conditions for applicability are not met, for operator 1 requires a v between P and Q, while actually there is a ⊃. Hence a new type 1 goal is created to change the ⊃ into a v. Operator 6, which has this function, is found, and the type 2 goal of applying it is set up and achieved. The transformed expression (2) now satisfies the conditions for applying operator 1. This is now applied, achieving the type 2 subgoal, and yielding expression (3). A similar but simpler sequence of events leads to expression (4)—at which time the problem-solver notes that it has eliminated all differences between the initial and terminal expressions, and hence has solved the original problem. Reference back to the protocol will show how closely this program models the behavior of the subject.[6]

[6] Our aim here is to illustrate, and not to deal with the scientific problems of how well these programs explain the protocols. In the sketch of the program given in the text, we generate the expressions in the order in which the subject wrote them down. The protocol indicates clearly that he proceeded initially in the opposite order. To simplify the exposition, we have not tried to describe the program that would simulate the subject's behavior most closely, and we have taken the liberty of editing the protocols. At another time we will undertake a more systematic analysis of the protocols as evidence.

90

It will be observed that neither the goals nor the methods of the functional problem-solving program make reference to logic or any other subject matter. Simply by acquiring new definitions of the terms "expressions," "differences," and "operators," the problem-solver can use the functional heuristic to solve problems relating to quite different subject matter. We hope, in the near future, to test whether this heuristic will, in fact, solve trigonometric identities.

The Heuristics of Planning

Another class of heuristics of great generality that increase the selectivity of solution generators are those that come under the rubric of "planning." Consider again a maze k steps in length with m branches at each choice point. Suppose that, instead of cues at each choice point, there were a cue at every second step to mark the correct path (see Figure 6). Then the task of traversing the maze successfully could be divided into a number of subtasks—specifically, the tasks of reaching successively each of the choice points that were marked by the cues.

Such a set of subtasks would constitute a plan. In place of the original task of traversing a maze k steps in length, the problem solver would now have the task of traversing $(k/2)$ mazes each two steps in length. The expected number of paths that would have to be searched to solve the first problem is, as before $\frac{1}{2}m^k$. The expected number of trials to solve the second problem is $\frac{1}{2}(k/2)m^2$.

If, as in the figure, the original maze were six steps in length with two alternatives at each choice point, the average amount of search required would be reduced from thirty-two trials to six—to which would have to be added the effort required to find the plan.

We use such a planning technique whenever we take a cross-country trip. First we sketch a general route from major city to major city; then, taking these cities as subgoals, we solve the subproblem of reaching each from the previous one.

We have devised a program of this kind to describe the way some of our subjects handle O. K. Moore's logic problems, and perhaps the easiest way to show what is involved in planning is

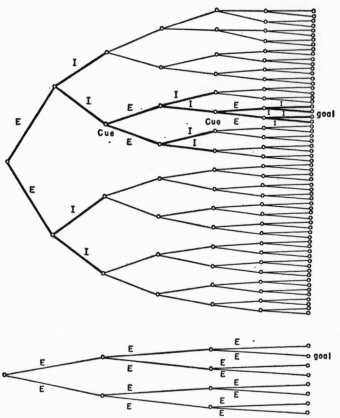

FIGURE 6. Problem space (top) and planning space (bottom) for a simple task. The plan is used to find the cues in the larger maze; then only the darkened paths in the maze need be explored. The steps marked E are essential, and those marked I are inessential—see text.

to describe that program. On a purely pragmatic basis, the twelve operators that are admitted in this system of logic can be put in two classes, which we shall call, respectively, "essential" and "inessential" operators. Essential operators are those which, when applied to an expression, make "large" changes in its appearance —change "$P \lor P$" to "P," for example. Inessential operators are those which make "small" changes—e.g., change "$P \lor Q$" to "$Q \lor P$." (See Appendix.) As we have said, the distinction is purely pragmatic. Of the twelve operators in this calculus, we have classified eight as essential and four as inessential. Roughly speaking, the inessential operators are those that change the order of the symbols in expressions, or change the connectives ("∨" to "•", for example) but make no other changes.

Next, we can take an expression and abstract from it those characteristics that relate only to inessential changes. For example, we can abstract from "*P* ∨ *Q*" the expression (*PQ*), where the order of the symbols in the latter expression is regarded as irrelevant [i.e., (*PQ*) is treated as identical with (*QP*)]. Clearly, if inessential operations are applied to the abstracted expressions, the expressions will remain unchanged, while essential operations can be expected to change them [e.g., the operator that will change "*P* ∨ *P*" to "*P*" will change (*PP*) to (*P*)].

We can now set up a correspondence between our original expressions and operators, on the one hand, and the abstracted expressions and essential operators, on the other. Corresponding to the original problem of transforming *a* into *b*, we can construct a new problem of transforming *a′* into *b′*, where *a′* and *b′* are the expressions obtained by abstracting *a* and *b* respectively. Suppose that we solve the new problem, obtaining a sequence of expressions, *a′c′d′* . . . *b′*. We can now transform back to the original problem space and set up the new problems of transforming *a* into *c*, *c* into *d*, and so on. Thus, the solution of the problem in the planning space provides a plan for the solution of the original problem.

Let us examine (Figure 7) an actual example of the application of the planning heuristic to the O. K. Moore problems. This example follows the protocol of one of our subjects and shows quite clearly that he used the planning heuristic in precisely this way to solve the problem in question. The left-hand side of Figure 7 shows the sequence of expressions the subject wrote down in solving Moore's problem A4. The subject was given the expressions in lines (1) through (4) and told to derive the expression in line (11). He carried through the derivation in seven steps, the prior expressions and rules used in each step being given to the right of the derived expression.

93

		PROOF		PLAN	
Step	Expression	Justification	Expression	Justification
(1)	PvQ	Given	PQ	Given
(2)	−R⊃−Q	"	RQ	"
(3)	S	"	S	"
(4)	R⊃−S	"	RS	"
(5)	S⊃−R	Rule 2 on (4)		
(6)	S⊃−Q	Rule 12 on (2), (5)	SQ	Rule 12 on (2), (4)
(7)	−Q	Rule 11 on (3), (6)	Q	Rule 11 on (3), (6)
(8)	−P⊃Q	Rule 6 on (1)		
(9)	−Q⊃P	Rule 2 on (8)		
(10)	P	Rule 11 on (7), (9)	P	Rule 11 on (1), (7)
(11)	PvT	Rule 9 on (10)	PT	Rule 9 on (10)

FIGURE 7. Solution of Problem A4 by Subject 8.

The subject's protocol shows, however, that prior to obtaining the rigorous derivation, he had worked out a complete plan for the proof. The plan is shown, in terms of abstracted expressions, in the right-hand half of the figure. The planning activity took place immediately after the problem was presented to the subject, and before he instructed the experimenter to write down any transformations of the expressions given him as premises. Here is the protocol segment that discloses the planning activity:

S. Well, one possibility right off the bat is when you have just a *P* ∨ *T* like that (the problem expression) the last thing you might use is that rule 9. I can get everything down to a *P* and just add a ∨ *T*. So that's one thing to keep in mind. . . . I don't know if that's possible; but I think it is because I see that expressions (2) and (4) are somewhat similar. If I can cancel out the *R*'s that would leave me with just an *S* and *Q*; and if I have just an *S* and *Q*, I can eventually get—expression (3)—get the *S*'s to cancel out and end up with just a *Q*. And if I end up with just *Q*, maybe the *Q*'s will cancel out; so you see all the way down the line. I don't know, it looks too good to be true, but I think I see it already.

At this point the subject has already constructed a four-step plan, which will lead him, as he executes it, to two subproblems of filling in the gaps (the other two subproblems are trivial, since they are solved simply by the translation of the abstracted expressions back into the original space). One of these subproblems is three steps in length, the other is two. Thus, for the original seven-step maze, the subject has substituted a four-step maze, a three-step maze, and a two-step maze.

To complete our illustration, let us see how the subject goes about solving the first subproblem—eliminating the R between expressions (2) and (4):

S. (Immediately following previous excerpt) Expressions (2) and (4)—we'll have to do something with them. If I invert expression (4)—apply rule 2 to it—I will have $(S \supset -R)$. Good. O.K. Apply rule 2 to expression (4).

E. That gives (writing): (5) $S \supset -R$.

S. Now apply rule 12 to expressions (2) and (4)—(2) and (5), I mean.

E. That gives (writing): (6) $S \supset -Q$.

S. Right. I got rid of the R's. Now. . . .

It will be observed that only rules 9, 11, and 12 are used in the derivation of the plan. All of these are essential rules. Rules 2 and 6, both of which are inessential, are used to solve the subproblems.

We can estimate how much reduction the planning heuristic accomplishes in the size of the maze to be searched. The number of alternative operations at each step is of the order of 10. (Because we distinquish between essential and inessential operations, it may be smaller when the planning heuristic is used than when the problem is solved without it, but we will ignore this additional source of efficiency of the planning heuristics.) If m is 10, then the average number of paths to be searched without planning is $\frac{1}{2} 10^7 = 5,000,000$. With planning, the number of paths is $\frac{1}{2} \cdot 10^4 + \frac{1}{2} \cdot 10^3 + \frac{1}{2} \cdot 10^2 = 5,550$. The search required in the first case is larger by a ratio of 900:1.

Of course these ratios assume that no other selective heuristic—apart from the planning heuristic—is employed. If the planning heuristic were superimposed, for example, on the functional analysis heuristic, the latter would reduce m to a much smaller number; hence there would be much less search either with or without planning. Suppose, for example, that the functional analysis heuristic reduced m to 4. Then the search without planning would involve $\frac{1}{2} \cdot 4^7 = 8,192$ paths; the search with planning would require $\frac{1}{2} \cdot 4^4 + \frac{1}{2} \cdot 4^3 + \frac{1}{2} \cdot 4^2 = 168$. The savings ratio is now *only* 49:1.

The subject, understandably, was pleased with his heuristic. His comment on solving the problem was "See, I'm acquiring an insight." Since his protocol gives evidence of other bits of heuristic in addition to the ones we have been discussing, his value of m was probably 2 or less, and the total number of paths he searched was probably less than a dozen. The combination of heuristics he used, simple though they were, secured him a saving over blind trial and error of a factor of perhaps 500,000. These rough statistics give us a good picture of the reason for the "aha!" that goes with "insight" into the problem structure (which we would translate, "acquisition of an additional piece of heuristic").

Summary: The Nature of Heuristics

In this section we have seen that the success of a problem-solver who is confronted with a complex task rests primarily on his ability to select—correctly—a very small part of the total problem-solving maze for exploration. The processes that carry out this selection we call heuristics. We have seen that most heuristics depend on a strategy that modifies subsequent search as a function of information obtained in previous search; and we have discussed at some length several of the most significant and powerful classes of heuristics that we have encountered in our attempts to simulate human problem-solving.

Among the heuristics we examined were: processes for working backward from the problem solution, selection heuristics, functional or means-end analysis, and planning. We provided operational meanings for these terms by sketching out what the actual processes would be in the Logic Theorist and in a chess-playing machine. We referred to our evidence from protocols of human subjects that such processes actually do occur in human problem-solving behavior. We also constructed quantitative estimates of the reduction in search that results from the selectivity of these heuristics, and used the estimates to account for the ability of humans—and of machines simulating them by using the same processes—to solve the particular problems in question.

SOME CONDITIONS OF CREATIVITY

In the remaining pages of this paper we shall use the theory of problem-solving developed in preceding sections to cast light on three topics that are often discussed in relation to creativity:

1. the use of imagery in problem-solving;
2. the relation of unconventionality to creativity;
3. the role of hindsight in the discovery of new heuristics.

These three topics were chosen because we think our theory has something to say about them. We have not tried to include all the traditional topics in the theory of creative activity—we do not, for example, discuss the phenomenon of incubation—nor will we try to treat definitively the topics we have included. We are still far from having all the mechanisms that will be required for a complete theory of creativity: these last pages are necessarily extrapolations and are more speculative than the earlier sections.

PLANNING AND IMAGERY

Among the issues that have surrounded the topic of imagery in the literature on thinking the following have been prominent:

1. What internal "language" is used by the organism in thinking? To what extent is this "language" related to the sense modalities, and is the thinking represented by elements that correspond to abstract "symbols," or to pictures, or to something else?

2. To what extent do the internal representations, whatever their nature, involve generalization and abstraction from that which they represent?

Using the example of planning we have been considering, we believe some clarification can be achieved of both issues.

97

Some Comments on Representation

How are the objects of thought represented internally? We are asking here neither a physiological nor a "hardware" question. We wish an answer at the level of information processing, rather than at that of neurology or electronics. In a state description of an information processing system, we can talk of patterns of elementary symbols. These symbols may be electric charges, as in some computer memories, or they may be the cell assemblies of Hebb's theories, or they may be something quite different. We are not interested in what they are made of. Given that there are some such patterns—that the system is an information processing system—our question is in what way the patterns within mirror, or fail to mirror, the patterns without that they represent.

Let us take a simple example from logic. We may write on a piece of paper the expression " $(p \lor q) \supset p$." What would it mean to say that the "same" expression was held in memory by the Logic Theorist? With the present program it would mean that somewhere in memory there would be a branching pattern of elementary symbols (or the internal counterparts of elementary symbols) that would look like:

Of course, there would not literally be mounds of ink like " p," but there would be internal elementary patterns in one-one correspondence to these. Note, however, that the correspondence between the internal and external representations as a whole is far more complicated than the correspondences between elementary symbols. The external representation of the expression in the illustration is a linear array of symbols; the internal representation has branches that make it topologically distinct from a linear array. The external representation uses symbols like " (" and ")"; these are absent from the internal representations— the grouping relations they denote being implicit in the branching structure itself (i.e., the cluster $p \lor q$, which is enclosed in parentheses in the external representation, is a subtree of the entire expression in the internal representation).

The implicitness of certain aspects of the internal representation goes even deeper than we have just indicated. For the tree structure we represented on the paper above by connecting symbols with lines is represented within the computer memory by the fact that there are certain information processes available that will "find the left sub-tree" and "find the right sub-tree" of such a tree structure. The actual physical locations of these elements in memory can be (and usually are) completely scattered, so long as these information processes have means of finding them.

Let us take another example. If we wish to represent on paper the concept of a pair of elements, P and Q, abstracted from the order of the pair, we can write something like: (PQ), and append it to the statement that (PQ) is equivalent for all purposes with (QP). In an internal representation, order-independence of the terms of the pair might be secured in a quite different way. Suppose that the symbols P and Q were stored (in some order) on a list in memory, but that the only information processes available for dealing with lists were processes that produced the same output regardless of the order of the items on the list. Suppose, for example, that the "print list" process always alphabetized the list before printing. Then this process would always print out " (PQ)" regardless of whether the items were stored on the list as PQ or QP. In this case, the order-independence of the information processes applicable to the lists would be an implicit internal representation of the equivalence of (PQ) with (QP).[7]

The main lesson that we learn from these examples is that the internal representation may mirror all the relevant properties of the external representation without being a "picture" of it in any simple or straightforward sense. It is not at all clear whether a human subject would be aware that his internal representation of a logic expression "carried" the information about the ex-

[7] A simple example of this in humans is well known to teachers of matrix algebra. Since all the elementary arithmetic and algebraic systems that students have encountered previously contain the commutative law, students must be *taught* that the matrix product AB is not equivalent to the product BA.

99

pression in quite a different way from the string of symbols on paper, or that, if he were aware, he could verbalize what the differences were.

A similar point has been made in discussions of "encoding." Our examples show, however, that encoding may involve something far more complex than translating a string of symbols in one alphabet into another string of symbols in another alphabet. The encoded representation may not be a string at all, and there may be important differences in what is explicit and what implicit in the two representations.

Representation and the Sense Modalities

Since the internal representation of information need not be a simple mapping of what is "out there," or even of what is received by the sense organs, it is not easy to know what is meant by saying that a particular internal representation is or is not "visual" or "auditory." Is the internal branching structure that represents the logic expression inside the Logic Theorist a visual image of the string of symbols on paper or is it not?

There is an obvious fallacy in saying that it is, not just because the spatial (or even the topological) relations are not the same in the two. The internal representations we carry around in our heads of even the most visual of pictures cannot possibly have the same metrical relations within (and possibly not even the same topologic relations) as without.

We believe that the explanation of why some memories are visual, some auditory, and some verbal lies in a quite different direction from a simple "mapping" theory. Since our explanation rests on considerations that have not even been touched upon in the present paper, we cannot discuss it at length. However, a very brief statement of it may help us understand the role of imagery in creative thought.

We will assert that an internal representation is visual if it is capable of serving as an input to the same information processes as those that operate on the internal representations of immediate visual sensory experiences. These information processes that can be applied to visual sensations literally serve as a "mind's eye," for they can operate on memories that have been encoded in the same way as sensory inputs, and when they are so applied produce the phenomena of visual imagination. Since there must be processes that can deal with sensory inputs, there is nothing mysterious in the notion that these same processes can deal with inputs from memory, and hence nothing metaphysical or nonoperational about the concept of "mind's eye" or "mind's ear."

But the mind's eye is used not only to process inputs that "nature" coded in visual form. Often we deliberately construct visual representations of abstract relations (e.g., we draw boxes to represent states of a system, and arrows connecting the boxes to represent the processes that transform one state into another). What can be the advantage of the imagery? The advantage lies in the fact that when we encode information so as to be accessible to visual processes, we have automatically built into the encoded information all the relations that are implicit in the information processes that constitute the mind's eye. For example, when we represent something as an arrow, we determine the order in which the items connected by the arrow will be called into attention.

We are led in this way to the concept of systems of imagery. A system of imagery comprises a set of conventions for encoding information, and coordinated with these a set of information processes that apply to the encoded information. As we have seen, the information processes for interpreting the encoded information may be just as rich in implicit conventions as the processes for encoding. It is the fact that the encoding makes available the former as well as the latter that sometimes makes it useful to represent information in a modality for which we have a rich and elaborate system of imagery.

Abstraction and Generalization

Bishop Berkeley founded his epistemology on the personal difficulty he experienced in imagining a triangle which is "neither oblique nor rectangle, equilateral, equicrural nor scalenon, but all and none of these at once." Hume, on the other hand, found this feat of imagination perfectly feasible!

The Logic Theorist would have to take Hume's side

101

against Berkeley. For in the planning program the problem-solver has the capacity to imagine a logic expression comprised of two variables joined by a connective, in which the connective is neither v nor • nor ⊃, but all and none of these at once. For this is precisely what the representation (PQ) stands for and the way in which it is used by the planning processes.

Once we admit that the relation between the object sensed and its internal representation is complex, there is no difficulty in admitting as corollary that the internal representation may abstract from all but a few of the properties of the object "out there." What we call "visual imagery," for example, may admit of colorless images even if all light that falls on the retina is colored.

The fact that the planning heuristic of the Logic Theorist possesses generalized or abstracted images of logic expressions does not prove, of course, that humans construct similar abstractions. What it does prove is that the notion of an image of a triangle "neither oblique nor rectangle, equilateral, equicrural, nor scalenon, but all and none of these at once" is not contradictory, but can be given a straightforward operational definition in an information processing system. Finally, since the information processes that can operate on the abstracted expressions in the Logic Theorist are of the same kind as those that operate on the full-bodied expressions, we would be forced, by any reasonable criterion, to regard the two images as belonging to the same modality.

The Uses of Imagery

We have already hinted at the uses of imagery, but we would like now to consider them a little more explicit. In order for us to think about something, that something must have an internal representation of some kind, and the thinking organism must have some processes that are capable of manipulating the representation. We have called such a combination of representation and processes a system of imagery.

Often, the term image is used somewhat more narrowly to refer to those representations that correspond to one or another of the sense modalities. Thus, we have visual images, auditory images, and tactile images, but we would not, in this narrower usage, speak of "abstract images"—i.e., representations and processes not used to represent any of the sensory inputs.

When a particular representation is used for something, a large number of properties are imputed implicitly to the object represented because these properties are imbedded in the information processes that operate on representations of the kind in question. Thus, if we represent something as a line, we are likely —because that is the way our visual imagery operates—to impute to it the property of continuity.

Herein lie both the power and the danger of imagery as a tool of thought. The richer the properties of the system of imagery we employ, the more useful is the imagery in manipulating the representation, but the more danger there is that we will draw conclusions based on properties of the system of imagery that the object represented doesn't possess. When we are aware of the danger—and are conscious that we have encoded information into a system of imagery with strong properties—we are likely to call the image a "metaphor."

Often we are not aware of the danger. As has often been observed, Aristotle's logic and epistemology sometimes mistook accidents of Greek grammar for necessary truths. From this standpoint, the significance of modern mathematics, with its emphasis on rigor and the abstract axiomatic method, is that it provides us with tests that we can apply to the products of thinking to make sure that only those assumptions that we are aware of are being used.

The imagery used in the planning heuristic drastically reduces the space searched by the solution generator by abstracting from detail. This is probably not the only function of imagery for humans, although it is the one best documented by our present programs. We think there is evidence from data on human subjects that, even in those cases where there is not a rich set of processes associated with the representation, imagery may provide a plan to the problem-solver at least in the sense of a list of the elements he is dealing with and a list of which of these are related.

103

Summary: Imagery

We have applied our problem-solving theory to the classical problem of the role of imagery in thought. Although our analysis of imagery is admittedly speculative, it provides a possible explanation of the relation of internal representations to the sense modalities, and provides an example from one of the computer programs of generalization or abstraction, and of an abstract "visual" image. Finally, the theory shows how images of various kinds can be used as the basis for planning heuristics.

UNCONVENTIONALITY AND CREATIVITY

Thus far, our view of the problem-solving process has been a short-range one. We have taken as starting point a system of heuristics possessed by the problem-solver, and have asked how it would govern his behavior. Since his initial system of heuristics may not enable the problem-solver to find a solution in a particular case, we must also understand how a system of heuristics is modified and developed over time when it is not adequate initially.

Change of Set and Learning

Although all adaptive change in heuristics might be termed "learning," it is convenient to distinguish relatively short-run and temporary changes from longer-run, more or less permanent changes. If we use "learning" to refer only to the latter, then we may designate the former as "changes in set."

There is a basis for the distinction between set change and learning in the structure of the problem-solving organism. The human problem-solver (and the machine simulation) is essentially a serial rather than a parallel instrument, which because of the narrow span of its attention, does only one or a few things at a time. If it has a rich and elaborate system of heuristics relevant to a particular problem, only a small part of these can be active in guiding search at any given moment. When in solving a problem one subsystem of heuristics is replaced by another, and the search, as a consequence, moves off in a new direction, we refer to this shift as a change in set. Change in set is a modification of the heuristics that are actively guiding search, by replacing them with other heuristics in the problem-solver's repertoire; learning is change in the repertoire of heuristics itself.

Stereotypy

A major function of heuristics is to reduce the size of the problem space so that it can be searched in reasonable time. Effective heuristics exclude those portions of the space where solutions don't exist or are rare, and retain those portions where solutions are relatively common. Heuristics that have been acquired by experience with some set of problems may be exceedingly effective for problems of that class, but may prove inappropriate when used to attack new problems. Behaviorally, stereotypy is simply the subject's persistence in using a system of heuristics that the *experimenter* knows is inappropriate under the circumstances.

It is a very common characteristic of puzzles that the first steps toward solution require the solver to do something that offends common sense, experience, or physical intuition. Solutions to chess mating problems typically begin with "surprising" moves. In the same way, a number of classical experiments with children and animals show that a simple problem of locomotion to a goal can be made more difficult if a barrier forces the subject to take his first steps away from the goal in order ultimately to reach it. When the task has this characteristic, the problem-solver is obviously more likely to succeed if his repertoire of heuristics includes the injunction: "If at first you don't succeed, try something counter-intuitive."

Is Unconventionality Enough?

It sometimes seems to be argued that people would become effective problem-solvers if only we could teach them to be unconventional. If our analysis here is correct, unconventionality may be a necessary condition for creativity, but it is certainly not a sufficient condition. If unconventionality simply means rejecting some of the heuristics that restrict search to a limited subspace, then the effect of unconventionality will generally be a return to relatively inefficient trial-and-error search in a very much larger space. We have given enough estimates of the sizes of the spaces involved, with and without particular heuristics, to cast suspicion on a theory of creativity that places its emphasis on increase in trial and error.

Let us state the matter more formally. Associated with a problem is a space of possible solutions. Since the problem-solver operates basically in a serial fashion, these solutions must be taken up and examined in some order. If the problem-solver has no information about the distribution of solutions in the space of possibilities, and no way of extracting clues from his search, then he must resort to a solution generator that is, to all intents and purposes, "random"—that leads him to solutions no more rapidly than would a chance selection. At some later stage the problem-solver learns how to change the solution generator so that—at least for some range of problems—the average search required to find a solution is greatly reduced. But if the modified generator causes some elements in the solution space to be examined earlier than they would otherwise have been, it follows that the examination of others will be postponed.

The argument for unconventionality is that at some point a class of problems may be faced where the generator looks at just the wrong elements first, or even carefully filters out the right ones so that they will never be noticed (as in the chess example of queen sacrifices). A return to the original trial-and-error generator would eliminate this perverse blindness of the generator, but at the expense of reinstating a search through an enormous space. What is needed in these cases is not an elimination of the selective power of a solution generator, but the replacement of the inappropriate generator by an appropriate one.

We have neither the data nor the space to illustrate this point from classical instances of scientific creativity, but we can give a simple example from chess. A chess novice is always stunned when his opponent demolishes him with a "creative" unconventional move like a sacrifice of a major piece. The novice has carefully trained himself to reject out of hand moves that lose pieces (and kicks himself for his oversights). If he tries to imitate his more experienced opponent, he usually loses the sacrificed piece.

Clearly the opponent's secret is not simply that he is willing to be unconventional—to consider paths the novice rejects. The secret is that the experienced player has various additional pieces of heuristic that guide him to promising "unconventional" moves by giving him clues of their deeper and less direct consequences. It is the possession of this additional selectivity that allows him, in appropriate positions, to give up the selectivity embodied in the novice's rule of always preserving major pieces. The evidence we possess on the point indicates rather strongly that the amount of exploration undertaken by the chess master is no greater than that undertaken by relatively weak players (de Groot, 1946). He does not generate more solution possibilities; he does generate them in a different sequence.

Nature Abhors a Vacuum

We see that set change in particular, and unconventionality in general, are likely to facilitate the solution of a problem only if the problem-solver has an appropriate new heuristic to replace the inappropriate heuristic that has been "blinding" him. Accordingly, to understand the success of effective and creative problem-solvers we must examine not only the motivational and attitudinal factors that enable them to change an initial set or to violate accepted conventions; we must pay equal attention to the richness of their systems of heuristics that makes any particular piece of heuristic dispensable, and to their learning processes that generate new heuristics to fill the vacuums created by the rejection of the ones previously used.

LEARNING BY HINDSIGHT

Our experience with the simulation of learning has been much more limited than our experience with the simulation of problem-solving. The chess-playing program is, to date, entirely a performance program; and only a few experiments have been carried out with learning heuristics for the Logic Theorist. Nevertheless, from these explorations and from our theoretical model we can draw some implications about learning processes that help

107

us understand how the creative problem-solver can gradually improve his heuristics.

In the next two sections we will describe two kinds of learning that have actually been tested with the Logic Theorist. Both kinds of learning involve "hindsight," and in the third section, we shall undertake a more general analysis of the role of hindsight in the acquisition of new heuristics.

Memory of Specific Results

The simplest kind of learning in a maze is to remember the path to a solution so that the same solution can be reached at once in a later trial. There is no difficulty in programming a machine for this kind of learning, provided that its memory is large enough, and little enough difficulty for a human. Thus it is probable that most high school geometry students, unless they have an enlightened teacher, focus their energies on memorizing theorems and their proofs.

The Logic Theorist stores in memory the theorems it has proved (it could also remember the proofs themselves, but at present is not programmed to do so), and hence can use these as starting points in exploring new parts of the maze.

One should not underestimate the enhancement of problem-solving power that can be obtained even with this "routine" kind of learning, particularly if the teacher is careful to present tasks to the problem-solver in an appropriate order. We have already seen how much the search for a long proof can be reduced if a plan is provided first; but a plan consists simply in dividing the original problem into a series of smaller problems— marking the path the problem-solver is to follow. Exactly the same effect can be secured if the subproblems generated by the planning heuristic are instead provided by the teacher.

On the other hand, storage of specific information about paths in the maze is not always helpful in subsequent problem-solving. We have conducted some experiments with the Logic Theorist in which a theorem is presented for proof (a) after all previous theorems have been stored in memory, and alternatively (b) after a carefully selected small set of "powerful" theorems has been stored in memory. In a considerable number of cases, the program proves the theorem more quickly, and with far less search, in the second condition than in the first. For example, in one case (Theorem *2.48 of *Principia Mathematica*) the Theorist achieved a three-step proof when it had in memory only the axioms and one prior theorem (*2.16) in one-third the time it took to find a two-step proof when it held in memory all prior theorems. We are reminded by this example of the blinding effects of excesses of pedantry on human problem-solvers also. A small arsenal of good general-purpose weapons may be much more effective than a storehouse of specific, narrowly useful ones.

A graphical impression of the qualitative difference that is produced in the Logic Theorist's problem-solving behavior when different numbers of prior theorems are held in memory can be obtained from Figure 8. The upper half of the figure shows the maze of subproblems the Theorist explored while proving Theorem *2.17 with all axioms and prior theorems (twenty in all) held in memory; the lower half shows the maze explored while proving Theorem *2.17 with only the axioms and five theorems (ten in all) held in memory. In the former case, twenty-three branches had to be explored to find a three-step proof; in the latter case only eleven branches to find the same proof.

Differentiation: Specialized Methods

As the problem-solver accumulates a larger and larger store of results and techniques, his problem of selection becomes more difficult unless he acquires at the same time additional clues on the basis of which to differentiate parts of the problem space in order to use special techniques under special circumstances. We have developed one example in the Logic Theorist of a process for learning specialized techniques. The Logic Theorist uses four basic methods of attack on problems. In each method it employs theorems already proved as its "raw materials." It turns out, empirically, that some theorems are used principally in connection with certain methods, other theorems with other methods. The Logic Theorist, when it has used a particular theorem in connection with a particular method to solve a problem, associates the theorem with that method. The next time it has occasion to use the same method, it tries theorems that have

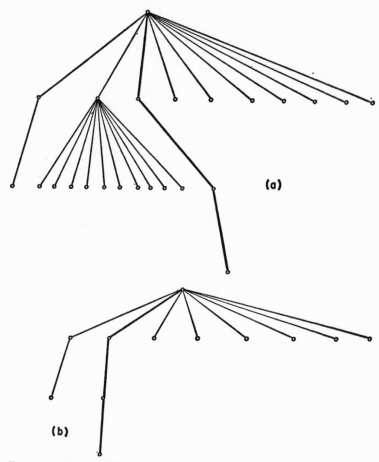

FIGURE 8. (a) Subproblem maze of *2.17 with 20 axioms and theorems in memory, and (b) subproblem maze with 10 axioms and theorems in memory.

had a history of success with that method before it tries the other theorems.

To study the effects of introducing this learning of associations between particular methods and particular theorems, we performed the following experiment. As a *pre-test,* we instructed the Logic Theorist to attempt in sequence the first fifty-two theorems in Chapter 2 of *Principia Mathematica,* allowing it, when attempting a particular theorem, to use all prior theorems (whether it had succeeded in proving them or not), but not to use the special methods learning program. Then, we erased the results of this experience from memory, and as a *test* of the learning, instructed the Theorist to attempt the same fifty-two theorems, this time using the special methods learning program. The main result of the experiment can be seen by comparing the times required by the program to obtain proofs for the twenty theorems that were proved in both pre-test and test and whose proofs were not trivial. (We disregard eighteen additional theorems proved on both runs, but having trival, one-step proofs.)

The abcissa of each point in Figure 9 shows the time re. quired to prove a theorem in the pre-test; the ordinate of that point, the time to prove the same theorem in the test run. The remarkable fact about this scatter diagram is that it consists of two straight lines, each containing about half of the points. For the points on the upper line, almost twice as long was required to discover a proof on the test run as on the pre-test; for the points on the lower line, less than half as long was required on the test as on the pre-test.

Closer examination of the machine's protocols provides a simple explanation. In the test run, the program tried its special high-priority theorems first. Only when these failed—i.e., when the problem was of a new "type" that did not yield to any methods that had worked on previous problems—did the program fall back on its full store of available theorems. The additional time required in the test run for these problems was the time spent in the futile attempt to use the special theorem lists it had learned. On the other hand, where a problem yielded to proof by a method that had worked on a previous problem, this was soon discovered in the test run with a corresponding large improvement in performance. Comparison of the mazes for pre-test and test runs of the latter group of problems reveals the characteristic difference— quite similar to that in Figure 2—between shallow, widely branching trees involving much search in the former case, and deep, sparsely branching trees in the latter.

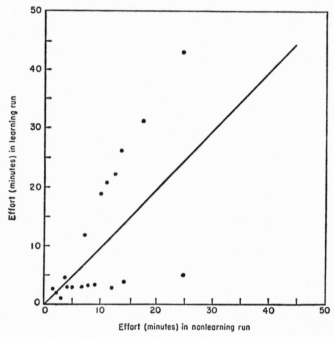

FIGURE 9. Effect of special methods learning on performance.

The Contribution of Hindsight to Heuristics

The learning programs we have mentioned have two important characteristics in common: (1) they consist in a gradual accumulation of selective principles that modify the sequence in which possible solutions will be examined in the problem space; (2) the selective principles are obtained by hindsight—by analysis of the program's successes in its previous problem-solving efforts. We believe that both of these characteristics are to be found in most of the important learning processes in humans. Since we have already discussed the first at length, we will turn next to some comments on the second.

Creative problem-solving is mysterious because it is hard to see how needles are found in haystacks without interminable search. We have tried to dispel the mystery of the performance by

112

exhibiting devices that are capable of narrowing search to a very small part of the haystack. In one sense, however, this only pushes the mystery back. We can now regard the task of learning an effective problem-solving heuristic as itself a problem-solving task. The space of possible heuristics for problem-solving is a space that must be enormous, even as problem spaces go. How do we find solutions in that space? How do we learn effective heuristics?

We must be careful not to overexplain the phenomenon by discovering learning mechanisms far more powerful than would be needed to account for the historical facts of scientific discovery. One of the key heuristics that underlie physical intuition in dynamics is the notion that forces produce changes in velocity (rather than producing velocities). Evidence from which this idea might be derived is available to anyone with eyes. Yet at least hundreds of man-years of search by highly intelligent men were required to discover this idea, and even after it was enunciated by Galileo another century of work was required before even the most intelligent scientists had cleared it of all obscurity and confusion. We have an even better-documented case in chess, where the game had a large literature and numbers of professional players for two centuries or more before Steinitz discovered some of the principles of positional play. From these and other examples we might conclude that the spaces that have to be searched to find important new heuristics are indeed large, and that the heuristics available for searching them are not generally very effective.

With this caution we can return to the question of how learning takes place—granted that it doesn't take place very often or very fast. Let us suppose that the Logic Theorist solves a difficult problem, and that it retains for a time in memory not only the correct path (the proof) that it finally discovered but also a record of the other paths it tried. One could then program it to re-examine some of the choice points at which it had not selected the correct branch of the first trial to look for relations between the state description at that point and characteristics of the correct branch. It could also be programmed to examine expressions just beyond the choice point along correct and incorrect paths in order to determine whether there were consistent differences between the expressions along the correct paths and those along the incorrect. Whatever differentia were discovered by such a program between correct and incorrect paths could be incorporated in the path generator. With the use of such procedures, a single successful experience of solving a problem after much trial-and-error search could become the basis for a great deal of learning.

More formally, suppose we wish to search a space of possible clues to determine which of these clues should be incorporated in a solution generator for maze paths. In terms of our general problem-solving theory we need a clue generator and a clue verifier. Hindsight contributes nothing to the construction of the clue generator, but it provides a cheap and effective verifier, since any possible clue we generate can be tested at once against a considerable number of instances.

We wish to offer a final comment on the "hindsight" aspects of learning. Suppose that, in terms of available computing power, the problem-solving organism can afford to explore only a few hundred paths in searching any particular problem space. Then an effective strategy for dealing with a large class of problems would be to abandon problems that did not yield solutions after moderate effort had been applied, to do learning by hindsight on the easier problems that proved solvable, and thus gradually to add to the number of problems that could be handled successfully.

Assume that we have a class of problems with an initial value of $m = 10$. Then, if the problem-solver had a limit of 500 paths per problem, he would only be able to solve problems of length $k-2$ or less. As learning proceeded, however, the new heuristic would reduce the effective value of m. By the time that m had been reduced to 6, problems of length 3 could be solved; when m reached 2, problems of length 8 could be solved; and reductions of m below an average level of 2 would increase very rapidly the lengths of the problems that could be handled.

CONCLUDING REMARKS

In this chapter we have treated creative activity as problem-solving activity characterized by the novelty and difficulty of the task. We have proposed an explanation for creative problem-solving, developing this explanation along three parallel lines: (1) by constructing an abstract model of problem-solving behavior that provides operational meaning to such concepts as "problem difficulty" and "power of a heuristic"; (2) by specifying programs for digital computers that simulate human problem-solving behavior, and using the abstract model to understand the effectiveness of the programs for solving problems; and (3) by re-examining some of the classical problems in the literature of problem-solving and creativity to see what light the theoretical model, the computer programs, and data on human behavior cast on them.

The main results of our investigations up to the present time are embodied in a number of computer programs, some of which have actually been run on a machine, some of which are coded but have not been run, and some of which are specified at the level of flow diagrams. The computer programs that we have referred to specifically here include: (1) the original program of the Logic Theorist, adapted to proving theorems in Whitehead and Russell's *Principia Mathematica;* (2) a learning program that modifies this basic program, permitting the Logic Theorist to learn to use special methods for special classes of problems; (3) a revision of the Logic Theorist that adapts it to solving logic problems in the form used by O. K. Moore in his experiments with human subjects and that incorporates a program for functional means-end analysis; (4) a supplement to this last program that gives it the capacity to construct plans; (5) a program for a chess-playing machine. A number of other programs that are in process of construction by members of the Carnegie-RAND group and by others are not specifically mentioned here, but have provided some of the background for our theorizing.

Data obtained by comparing in detail the operation of these programs with the behavior of human subjects are limited. We have now accumulated human protocols that will permit such comparison for both the logic and chess programs, but our main tests of the theory have so far been of a grosser sort. We would chiefly rely on the fact that we have specified programs enabling mechanisms to solve complex problems so large that they would not yield to a brute-force approach, using even the most powerful computers. The success of these programs in obtaining problem solutions is the primary evidence for the theory of the problem-solving process that underlies their design.

We should like to stress our specific findings less than the methodology we have described for understanding the human mind. The use of computer programs to simulate information processes allows us to study the behavior of systems of great complexity—far greater complexity than can be handled reliably with either verbal or classical mathematical techniques. We have constructed a theory of human thinking in terms of its underlying information processes, and we have indicated how the theory can give precision to topics that, however important, have in the past been discussed in exceedingly vague terms. We have, for example, identified in the program of the Logic Theorist notions like "grasp of problem structure," "visual image," "abstraction," and "set."

Some of the programs we have described perform work that is considered difficult, and even mildly creative, when it is done by humans. Although these programs fall considerably short in performance of the highest levels of creativity of which humans are capable, there is every reason to suppose that they are qualitatively of the same genus as these more complex human problem-solving processes. In another place, we have predicted that within ten years a computer will discover and prove an important mathematical theorem, and compose music that is regarded as aesthetically significant. On the basis of our experience with the heuristics of logic and chess, we are willing to add the further prediction that only moderate extrapolation is required from the capacities of programs already in existence to achieve the additional problem-solving power needed for such simulation.

116

REFERENCES

de Groot, A. D., *Het Denken van den Schaker* (Amsterdam: Noord-Hallandsche Uitgevers Maatschappij, 1946); *Thinking in Chess* (Rijswijk Z-H: Mouton & Co., to be published 1962 or 1963).

Dineen; G. P., "Programming Pattern Recognition," Proceedings of the Western Joint Computer Conference, Institute of Radio Engineers (1955), pp. 94–100.

Duncker, K., "On Problem-Solving," *Psychol. Monogr.*, 58, 270 (1945).

Johnson, D. M., *The Psychology of Thought and Judgment.* (New York: Harper, 1955).

Moore, O. K. and Scarvia Anderson, "Search Behavior and Problem Solving," *Amer. Sociol. Rev.*, 19 (1954), 702–714.

Newell, A. and J. C. Shaw, "Programming the Logic Theory Machine," Proceedings of the Western Joint Computer Conference, Institute of Radio Engineers (1957).

———, ———, and H. A. Simon, "Empirical Explorations of the Logic Theory Machine: A Case Study in Heuristic," Proceedings of the Western Joint Computer Conference, Institute of Radio Engineers (February 1957).

———, ———, and ———, "Elements of a Theory of Human Problem Solving," *Psychol. Rev.*, 65 (1958a), 151–166.

———, ———, and ———, "Chess-playing Programs and the Problem of Complexity," *J. Res. and Development* (IBM), 2 (1958b), 320–335.

——— and H. A. Simon, "The Logic Theory Machine," IRE Transactions on Information Theory, Vol. IT-2, No. 3 (September 1956).

Patrick, Catherine, "Creative Thought in Poets," *Arch. Psychol.*, 178 (1935).

———, "Creative Thought in Artists," *J. Psychol.*, 4 (1937), 35–73.

Polya, G., *Mathematics and Plausible Reasoning* (Princeton, N. J.: Princeton University Press, 1954).

———, *How to Solve It* (New York: Doubleday, 1957).

Selfridge, O. G., "Pattern Recognition and Modern Computers," Proceedings of the Western Joint Computer Conference, Institute of Radio Engineers (1955), 91–93.

Wallas, G., *The Art of Thought* (New York: Harcourt, 1926).

Whitehead, A. N. and B. Russell, *Principia Mathematica* (Cambridge, England: University Press, 1925–1927).

117

APPENDIX

It may be helpful to the reader, in following the specific examples in the text, to have a brief description of the problem-solving task involving logic expressions that was designed by O. K. Moore and Scarvia B. Anderson.

A logic expression is a sequence of symbols of two types: (1) variables—P, Q, R, and so on—and (2) connectives—not (–), and ($\cdot$), or ($\vee$), and implies ($\supset$). An example from the text is $R \cdot (-P \supset Q)$, which may be interpreted as "R and (not P implies Q)." The subjects are not provided with this interpretation, however, but are told that the expressions are code messages and that the connectives are named "tilde" (–), "dot" ($\cdot$), "wedge" ($\vee$), and "horseshoe" ($\supset$).

The following rules are provided for transforming one or two given logic expressions into a new expression (recoding expressions). We will state them here only approximately, omitting certain necessary qualifications.

One-Line Rules

1. $A \vee B \Longleftrightarrow B \vee A$
   $A \cdot B \Longleftrightarrow B \cdot A$
2. $A \supset B \Longleftrightarrow -B \supset -A$
3. $A \vee A \Longleftrightarrow A$
   $A \cdot A \Longleftrightarrow A$
4. $A \vee (B \cdot C) \Longleftrightarrow (A \vee B) \vee C$
   $A \cdot (B \cdot C) \Longleftrightarrow (A \cdot B) \cdot C$

5. $A \vee B = -(-A \cdot -B)$
   $A \cdot B = -(-A \vee -B)$
6. $A \supset B \Longleftrightarrow -A \vee B$
   $A \vee B \Longleftrightarrow -A \supset B$
7. $A \vee (B \cdot C) \Longleftrightarrow (A \vee B) \cdot (A \vee C)$
   $A \cdot (B \vee C) \Longleftrightarrow (A \cdot B) \vee (A \cdot C)$
8. $A \cdot B \Longrightarrow A$
   $A \cdot B \Longrightarrow B$
9. $A \Longrightarrow A \vee X$, where X is any expression

The rules can be applied to complete expressions, or (except rule 8) to subexpressions. Double tildes cancel—i.e., $-- A \Longleftrightarrow A$, but this cancellation is not stated in a separate rule.

Two-Line Rules

10. If A and B are given, they can be recoded into $A \cdot B$.
11. If A and $A \supset B$ are given, they can be recoded into B.
12. If $A \supset B$ and $B \supset C$ are given, they can be recoded into $A \supset C$.

Subjects were instructed in the use of these rules, then were given problems like those described in the text. They were asked to think aloud while working on the problems, and each time they applied a rule to recode one or two given expressions, the new expression was written on the blackboard by the experimenter, together with the numbers of the expressions and rule used to obtain it.

By inspection of the rules it can be seen that in the planning space, where connectives and the order of the symbols are disregarded, rules 1, 2, 5 and 6 would leave expressions unchanged. These are the inessential rules; the others, in altered form, become the essential rules. Rule 8, for example, becomes simply: $AB \Rightarrow A$.

4

CONFORMITY AND
CREATIVE THINKING

RICHARD S. CRUTCHFIELD
University of California, Berkeley

In his essay "Self-Reliance," Emerson (1841) comments on the antipathy of conformity and creativity. "The virtue in most regard," he writes, "is conformity. Self-reliance is its aversion. It loves not realities and creators. . . ."

Two key words in this passage offer a clue to the inherent opposition of conformity and creative thinking. One word is "self-reliance." Conformity, involving loss of self-reliance, undermines the person's creative powers by weakening his trust in the essential validity of his own processes of thought and imagination.

The other word is "realities." Conformity inhibits the person's ability to sense and grasp basic reality, and the loss of this contact with reality is fatal to creative thinking. In short, conformity tends to destroy creativity by alienating the creator both from reliance on his own thought processes, and from contact with basic reality.

We shall try to throw some light on the particular processes through which conformity pressures on the individual do in fact produce their detrimental effects. The first general point to be made is that conformity pressures tend to elicit kinds of *motivation* in the individual that are incompatible with the creative process. The second general point, for which empirical evidence will presently be provided, is that high susceptibility by the individual to conformity pressures tends to be associated with certain *personality traits* that are detrimental to creative thinking.

MOTIVATIONS OF THE CREATIVE ACT

Consider the following questions about the motivations of the creative act and the essential requirements for its success: What motives impel the creative act? Is the creative act merely a means in the service of other ends, or is it sought as an end in itself? How does the nature of the motivation for a given creative act affect the likelihood of its achievement?

It seems perfectly clear that the underlying motivations are many and complex, varying widely with the nature of the situation and the nature of the person. The person may be driven to create by needs for material gain, such as money or promotion in his job. He may be driven by needs for status or for affiliation with others. He may be driven by needs for self-enhancement or self-defense. In all these cases, the particular need has merely extrinsic and arbitrary relation to the inherent nature of the specific creative task. The achievement of the creative solution is a *means* to an ulterior end, rather than the end in itself. We may refer to such cases as ones of *extrinsic, ego-involved* motivation for creative thinking.

In clear contrast is that motive which has to do with the intrinsic value in the attaining of the creative solution itself. Here the problem is perceived as inherently challenging, the person is "caught" by it and compelled to be immersed in it, and with achievement of a solution the creator is "by joy possessed." Like Harlow's monkeys, who solve problems for the "fun"

121

of it (1950), the creative man may invent a new device, paint a picture, or construct a scientific theory for the sheer intrinsic pleasures involved—pleasures in the creative process, in the attaining of a solution, and often also in the aesthetic satisfactions of achieving an "elegant" solution. This, then, is the kind of motivation in which the creative act is an *end*, not a means. We may refer to this as *intrinsic, task-involved* motivation for creative thinking.

In order to clarify the meaning of such intrinsic motivation, we should emphasize what it is not. For one thing, task-involvement in the creative act is not the same as the person's seeking to achieve "creativity" *per se* as his goal. The latter is merely a form of ego-need in which the person strives to create in order to fulfill a certain self-conception—or a conception by others—that he is a "creative person." Such deliberate strivings to be "creative" are not likely to be conducive to genuine creativity. The person who is too self-consciously bent on being a "creator" is not apt to succeed. His primary fixation is upon the outer shell of the creative act, rather than upon the inherent challenge it offers. Just because such strivings to be "creative" are mainly in the service of persistent ego demands they often become insatiable, even though they may be unrealistically related to the person's particular talents and situation. The person who develops such insatiable and unrealizable cravings to be recognized as "creative" may, as a consequence, come to be especially sensitive to and dependent upon the standards and values dictated by his particular "creativity" reference group. And this increased susceptibility of the person to conformity pressures from the group may serve further to inhibit the very creativity that he insatiably seeks.

Nor can we regard a *need for self-expression* as being properly in the nature of intrinsic, task-involved creative motivation. The person who sets out to create something in order to "express himself" is unlikely to create notably. The aim is too self-conscious, too ego-oriented. To be sure, the genuine creative act is necessarily expressive of the person—this is indeed one of the main points we wish to stress—but this is not a matter of its being explicitly directed at *self*-expression. The truly creative act reflects a spontanous, unpremeditated, outwardly manifested expression of the person's processes.

Although up to this point we have sharply separated the extrinsic, ego-involved and the intrinsic, task-involved motivations for creativity, we must not overlook their intimate functional connection. Task-inspired creative activities readily arouse and enlist accessory ego-needs which can help sustain the person's contact with and efforts on the task, or may divert him from its achievement. Conversely, ego-involved motives often pave the way for the emergence of the intrinsic motives in the creative task itself. For a person to be properly "caught" by a problem, fully immersed in it, usually requires that he be sufficiently exposed to it and kept in contact with it until its "autonomous forces" take over. It is often the needs for self-enhancement or self-defense, the needs for status and prestige, the needs for social affiliation, the needs for material gain, that first bring him to grips with the problem.

It is in this sense that necessity is the mother of invention. But necessity alone is not sufficient to bring about the creative solution—indeed, too much necessity may only inhibit. What is also required is the *father* of invention—unduly neglected in many accounts of the creative process. Jerome Bruner comments on a possible solution of this ancient paternity question:

> Most recently E. M. Forster has suggested that the father was Pan, and practically every writer that I have come upon who has posed this question for himself—and this includes many—has had the idea that somehow it was a wayward minstrel, that it was play- fulness, the playful aspect of the male as compared with the exigent characteristic of the female.

The crucial significance of the distinction between ego- involved and task-involved motivations for the creative act can be expressed in the hypothesis that the quantity and quality of crea- tive acts will, in general, be higher under conditions of task- involvement than under conditions of ego-involvement.

Consider for a moment the essential requirements for crea- tive thinking, and how they may be affected by motivational fac- tors. In brief, the creative solution involves the emergence of a new and "fitting" organization of the elements of the problem. Almost invariably this first necessitates the setting aside of a previous and inadequate organization. To achieve this the creator must break free of the powerful constraints of habitual thought, of stereotyped perception. Barriers to creative solution often occur just at this point where the person fails to overcome these powerful constraints.

There is a large body of laboratory and clinical evidence indicating that ego-involvement, as compared with task-involvement, is detrimental to cognitive functioning. When there is intensely aroused motivation, especially when it is predominantly ego-involved with widespread emotional reverberations in the person, adaptive cognitive processes tend to become more inflexible. Like Maier's frustrated rats in the discrimination box (1940), the anxious person becomes more strongly fixated upon habitual modes of perception and thought, less capable of putting aside these inadequate organizations of the problem to prepare the way for cognitive restructuring.

But even being able to gain freedom from the constraints of the old is not alone sufficient to guarantee a creative solution. There must also, of course, be the production by the person of something original and "fitting," appropriate to replace the old. Exactly *how* such original ideas come into being is still an unsolved mystery. It most often seems to the person that the new idea simply "spontaneously emerges," and that it cannot be arbitrarily "forced." This offers another clue to why intense motivation, especially that which is ego-involved, may be detrimental to creative thinking.

It may be suggested that one source of original ideas lies in the ready accessibility to the thinker of many rich and subtle "physiognomic" attributes of the percepts and concepts in his mental world and to the metaphorical and analogical penumbras extending out from their more explicit, literal, or purely logical features. For it is partly through a sensitivity to such physiognomic and metaphorical qualities that new and "fitting" combinatorial possibilities among the elements of a problem may unexpectedly emerge. What is often required is the kind of fresh, spontaneous, childlike mode of perception that sometimes vividly characterizes the man of genius, an ability where necessary to go beyond the stereotyped and narrower kind of "objective" reality which is denuded of metaphorical and physiognomic qualities.

124

This openness to contact with fullest reality, essential for creativity, is presumably diminished through the effects of certain kinds of motivational states, especially those of intense ego-involvement. Under these conditions the self occupies a predominant place in the psychological field, and the person's defenses are actively engaged. The result tends to be a constriction of the range of immediate experience, a reduction in spontaneity, an isolation of cognitive processes from their natural affective contexts, a defensive over-intellectualization, and so forth.

To recapitulate: in problem-solving, it appears that extrinsic, ego-involved motivations, as contrasted with intrinsic, task-involved motivations, are detrimental both to the ability of the creator to free himself from the constraints of old ways of thought and to his capacity to produce original insights.

In the light of this, part of the reason that *conformity* pressures may be expected to be injurious to creative thinking now becomes somewhat clearer. The outer pressure and inner compulsion to conform arouse extrinsic, ego-involved motives in the problem solver. His main efforts tend to become directed toward the goals of being accepted and rewarded by the group, of avoiding rejection and punishment. The solution of the problem itself becomes of secondary relevance, and his task-involved motivation diminishes. In being concerned with goals extrinsic to the task itself, and particularly as rendered anxious about potential threats in the situation, his cognitive processes become less flexible, his insights less sensitive.

Moreover, as we shall now see, persons who are especially susceptible to conformity pressures, and to the extrinsic motivations they evoke, tend to have other personality characteristics that are deleterious for creative thinking.

THE NATURE OF CONFORMITY

The term *conformity* as used in this discussion is to be understood as having only the meaning explicitly defined in the following way. When an individual is required to express a judgment in a group situation, and when his own private conviction on the matter is clearly at variance with the expressed consensus of the rest of the group, he is thereby placed in a conflict. There are two main courses of action open to him: he may announce his own deviant judgment, thus remaining *independent* of the group consensus; or he may express agreement with the group judgment, thus *conforming*. Therefore conformity, as discussed here, is not mere conventionality or social uniformity of behavior. Its essence is that the individual yields to the pressure of contrary group opinion. This need not imply that the group tries actually to force the individual to comply; the conformity may occur only out of the individual's inner compulsion to agree with the group.

There are important differences in type and nature of conformity behavior under varying circumstances and in different persons. In one basic type of conforming the person is brought to comply with the group through a weakened conviction about his own judgment, a readiness to assume that the group is right and he is wrong. Conforming in this case involves some degree of shift of the individual's private judgment, as well as of his outwardly expressed judgment, toward that of the group. In another main type of "expedient" conformity, the person chooses deliberately to express outward agreement with the group even though his inner judgment remains uninfluenced.

There are also important differences in the nature of several forms of noncomformity behavior, where the person is not induced to express agreement with the group view. There are cases of "true" independence in which the person is, through strong inner conviction and self-confidence, capable of holding to and expressing his own independent judgments unimpaired by the opposition of the group opinion. And there are other cases in which resistance to the group pressure is not this "true" independence, but is in the form of a reaction against the group— the person *is* actually influenced by the group pressure, but in a contrary direction. His motivation is not for the firm, independent adherence to what his judgmental processes seem validly to tell him; instead it involves a repudiation of or attack upon the group, a deliberate dissent that may better be termed *counter*formity than nonconformity.

Bearing in mind these considerations about the nature

and meaning of conformity, we turn now to a review of the results of a series of studies that I have carried out during the past few years at the Institute of Personality Assessment and Research in Berkeley (Crutchfield, 1955, 1959). These studies have made use of an experimental technique for the standardized measurement of conformity tendencies in the individual.

MEASUREMENT OF CONFORMITY TENDENCIES

In this technique persons are tested in groups of five, without knowledge of the purpose of the task. They are required to make individual judgments of a series of stimuli presented to the group by the experimenter. Although the five persons sit together during the task, they are not permitted to speak with one another. Instead they can communicate only indirectly by means of an electrical signal network.

The five persons sit side by side in five partly closed booths, each person facing his own switchboard. Slides are projected on the wall in front of the group, each slide presenting stimuli to be judged. For example, one item is to judge which of two simple geometrical figures is the larger. Each person signals his individual judgment by closing one of a row of numbered switches on his board. Also displayed on his board are signal lights which flash on to let him know the judgments being made by each of the other four group members. The persons are instructed that they must wait their proper turn before signalling their judgments, the serial order of responding being designated by the letter of the booth. Thus, the person in booth *A* is to go first, then the person in booth *B*, then *C*, then *D*, and finally *E*.

Now, though this is how the five persons are led to understand the situation, they are actually being grossly deceived by the experimenter. The sequence of flashing lights on each of the boards is not really produced by the responses made by the other group members. The signals are in fact manipulated entirely by the experimenter through a master switchboard. There is really no connection at all among the five switchboards of the subjects.

127

Through this deception, the experimenter is able to counterfeit plausible sequences of judgments on the subjects' boards, thus convincing them that they are observing the authentic judgments of their fellows. Identical false information is fed simultaneously to all five boards; this is possible because all five boards are labelled as *E*. In short, the technique enables the experimenter to confront all five persons at each step throughout the test session with a same standard series of faked "group" judgments.

At certain points throughout the series of slides, group pressure is applied. This is done simply by making it appear that all the first four members to respond—*A, B, C,* and *D*—agree on an answer which is really wrong. For example, one of the slides calls for a judgment of the relative areas of a circle and a star figure, the circle being clearly the larger. The experimenter makes it appear that each of the first four members judged the *star* as the larger, though to each of five naive subjects it would normally seem obvious that the circle is the larger. Confronted by this sharp discrepancy between his own perception and that of the group, the person may make one of two possible responses: he may independently give the correct answer as he really sees it, despite the unanimous group consensus against him, or he may conform to the false group consensus.

During a test session as many as fifty such critical pressure items are exposed. The stimuli vary widely in type, ranging from easy perceptual judgments and matters of objective fact and logic to complex attitudes and opinions on difficult issues. Thus, it is possible to establish not only a total conformity score for each person but also sub-scores pertaining to the extent of conformity on varying types of judgments—objective versus attitudinal, easy versus difficult, important versus unimportant, and so forth.

FINDINGS ON CONFORMING BEHAVIOR

This standard measurement technique has been administered to more than 600 persons, varying in age, education, occupation, social class, intelligence, and personality characteristics,

128

under a number of systematically varied experimental conditions. These individuals were assessed by the Institute in studies of superior professional and academic groups.

It is found that these various populations of persons differ markedly in the average amount of conformity behavior induced in them by the test procedure. The comparative percentage scores presented in Table 1 are based on a standard set of twelve objective items, including judgments of visual stimuli, of vocabulary terms, of completions of arithmetic series, and so forth. Some of the items are easy, some are difficult or ambiguous, others are of intermediate difficulty. The range of possible scores runs from zero per cent conformity to 100% conformity, that is, from yielding to the false group consensus on none of the items to yielding on every one of the twelve items.

TABLE 1. Comparative Conformity Scores among Various Groups

Group	Number of Persons	Average Conformity Score *	Range of Individual Conformity Scores
Males			
Military officers	50	33%	0–100%
College sophomores	53	26%	0–100%
Senior honors students in engineering	30	20%	0– 83%
Research scientists in industry	45	14%	0– 58%
Females			
College sophomores	80	38%	0–100%
College seniors	24	32%	0– 83%
College alumnae	50	22%	0–100%

* The conformity score is the percentage of items out of a standard set of 12 objective-type items on which there was yielding to the group pressure of a false answer.

Among male samples, the most conforming of those studied is a group of fifty military officers, whose average yielding score is 33%. In descending order of conforming, then, come college sophomores (26%), and senior honor students in engineering (20%). Most independent of all is a group of high-level research scientists working in industry, whose average conformity score is only 14%.

RICHARD S. CRUTCHFIELD

Among female samples, the most conforming of those studied are college sophomores (38%). Considerably less conforming is a group of college seniors (32%). And least conforming of all is a group of middle-aged alumnae from a prestige women's college (22%).

These comparative conformity scores seem to be reasonably consistent with what we would expect to be the relative levels of creative ability of these groups, the relationship, of course, being inverse. Thus, among males the well-selected research scientists, who show themselves the most independent in the conformity test procedure, are presumably relatively the highest in creativity. The senior honors students might be expected to come next highest in creative ability and the unselected college sophomores considerably lower. Military officers, it would seem reasonable to guess, are not mainly selected for creativity.

Among the female samples, too, the relationship appears consistent, with the most conforming group—the unselected sophomore women—presumably being lowest in creative ability.

There appears, moreover, to be a significant though not pronounced tendency for females to be more conforming than males in the test procedure. The most direct comparison available is that between the male and female college sophomore (26% versus 38%). This difference in conformity in favor of the male would appear to be consistent in direction with the common assertion that males are, on the average, more creative than females. But it should be emphasized that such simple comparisons of the average conformity scores of female and male subjects are of questionable value. Although the details cannot be given here, there appears to be convincing evidence from the analysis of the conformity behavior in the test procedure that the processes underlying conformity to group pressure in males are strikingly different from what they are in females. For example, patterns of personality correlates of conformity behavior differ markedly in many respects for the two sexes.

Indeed, not only is such simple comparison of average conformity scores in males and females of dubious value for inferences about the relation of conformity and creativity; so too

130

are the kinds of comparisons we have made above among the various male samples and female samples themselves. It is quite clear that these various groups differ in a great many other respects; the parallelism observed between average amount of conformity and the judged level of creative ability of the groups may be mere artifact.

A better approach is through the comparison of individuals *within* each of these groups. Shown in Table 1 is the range in individual conformity scores for each sample studied. It will be seen that even more striking than the differences in average conformity scores among the various groups are the enormous individual differences within each group. In every sample there are some individuals who show zero conformity and some who show almost complete conformity on the twelve test items. (The one partial exception is the group of research scientists in which the highest conformity score is 58%.) It should be noted that in the standard test procedure the individual is always tested with four of his peers. Hence, the individual conformity scores are properly comparable in that each person is alike subjected to the pressure of group opinion which he believes to come from other persons of his own status.

PERSONALITY CORRELATES OF CONFORMITY

Inasmuch as there proves to be a considerable degree of individual consistency in the level of conformity manifested over a wide range of items, it is feasible to correlate conformity scores with the great variety of personality variables measured in assessment, and thus to ascertain some features of the personality of the typical conforming person, and of the typical independent person. Without mention of detailed findings in the particular studies, we can briefly summarize those of the personality characteristics found to be significantly associated with conformity that have obvious relevance for the creative process. It should be mentioned that the evidence for each of these main personality characteristics is based not on a single measure but on multiple measures, including objective test scores, and on ratings by the

131

assessment staff made in complete ignorance of the subject's performance in the conformity procedure.

Intellectual functioning. The conformists prove to be significantly less intelligent than the independent persons. Moreover, they show tendencies toward rigidity of cognitive processes and poverty of ideas, as contrasted with the greater cognitive flexibility and ideational fluency found in the independent persons.

Motivational and emotional functioning. The conformists are clearly lower in ego-strength and in ability to cope with stress. They exhibit more emotional constriction, lack of spontaneity, repression of impulse, and tendency toward indirect expression of hostility. They are more anxious.

Self-conception. The conformists are inclined toward pronounced feelings of personal inferiority and inadequacy. They lack self-confidence. Moreover, they tend to be less insightful and realistic in their self-conceptions than are the independent persons.

Relations with others. The conformists exhibit a strong sociocentric orientation, and an intense preoccupation with other people, as contrasted with the more self-contained, autonomous attitude of the independent persons. The interpersonal behavior of the conformists tends to show far more in the way of passivity, suggestibility, and dependence toward others, while at the same time there is considerable evidence of disturbed and distrustful attitudes toward other people. Moreover, the conformist proves to be inferior to the independent person in social acuity, that is, in his ability to judge other people's reactions correctly.

Personal attitudes and values. The conformists express attitudes and values of a far more conventional and moralistic nature than do the independent persons. Often this is coupled with a somewhat rigid and authoritarian outlook.

It seems undeniable that the differentiated pictures of the personalities of the conforming individual and the independent individual revealed in the above findings bear remarkable resemblance to many of the critically distinguishing features that are commonly thought to set off the noncreative from the creative person. Here then is strong supporting evidence for the antithetical relationship of conformity and creativity.

Even more direct evidence on the point is emerging from a number of current studies, which are part of a program of research on creativity [1] at the Institute of Personality Assessment and Research. The data reported here pertain only to that limited aspect of these studies bearing directly on the conformity-creativity question.

STUDIES OF CREATIVE PERSONS

The first study involves the intensive personality assessment of forty-five research scientists working in industrial laboratories on such problems as missile development.[2] These men were all engaged in full-time research activities, and information collected following the assessments indicate that they represent a range of moderate to high creativity as scientists. Twenty-eight of them hold Ph.D.'s in physics, mathematics, or engineering. Their ages range from twenty-five to fifty-four. As one part of the intensive assessment the standard conformity procedure was administered. As we have already indicated in discussing group differences, the average amount of conforming in these research scientists was relatively low, being only 14% on the standard set of twelve objective items. Yet even within this superior group the range of individual differences in conformity is large, with some of the scientists conforming to as many as seven of the twelve bogus group judgments and others conforming to none.

We can ask, then, how these wide individual differences in conformity scores may relate to differences in the degree of creative ability. For obviously, even though the general level of creativity in these scientists is unquestionably high, there are doubtless still some differences among them in the amount manifested. One preliminary approach to the question is through use of the assessment staff's rating of "originality" on each man. Shown in Table 2 are the average conformity scores for the seventeen men rated highest in originality and for the seventeen men rated lowest in

1 Supported in part by a grant from the Carnegie Corporation of New York.
2 The study is under the direction of Harrison G. Gough. For a preliminary description of the study, see Gough and Woodworth (1960).

originality. (Those falling just in the center of the rating scale have been omitted.) The difference is in the hypothesized direction, the more "original" scientists being the less conforming.

TABLE 2. Relation of Conformity Scores to Ratings of Creativity

Group	Number of Persons	Average Conformity Score *
Research scientists in industry		
Those more highly rated on "originality"	17	10%
Those less highly rated on "originality"	17	18%
Senior college women		
Those nominated as high in "creativity"	12	23%
Those not nominated as high in "creativity"	12	41%

* The conformity score is the percentage of items out of a standard set of 12 objective-type items on which there was yielding to the group pressure of a false answer.

The second study is of twenty-four seniors at Mills College.[3] The faculty was asked to nominate those senior women regarded as outstanding in creative ability. Twelve of those nominated—whose fields of study varied from the sciences to the humanities—participated in an intensive personality assessment. A comparison group of twelve seniors, matched with the creative group for field of study, was selected at random from the rest of the senior class, and similarly assessed. The standard conformity test procedure was included in the assessment. As Table 2 shows, the average conformity score in the "creative" group is markedly lower than in the comparison group. It should be noted that this difference cannot be ascribed simply to differences in intellectual capacity; the "creative" and the comparison groups do not differ significantly in intelligence test scores.

The third study is of forty American architects, nominated as being among the most highly creative in their profession.[4] A "conformity" scale was empirically constructed of those items of a personality inventory significantly differentiating between the architects who yielded most to the experimental group pressure

[3] The study is under the direction of Ravenna M. Helson.
[4] This study is under the direction of Donald W. MacKinnon. For an account of some of the findings of the study, see MacKinnon (1962).

and those who yielded least. When this "conformity" scale was then administered to a sample of eighty-four architects *not* nominated for creativity, the mean score was found to be significantly higher than that in the sample of forty creative architects. Creativity in architects, clearly, is related to the ability to resist group pressure.

Taken together, these findings from current studies of creative persons and the other findings on personality attributes of conformists offer consistent evidence for a significant empirical relationship between conformity tendencies in the person and lack of manifest creativity. How may we account for this relationship?

CREATIVITY AND THE CONFORMIST

We have already indicated one probable basis of the inhibition of creativity in the conformist. The motivations that are aroused in him by the outer pressure and inner compulsion to conform are ego-involved motives.

Moreover, as we have previously seen, the extreme conformist tends generally to be more anxious, insistent on securing a safe and stable environment, desirous of avoiding uncertainty and ambiguity at any cost. He seeks strong anchors in his world, and the group is usually prepared to offer him such strong anchors in the form of undeviating acceptance of its judgments and its established beliefs.

We have also seen that the extreme conformist tends to be assailed by doubts concerning himself and his personal adequacy. This makes him timid about expressing his ideas when they diverge from the group's, hesitant to expose them to critical group scrutiny. Faced with a choice between the validity of his own thought processes and those of others, he tends to default on his own and to defer to the others. He is readily demoralized in the face of what seems to him the superior wisdom of the group; that he sometimes finds himself out of step with the group judgment serves as added proof of his own inadequacy and may further attack his sense of personal worth and resolution.

Being anxious and insecure, lacking basic self-confidence, the conformist may fear the challenge that creativity offers, fear that he will not measure up to what it requires of his abilities. He may therefore seek to avoid exposing himself nakedly to the actuality of the creative try. In such cases, group pressures toward conformity may even sometimes be in an underlying way really *welcome* to him, in that they reinforce his defenses against the creative try. Such "escape from creativity" can be especially pronounced when the entire group shares something of this fear of the creative act. For its standards may then tend to become the standards of *not creating*. Just as industrial piece-work groups can impose reduced norms of quantity output on all the members in the interests of maintaining rate scales, so can other kinds of higher-level groups working on more complex tasks come insidiously to impose negative sanctions that inhibit the creativity of all the members (a phenomenon not unknown even in academic institutions).

So far we have been discussing that principal type of conformist who lacks ego-strength, is anxious and suggestible, is overly dependent on the emotional support of other people. But what about the effects of conformity on creativity in another, quite different kind of person—one who is brought by group pressure to express *outward* agreement with the group, while his private judgment remains unaffected? These "expedient" conformers are presumably not prevented in their inner thinking from seeking for creative solutions, despite the group pressure. But there may nevertheless be some deleterious effects of the group pressure on their creativity. For one thing, when working in the group setting within which much of an individual's creative activity takes place, the expedient conformist avoids exposing his deviant view to the group, thereby causing both a loss of his potentially productive ideas to the group as a whole, and a handicap to his own thinking through the inability to validate or correct his ideas with the aid of the group's appraisal.

Moreover, it would seem likely that the repeated act of outer acquiescence may in due course be accompanied by a growing disposition to conform inwardly as well. In Festinger's (1957) term, the "cognitive dissonance" between one's outer behavior and one's inner belief causes changes directed toward reducing this dissonance. If the strong disposition of the expedient conformist toward outward agreement with the group cannot readily be changed, then the inner judgment may have to yield.

On the other hand, the fate of the privately-held deviant opinion depends greatly upon what psychic supports the person may find for his view among other people, and upon what other group outlets for expression he may have. Asch (1952) has found, for example, that yielding to group pressure is significantly lessened if the dissident individual believes that he has the support of at least one other member of the group. And it has often been pointed out that because of the support of his other group identifications—with both actual and reference groups—the dissident individual may be able to hold fast to his views even though they are unpopular in the immediate group where he is under pressure.

CREATIVITY AND THE COUNTERFORMIST

Group pressures may also, we have earlier said, have quite the reverse effect from that of inducing conformity. Some individuals are driven to react *negatively* to the group, to rebel against it, to repudiate its standards. They are actively contrasuggestible. We may call them *counterformists,* in order to distinguish them both from conformists and from those nonconformists whom we have termed "true independents." The motivations impelling the counterformist involve needs for defending his personal identity, becoming emancipated from the group's authority, expressing hostile impulses toward others. All these are manifestly ego-involved motivations, and, as such, can be expected to impair his creative efforts.

Moreover, because of his compulsive drive to deviate from the group, the counterformist strives for "difference for difference's sake." He often deliberately seeks to acquire the discernible marks of the nonconformist—the Bohemian mode, the affectation of the bizarre and the outrageous. Thus, his creative efforts may often be directed at the mere superficial outer appearances of the creative act and product rather than at its inner requiredness, with a resultant loss of sensitivity to true creative merit.

Paradoxically, society or certain segments of society may, under some circumstances, choose to *reward* rather than to outlaw these deviant and dubious products of the counterformist. The painter with the new and "different" technique may become wildly fashionable; the purveyor of shockingly iconoclastic notions may become the momentary darling of society. Such rewards for deviation into what are essentially spurious creative acts are likely eventually to corrupt whatever genuine creative impulses the individual possesses. Thus, the group through assigning the counterformist an "official" and rewarded social role of dissident may sometimes in the end reenvelop him. This is one of society's ways of "decontaminating the deviant."

Finally, there is another important way in which extreme counterformity can impair the person's creative thinking. Through being driven to repudiate the group standards in order to serve his compulsive ego-needs, he is thereby led to an *alienation* of his own judgments from that reservoir of group thinking that may be valuable or indispensable for his own creative solutions. By indiscriminately rejecting everything that the group believes, he may end up as badly off as the utter conformist who indiscriminately accepts everything that the group believes. In our studies of conformity there is fragmentary evidence confirming this effect. Some subjects who prove to be highly contrasuggestible to the group pressure also come at later stages in the test series to be caught in the trap of stating judgments which deviate from the alleged group consensus *even on those items where the bogus group judgment is clearly correct.* In short, the counterformist can become fatally cut off from the social source of that *consensual* validation of creative productions which is essential to the creative process.

We have seen, then, that excessive conformity and counterformity alike can impair creativity. This is but one aspect of the larger question of how creativity is affected by the individual's relations to the group. Creative work necessarily occurs within a social context, stimulated by social requirements, evaluated by social standards. Hence, the group has the potentiality for favorable as well as for unfavorable influences on the creative processes of the individual. Being concerned mainly with the problem of the conformist (and the counterformist), our emphasis has naturally been upon the *negative* effects of the group. But we have also noted earlier that under the pressure of group opinion in the test procedure some individuals behave neither as conformists nor as counterformists; they demonstrate instead a capacity to arrive independently at their own judgments.

CREATIVITY AND THE INDEPENDENT THINKER

It is such a truly independent thinker who is best able to benefit from the favorable contributions of society and the group and to avoid the unfavorable. He succeeds in maintaining an optimal balance between self-reliance and group identifications, between his own views and the view of the group. On the one hand he escapes the oversocialization of the extreme conformist, involving as it does a susceptibility to the violation of the validity of one's own experience, a betrayal of one's own processes of thought and judgment. And, on the other hand, the truly independent person does achieve a sufficient degree of socialization, the absence of which in the extreme counterformist undermines his creative efforts by divorcing him from the essential resources of society's thinking. Indeed, the independent person is often highly conventional in those ways of social behavior that facilitate life in the group and yet do not impede his own aims. The truly independent person—in whom creative thinking is at its best— is someone who can accept society without denying himself.

Having begun with a passage from Emerson, whose concern was for the integrity of the self-reliant creator in opposition to the group, it may be fitting to end with a statement made by Albert Camus (1958) on the occasion of his acceptance of the Nobel Prize for Literature. Camus, too, saw the creator as one who must resist pressures to conform. Speaking of the role of the writer, he said:

> Whatever our personal frailities may be, the nobility of our call- ing will always be rooted in two commitments difficult to observe: refusal to lie about what we know and resistance to oppression.

139

RICHARD S. CRUTCHFIELD

But Camus was also fully conscious of the essential relation of the creator to his larger human society. He wrote:

> And the man who, as often happens, chose the path of art because he was aware of his difference soon learns that he can nourish his art, and his difference, solely by admitting his resemblance to all. The artist fashions himself in that ceaseless oscillation from himself to others, midway between the beauty he cannot do without and the community from which he cannot tear himself. This is why true artists scorn nothing. They force themselves to understand instead of judging. And if they are to take sides in this world, they can do so only with a society in which, according to Nietzsche's profound words, the judge will yield to the creator. . . .

REFERENCES

Asch, S. E., *Social Psychology* (Englewood Cliffs, N. J.: Prentice-Hall, 1952).

Camus, A., "Camus at Stockholm: The acceptance of the Nobel Prize," *Atlantic Monthly,* 201 (May 1958), 33–34).

Crutchfield, R. S., "Conformity and Character," *Amer. Psychol.,* 10 (1955), 191–198.

———, "Personal and Situational Factors in Conformity to Group Pressure," *Acta Psychologica,* 15 (1959), 386–388.

Emerson, R. W., *Essays* (Boston: J. Munroe, 1841).

Festinger, L., *A Theory of Cognitive Dissonance* (Evanston, Ill.: Row, Peterson, 1957).

Gough, H. G. and D. G. Woodworth, "Stylistic Variations among Professional Research Scientists," *J. Psychol.,* 49 (1960), 87–98.

Harlow, H. F., M. K. Harlow, and D. R. Meyer, "Learning Motivated by a Manipulation Drive," *J. exp. Psychol.,* 40 (1950), 228–234.

MacKinnon, D. W., "The Personality Correlates of Creativity: A Study of American Architects," *Proceedings of the XIVth International Congress of Applied Psychology,* 1962.

Maier, N. R. F., "Studies of Abnormal Behavior in the Rat, III: The Development of Behavior Fixation through Frustration," *J. exp. Psychol.,* 26 (1940), 521–546.

5

ON THE PSYCHODYNAMICS
OF CREATIVE
PHYSICAL SCIENTISTS

DAVID C. McCLELLAND
Harvard University

The persistent curiosity of the creative physical scientist presents a challenge to psychologists interested in human motivation. Why is it that some men spend their entire lives in an unceasing effort to penetrate the secrets of the universe? Certainly they must have brains and a good store of scientific knowledge to draw on, but so do many people in our day and age. Why are a few called to intense devotion to such a task? What turns them first to natural science? Is it a single common factor or several factors operating differently on different individuals? The path of least resistance is to believe that a series of "fortunate accidents," different for each case, turns a man toward science, but the psychologist is after all a scientist too; he is not likely to rest content until he has exhausted all possibilities of finding a common explanation for a common effect—namely, scientific curiosity. While there are, of course, many other fields of creative endeavor, the paper will be restricted largely to the motivational makings of physical scientists.

By now the psychologist has conducted an impressive number of investigations into the characteristics of physical scientists, nearly all summarized in one place: the report of a Research Conference on the Identification of Creative Scientific Talent held at the University of Utah in 1955 (Taylor, 1956). It is worth reviewing them briefly here to show the variety and extent of the research that is already available to anyone wanting to study the motivation of physical scientists.

Knapp (1952, 1956, 1957), with a variety of collaborators, has conducted studies on the collegiate origins of American scientists, on the characteristics of scientists in Thorndike's ratings of eminent men, and on the differences between science and nonscience concentrators in college in terms of various backgroud variables and the Blacky and Thematic Apperception Tests. Stein (1956) and his associates have been studying intensively the differences between creative and noncreative industrial chemists as reflected in a considerable variety of personality tests. Cattell and Drevdahl (1955) have compared factor scores on objective personality tests of physicists who are teachers, administrators, or researchers with the scores made either by the general public or by a college population on the same tests. McClelland (1956) has presented a content analysis of the answer keys of the Strong Vocational Interest Blank showing how physical scientists differ in their interests from men in general. Data of a unique kind have been summarized by Terman (1954), who followed the careers of a large number of intellectually gifted children for thirty years after he first identified them around the age of ten. Among his subjects he found fifty-one individuals who later went into basic research in one of the physical sciences. These he has compared with engineers, medical-biological scientists, those who majored in physical or biological sciences as undergraduates but who did not pursue them in life, social scientists, a group who majored in the humanities, and lawyers. The uniqueness of Terman's data lies in the fact that they are not retrospective, but consist of actual measurements taken at different periods in the individuals' lives, so that, for example, the peculiar characteristics of the future physical scientist can be singled out as they appear as early as age ten. Finally, Roe (1951, 1953a, 1953b) has made case studies which are especially valuable because her subjects were more eminent than any of the other scientists studied and because she investigated their life histories more intensively and completely than anyone has heretofore. She has published extensive summaries of the life history material, and performance data on ability, Rorschach, and Thematic Apperception Tests. While this list of investigations is not complete, it covers the major contributions of motivational import to the Utah conference, except for a number of less formal observations on the behavior of scientists presented by various participants. So anyone searching for the basic motivations of the physical scientist has a lot of material to draw on. Perhaps the facts are all there and all that needs to be done is to put them in the proper order and draw the correct inferences.

As a participant in the Utah conference, I felt that the picture of the creative physical scientist which was emerging from these data was fairly clear, yet no agreement was then reached as to his basic motivations. Perhaps a systematic study of the data for its motivational implications will now provide an hypothesis or two which can be tested by further research. Let us see if it will.

What are the characteristics of physical scientists that have been repeatedly confirmed in these various studies? Before listing them, it is well to be clear at the beginning just whom we are describing. Obviously the studies just mentioned used as subjects very different orders of "scientists"—all the way from those who had won the Nobel Prize to undergraduate majors in science. So it will be difficult, if not dangerous, to make generalizations that apply to all groups with equal force. One way of minimizing the difficulty is to try to select only those characteristics which are so striking that they apply (with variations, of course) to all scien-

143

DAVID C. MC CLELLAND

tifically oriented subjects but in greater degree to those who are more creative or more eminent. Another way of minimizing the danger of too-sweeping generalizations is to focus on experimental physical science—in particular on physics and chemistry. Theoretical physics and mathematics shade off in one direction from such a focus and the biological sciences in another, so that any statements made need not apply as fully to scientists in these areas. With these guidelines in mind, the following generalizations would appear to summarize fairly well the characteristics of physical scientists as they have been uncovered by investigations up to the present.

1. *Men are more likely to be creative scientists than women.* There are no women among Anne Roe's (1951, 1953b) eminent scientists, and very few in *American Men of Science*. No fact is more obvious than the differential yield for science of the two sexes, though it is saved from being trivial only by the further fact that women have not flocked to experimental physical science in increasing numbers as opportunities for higher education for women have been more nearly equalized. In other words, it may not be a social factor—lack of opportunity for women in science —but rather a personality factor—lack of interest in physical science among women—which accounts for the small number of female physical scientists.

2. *Experimental physical scientists come from a background of radical Protestantism more often than would be expected by chance, but are not themselves religious.* Historically modern science developed in close association with Puritanism. Merton (1949) has described the "point-to-point correlation" between "the principles of Puritanism and the attributes, goals, and results of science," and has shown that the original membership of the Royal Society of London was disproportionately Puritan in background in 1663. Knapp and Goodrich (1952) found that between World Wars I and II American scientists were graduated disproportionately more often from small Protestant colleges, particularly during the period in history when colleges were breaking away from religious orthodoxy. Roe's eminent scientists (1953b) included more individuals than would be expected from radical Protestant backgrounds (e.g., Quaker, Mormon), although her frequencies are not large enough to be very reliable. She fur-

144

ther found that her scientists were not personally religious, a fact supported in Terman's (1954) report that his scientists were less interested in religion than any of his other groups of comparable intellectual ability. In other words, scientists appear to come more often from a radical (thoroughgoing or strict) Protestant background and to reject it for science as a "way of life."

3. *Scientists avoid interpersonal contact.* They are less gregarious, more autonomous, prefer working with things to working with people. Evidence for this generalization comes from many sources. McClelland (1956) reports that of the ninety items which consistently differentiated scientists from nonscientists on the Strong Vocational Interest Blank, forty-seven could be classified as having to do with avoiding interpersonal contact. For example, scientists prefer being a lighthouse keeper to being a headwaiter, gardening to house-to-house canvassing, dealing with things to dealing with people. They would dislike significantly more than men in general being a lawyer, a politician, a reporter, a social worker, or a traveling salesman. They also dislike dramatics, public speaking, interviewing prospective customers, or bargaining. Cattell and Drevdahl (1955) report very similar findings also based on objective personality tests. Their research physicists are significantly high on Factor A (schizothymia) and Factor Q2 (self-sufficiency) as contrasted with a college group or with other professional groups. The items which make up these factors are very similar to the ones just mentioned (Cattell, 1957). Furthermore, the unsociability of scientists appears as early as age ten according to Terman's (1954) data. He found his future scientists rated lowest in sociability score based on a play and games test at age ten. Finally, significantly more of Stein's (1956) creative chemists are either high or low in nAffiliation (82%), as compared with his uncreative chemists (48%), when nAffiliation is measured by coding TAT's according to the technique initially developed by Shipley and Veroff (1952).[1] Clinical data

[1] I am grateful to Stein for lending me TAT's on forty-five of his industrial chemists to code for nAffiliation and also nAchievement and nPower (see below). Scores for nAffiliation were based on stories told to TAT cards #2, #6, #13MF, the blank card, and one specially constructed card showing two men sitting in a laboratory with a woman in a laboratory coat. Four of the twenty-two more creative chemists scored in the middle range of nAffiliation scores (5 to 9) as compared with twelve of the twenty-three less creative chemists ($\chi^2 = 5.61 \ p < .05$).

suggest that being either high or low on nAffiliation leads a person to avoid interpersonal contact, in the first instance because the person is "super-sensitive" to others, and in the second because he simply is not interested in others. What leads to normal gregariousness is the moderate amount of nAffiliation which characterized over half of Stein's uncreative chemists, and less than one-fifth of his creative ones. Outstanding scientists are anything but normally gregarious. They like being self-sufficient and like being alone, probably because people and human relations seem both difficult and uninteresting to them.

4. *Creative scientists are unusually hardworking to the extent of appearing almost obsessed with their work.* Roe (1951, 1953a, 1953b) in reporting on her eminent scientists remarks that the *one* characteristic all of them seemed to have had without exception is an intense devotion to their work (cf. also Kubie, 1953). There was never a question of putting in so many hours a day, a week, or a year. Instead they worked nights, weekends, holidays, all the time. In fact she wondered how they ever found time to be with their wives and families. Terman (1954) also reports that his physical scientists stated more often than any others that their work itself gave them the greatest satisfaction in life. A motive which is known to produce hard striving under certain conditions is nAchievement. Perhaps scientists are as a group especially high in the need for Achievement, as I have predicted elsewhere (McClelland, 1956). It gives me considerable satisfaction to report that the data do not support such a logical inference. My apparently quixotic pleasure derives from the fact that my own extensive work on nAchievement may have led some of my critics and friends alike to assume that I believe nAchievement is the root cause or motive force behind *all* energetic, successful behavior, or in simpler terms that all achievement is produced by a high nAchievement. If this were so—if overt behavior bore a one-to-one relationship to inner motivational determinants—it would obviously be more parsimonious to do without the concept of motivation altogether. So it actually underlines the need for a construct of motivation to discover a case where high achievement must be attributed to some motive other than nAchievement, as it is usually measured in fantasy.

146

The facts are not as extensive as they ought to be, but so far as they go they do not point to *n*Achievement as a crucial factor in the persistent striving of scientists. Figures comparing scientists and controls exist for stories told about two pictures from the Murray TAT: card #1 (boy with violin) and card #7 ("father and son"). Out of sixty-four stories told about the two pictures by thirty-two normal college students, 52% contained achievement imagery, whereas only 28% of the stories told by Stein's forty-five industrial chemists contained achievement imagery, and 47% of the stories told by thirty-nine of Roe's eminent scientists contained achievement imagery. A further analysis of the full *n*Achievement scores for Stein's chemists (based on TAT cards #1, #2, #6, #7, and two specially designed cards) demonstrates that the more creative ones average *lower* than the less creative ones, but are significantly more often in the middle of the *n*Achievement score distribution.[2] Apparently only a *moderate* amount of *n*Achievement favors success in industrial chemistry. The reason may be that too high *n*Achievement leads to considerable frustration in research because positive results are not obtained often enough and with sufficient regularity to please the person with high *n*Achievement, whereas very low *n*Achievement may simply lead to laziness. There is also the hint that while scientists in general are lower than the normal college population in *n*Achievement, the especially productive eminent scientists are somewhat higher than their colleagues. Still, even the eminent ones do not exceed the normal college population in *n*Achievement, and the explanation of their high achievement must be sought in some other motivational system.

5. *Scientists avoid and are disturbed by complex human emotions, perhaps particularly interpersonal aggression.* By its very nature science as an occupation glorifies objectivity, dispassionateness, or the impersonal search for truth. While personal biases and feelings have sometimes crept into scientific work, ideally they have no place in it. For most scientists avoidance of human emotion is far more than simply an ideal as far as their

2 Thirteen of the 22 more creative chemists have scores in the middle *n*Achievement range (0 to +4) as compared with 5 of the 23 less creative chemists ($\chi^2 = 6.5$, $p < .02$).

profession is concerned; it runs as a theme through much of their thinking in other areas of life. Knapp (1956) in particular found that science majors tell TAT stories significantly low in dramatic salience, in aggression, guilt or vindication, and in the tendency to bring the plot to a clear and decisive conclusion. Teevan (1954), reporting on the same subjects, found them the lowest on all variables on the Blacky Test, technically indicating that science majors are least disturbed of all students in psychosexual development, but more probably suggesting that they are unable to enter into the spirit of the test, which involves identifying with a little black dog. Instead they simply give bland, unemotional, objective responses which are hard to score for any disturbance. These findings might be discounted, since they deal only with undergraduate science majors, except that Roe (1951) reports very similar results based on the TAT's of her eminent scientists. She notes:

> The attitude they manifest with regard to family relations is rather an unusual one. Its chief aspect is of independence of parents, usually without conflict over it . . . a similar independence of other personal relations is generally noticeable. But here, particularly with respect to sexual relations, there is a strong tendency to evade an emotional situation, to give it distance in some way. . . . In most of the stories where aggression is clearly apparent, it is relegated to a fairly distant past, and as a rule the aggressor suffers severely for it.

Actually one of the most striking things about the way the eminent scientists reacted to the TAT is their marked dislike for the task. The test requires a response to a number of dramatic human situations and the scientists reacted by trying more or less strenuously to avoid responding to them at all in the usual manner. They found it extremely difficult to empathize with the characters pictured and to tell a dramatic story as they had been instructed to do. Instead they tended to block, to analyze various portions of the picture, to consider various possibilities of action, and to be unable to decide on any one of them. The following initial reaction of one physicist to the first card (boy with violin) is typical: "That is most objectionable. We will carry out an

148

analysis. I have all sorts of blocks because people are so unreasonable it always makes great difficulty for me." [3]

Veroff and others (1957), in a factor analysis of Thorndike's ratings of eminent men have also found that scientists differ from others chiefly in being significantly lower on *Choler* (Anger, Dominance, and Liking for Conflict). To oversimplify a little by way of summary: *scientists react emotionally to human emotions and try to avoid them.*

6. *Physical scientists like music and dislike art and poetry.* On the Strong Vocational Interest Blank they say more than others do that they would dislike being a poet or decorating a room with flowers, and that they like symphony concerts. Terman (1954) reports that liking for art is least common in his physical science groups and that interest in music among the physical science research group rises throughout life until it is highest of all by age forty. The attitude toward modern art is perhaps best expressed by the response of one physicist to a TAT picture when he said: "It's confusing enough to win a prize."

7. *Physical scientists are intensely masculine.* On all interest and attitude scales that differentiate between men and women, physical scientists score very high on masculinity. For example, Terman (1954) found 64% of his physical science research group score above the standard score of fifty on masculinity for the Strong Vocational Interest Blank. Only the engineers and those whose undergraduate major was science score higher, whereas lawyers, social scientists, and those majoring in the humanities score much lower. In general his scientists show a liking for nature and for outdoor sports when they are young, and for working with things rather than with people—all of which are typically male as contrasted with female interests.

Another aspect of their masculinity appears as a positive image of the father figure in the TAT stories combined with little or no rebellion or guilt over rebellion in the father-son relationship. Though difficulty is often present in the mother-son relation-

---

3 I am much indebted to Anne Roe for lending me the TAT's of some of the scientists in her group from which this and subsequent observations are drawn.

ship, Roe's eminent scientists portray the father as a benign and understanding influence. The following comments from stories to TAT card #7 are typical: "Father, though, is an understanding person and definitely makes a reconciliation"; "His father gave him wise counsel and took a less serious view of the situation." It is perhaps significant that while about one-half of Roe's cases picture the father in this way, none, or at the most one, of Stein's uncreative chemists give a similar response. While the relationship to the father seems to be respectful, it is also somewhat distant, as Terman's (1954) figures show. His research scientists report little oversolicitousness from their fathers, and also the *least* amount of affection and understanding between father and son. The science majors who did not continue in a scientific occupation report the *most* affection between father and son, a fact to which we must return later since in practically all other respects these two groups are very similar.

It is perhaps also worth reporting here that Stein's creative chemists show more nAchievement (mean $= .91$) in response to TAT card #7—the father-son picture—than do the uncreative chemists (mean $= .61$). The less creative chemists on the other hand show markedly more nAchievement to TAT card #2—the farm scene—where their mean nAchievement score is 1.09, as contrasted to the —.05 mean score for the more creative chemists. To put the same result in a different fashion, 56% of the more creative as contrasted with 22% of the less creative chemists gave more nAchievement to card #7 than to card #2 $\chi^2 = 3.97$, $p < .05$).

Since the figures in card #7 are male and in card #2 predominantly female, apparently nAchievement in more creative chemists is elicited by male figures, and in less creative chemists by female figures.

8. *Physical scientists develop a strong interest in analysis, in the structure of things, early in life.* One of the most striking things about the case histories of scientists is the early age at which their scientific interest appears. It is not just mathematicians—who are often child prodigies—but all kinds of natural scientists who typically develop a strong scientific interest between the ages of five and ten. Terman's (1954) results show that his future scientists had a scientific interest by the age of ten that was

easily recognized as dominant by the boys themselves, by their teachers, and by their parents.

That the nature of this interest is analytic is almost self-evident from the goal of physical science; this goal, in the words of one of Roe's theoretical physicists, is to discover the "connections of things," and to get at the "inner secrets of the world." That is, it is the scientist's job to take apart the real world as we perceive it and to discover what lies behind it, to work out the microstructure of reality.

What is required of them in their profession has been enthusiastically adopted by them in their entire attitude toward life. For example, Terman's (1954) physical science research group is highest in its interest in photography as an avocation, and photography is the method par excellence by which one "freezes" the flux of reality so that one can get a good look at its structure. As has already been suggested above, the task of telling stories to TAT cards was found to be particularly baffling by Roe's eminent scientists. The difficulty arises not only from a desire to avoid talking about human emotions but also from their obsessive concern with analysis or with what is "really" a *correct* interpretation of the pictures. The following comments are typical:

> "My wife says my most maddening trait is my unwillingness to guess." "You want some fiction this time? I'm utterly sunk on doing anything in fiction. You have found one of the blocks in my mental processes. It's virtually impossible to associate a tale of fiction with this. That's a process I've never attempted—to tell a story about an imaginary thing." [The examiner asked if he had ever told stories to his children.] "They were the ones I had learned. I don't ever remember telling them stories that I created. It would have to be something associated with the acoustics of the violin rather than the boy" [referring to TAT card #1]. "The youth certainly is meditating about the violin, possibly even dreaming that some day he will be able to make a violin that will be as good as the old Stradivarius; he is in deep meditation. What is this and what are the characteristics that make the violin outstanding? By a process of trial and error he finds that it is just the breaking down of the glue in the joints that makes it better than others, and he sees that he can probably make one as good, and by checking his results he probably makes one as good."

Note that here he hardly succeeds in telling a story at all but finally ends up with wondering how the violin is constructed. The intense concern with what is "really there" in the pictures is illustrated by these comments:

"I keep wondering whether the chin rest is on the right side or not, trying to figure out if he is left-handed."

"And the young man's ambition will push him along. The young man also needs a hair-cut."

They simply cannot let themselves go, in telling a tale of dramatic action, but are constantly brought up short by details which seem to require analysis and which do not fit into the story that has been started. Consequently it is not so surprising to discover that physical scientists are also conspicuously high in their tendency to make responses based on details in the Rorschach ink blot test and on the white background rather than the blot itself (Roe, 1956). It is the unusual which catches their attention and demands analysis. Furthermore, they are significantly low in their tendency to attribute movement to the static ink blots (Roe, 1956), again showing their preference for analysis, for "freezing" reality and trying to get at its structure, rather than for synthesis, for going beyond the blot and interpreting it in the way a person interested in dramatic action would.

So much for the facts in the case. There are others—such as that eminent scientists are more often first born (Roe, 1951)—but these appear to be the main facts from which the psychodynamics of the creative physical scientist must be inferred. It is time to stop, as the authors of mystery stories often do, and present a challenge to the reader. You have all the facts in your possession. All the clues have been presented. Now what is the solution? What motivational complex will account best for all the facts? Or are there several equally probable explanations? Or is there as yet not enough information to suggest a solution? Unfortunately the psychologist, unlike the mystery story writer, does not really know if there is a solution. He can only try to construct a hypothesis which fits the known facts and then try to check it with further observations. And this is what I, as one psychologist, attempted to do, although before going on to explain what I did, I should like to challenge the reader to try it himself—to try to find an explanation which will fit all eight of these generalizations. It is not so easy as it may appear, yet I will try to do it.

To begin with, a psychologist interested in psychodynamics assumes that certain conditions are necessary but not sufficient for the making of a scientist. Chief among these are, of course, a high level of intelligence and opportunity for contact with scientific knowledge through some system of education. Granted these preconditions, why is it that some boys develop a strong scientific interest and others do not? The fact that the interest develops so strongly early in life suggests that the key to the problem may lie in the family, because it is the main educational influence at this period in life.

In thinking of family relationships as a source of motivation, one is of course immediately reminded of Freud's insistence on the central role of the Oedipus complex. What could have happened to the little boy to turn him so strongly to the male role and away from contacts with people? One answer, in terms of the "passing" of the Oedipus complex, is obvious. The future scientist is simply a boy who resolves his guilt over love of his mother and hatred of his father by early and complete identification with his father, probably in the phallic period.

Such an explanation does a pretty good job of accounting for the facts just enumerated. It explains the strong masculine identification and the fact that scientists are more often men than women—because women are not troubled by the Oedipus complex. It could easily account for the avoidance of people, the dislike of human emotions, and the distaste for art and poetry—all because they are connected with the acute anxiety aroused by the boy's first important interpersonal relationship with his mother. That is, in psychoanalytic terms, one can assume that for the first three or four years of his life the future scientist, like most boys, develops an intense love relationship with his mother which produces acute anxiety arising simultaneously from the fear of the strength of his own impulses, from guilt over hatred of the loved father, and from fear of retaliation by the father. Normally a boy is supposed to defend himself against his anxiety by repression and identification with the father. Perhaps the future scientist differs in that he adopts the defense slightly earlier—in the phallic rather than the genital period—so that all his "symptoms" are more extreme than those of a normal boy. He is particularly marked by a tendency to avoid any cue associated with interpersonal relationships which may rearouse the original anxiety. So the scientist dislikes interpersonal contacts, human emotion, and even art and poetry, which frequently deal with human emotions. Finally he is analytic and hard-working because his sexual drive has been repressed earlier than usual and finds its substitute outlets in intellectual curiosity—or more specifically in "looking" and seeking to "penetrate the secrets of nature" which in classical psychoanalytic terms are pregenital, especially phallic, sexual activities. Freud (1916) traced Leonardo da Vinci's compelling scientific curiosity to the same libidinal source. In other words, the scientist does not mature fully, as far as the sexual instinct is concerned, because of the early passing of the Oedipus complex; instead he continues to find a good deal of his sexual satisfaction in phallic activities. He remains fixated somewhat at the level of "looking and knowing," as Kubie (1953) has indirectly suggested. In short, perhaps scientific drive and curiosity derive their energy from a slight perversion of the sexual instinct. And it is a fact, as Anne Roe reports (1953b), that young scientists are typically not very interested in girls, date for the first time late in college, marry the first girl they date, and thereafter appear to show a rather low level of heterosexual drive.

If such an explanation is to be considered seriously, it has at least three consequences which ought to show up in the behavior of scientists. First, they ought to be particularly shocked and upset by TAT card #13 which suggests the "primal scene" (a seminude woman on a bed, and a man in the foreground at the door of the room with head bowed). Certainly the scene evokes the intense analytic attitude characteristic of Roe's eminent scientists toward all the TAT pictures. For example, a theoretical physicist tells the following story:

> It doesn't look as if any crime had been committed, although I suppose that's a possibility, and yet this man looks as if he saw something very shocking which presumably he was responsible for. What could those books have to do with it? One of them might be

154

a Bible but there would not be two Bibles . . . well, what's going to happen? He's going away but I am very much puzzled about this gesture of grief or regret or whatever it is. There must be some explanation which I don't get.

It would not take very much clinical imagination to interpret this story as confirming the hypothesis. The scientist does not reveal the identity of the male figure in the picture. It may be himself. It may be his father. Either he or his father may have committed an act of sexual aggression (a crime?) against the mother and he is not sure whether he is sorry or not. The religious overtone may reinforce the fact that this is a moral situation, involving above all the commandment to "Honor thy father and mother." It could be regarded as particularly significant that the key response evoked by the obvious sexual content of the scene is one of "looking." "This man looks as though he saw something very shocking which presumably he was responsible for"—a sentence which sums up rather neatly the hypothesis under examination, namely, that the scientist is somehow continuing to look for some sexual secret in which he is personally involved.

A single story unfortunately cannot confirm a generalization, especially when it is subject to alternative interpretations. All that can be said with a fair degree of scientific caution about the reaction of the eminent scientists to this picture is that they see the woman significantly less often ($p < .05$) as the man's wife (13% of the cases) than do the uncreative chemists (60% of the cases). Perhaps they are repressing the "wife-mother" association because of its anxiety-provoking qualities for them, or perhaps they are just finding another way of playing down the emotional character of the scene, as they repeatedly attempt to do through analysis: "The bed isn't big enough" for a seduction scene. "There's no weapon for murder." "He might be sorry." "She can't be sick or her breasts wouldn't be bare." "He seems remarkably well groomed if they've just had a night of it."

A second consequence of the hypothesis is that scientists should defensively see their mothers as rejecting them. In other words, if they feel intense guilt over their love for their mother, a common method of defense against such impulses would be to see the mother as not loving but rejecting them. The evidence

155

here is more clearcut. On TAT card #6 (the "mother-son" picture), 90% of the eminent scientists see the mother and son as going their separate ways, versus 20%, or at the most 30%, of the uncreative chemists. The difference is significant at better than the 5% level, although the frequencies are very small. An ironic tale from a theoretical physicist depicts the relationship clearly: (He had a) "dear kind old mother who was extremely religious. . . . He decided there was a much more straightforward interpretation of the world to believe than these old wives' tales. . . . One day his mother took him to task for his view. . . . They had come to the parting of the ways. . . . It grieved him . . . but he couldn't be stifled by her clucking care." The key elements in the story are that the mother is trying to stifle him, that her solicitousness is unwelcome and tied up with religion, and that he had to get away from her and did so successfully. Among the uncreative chemists, even in the two or three stories where the mother and son parted, the son had to move away from home not because he wanted to but because of force of circumstances. The frequencies are small, and it is therefore especially important to note that in Terman's (1954) data the scientists in general report low admiration for the mother, little rebelliousness toward her, and little effort by her to resist their efforts at independence.

The general picture is one of distance between mother and son rather than of rebellion and conflict. In the physical science research group, the same distance appears between father and son, so that it may simply reflect the already-noted tendency of scientists to report themselves as self-sufficient.

So far as the first two consequences of the Oedipal explanation of the scientist's motivation are concerned, then, the evidence is unfortunately not clearcut either way. The most one could say is that it can be interpreted as confirming the hypothesis, but that one would certainly want more precise checks in the future. The third consequence is of even greater importance than the first two. It is that somewhere, somehow, scientists must reveal to the inquiring investigator hidden and disguised attraction to the mother or the mother figure. Obviously on the surface they show no such attraction, and in fact the hypothesis predicts that they would not, because of their great anxiety over it. But is there no method available to the psychologist for penetrating behind the more or less conscious negative attitude toward the mother to the unconscious or more primitive positive one? Unless such a strong attachment to the mother can be actually demonstrated, the hypothesis remains only indirectly confirmed by circumstantial evidence. After all, the key assumption is that scientists are fleeing from their mothers into masculinity because they love them so much and fear the consequences. Is there no way to demonstrate their secret love?

A research project [4] was designed by one of my students, Ellen Greenberger, to get at this problem. She took as her cue the historical fact noted previously that Protestantism was associated with the rise of science. Another characteristic of Protestantism, as contrasted with Catholicism, was the disappearance of female figures from religious imagery. Christ, the male mediator, became all-important for Protestants, whereas for Catholics the Virgin Mary and other female saints have played an increasingly important religious role. What became of the female, "mother" image in Protestantism? In half-seriousness theologians suggested at the time that "she" had entered the parish house; that, since the Protestant clergy was not celibate, it did not have the same need as the Catholic priesthood for dwelling on women in fantasy. True as this may have been for the clergy, it scarcely explains why the image of the Virgin Mary grew so much in importance for the average Catholic who *was* married, while it remained neglected by the average Protestant. One possible explanation is that Nature became a vivid mother-image substitute for Protestants, thus displacing and serving the same psychological functions as the image of Mary, Mother of God, does for Catholics. [Cf. Leonardo da Vinci whose portrayal of Her is interpreted by Freud (1916) as revealing his secret attachment to his mother.] Certainly Protestants, including the tough-minded Calvin, wrote lyrical appreciations of the beauties of nature which can readily be associated with a female, or mother, image. In fact their de-

[4] We are both much indebted to Rober H. Knapp for suggesting the technique (The Metaphor Test) and many of the ideas it was designed to study.

scriptions of nature—its fruitfulness, bounty, and beauty—are remarkably reminiscent of the paeans of praise directed toward nature by one of the best known scientists of all time, the Roman materialist Lucretius. In psychodynamic terms, what may have happened to Lucretius, and to boys reared in the radical Protestant tradition, is that the *early* passing of the Oedipus complex diverted the repressed sexual impulse toward a mother substitute —namely, nature. Consequently the passion that they feel for Nature, for being in it, and for investigating it, is ultimately a sexual passion which originates when they substitute Nature for Mother as an object of devotion. Certainly the substitution is an easy one not only for those reared in the Protestant tradition, since the metaphor of "Mother Nature" is very common and appears to be based on the association in the Western mind of life-giving, creative properties with both mother and nature.

So Greenberger reasoned that perhaps scientists could be lured into revealing their primitive yearnings for mother indirectly and in a nonthreatening way by asking them what metaphors they felt were most suitable for describing nature. She predicted, in accordance with the hypothesis, that they would prefer metaphors describing nature in positive feminine terms, thus revealing that their life-long intense concern with nature might at its root derive from its female connotations, from its capacity to serve in some way as a mother substitute in fantasy.

She therefore constructed a test containing fifty-nine different descriptions of nature to which subjects were asked to respond by marking how well the phrases described nature, on a scale from —2 (very poorly) to +2 (very well). No neutral or zero judgment was permitted because she felt that scientists might well respond to such a literary type of task by refusing to make judgments wherever possible. The descriptions included both positive and negative male and female images for nature, symbolic representations of a sexual relationship to nature, metaphors suggestive of pre-Oedipal experiences and maternal tenderness, and general abstract images of both a positive and negative character. She predicted that scientists more than control subjects would prefer descriptions picturing nature in positive female terms, descriptions suggesting a sexual relationship to nature (predominantly phallic) and possibly descriptions of nature in pre-Oedipal terms.

The test was administered to two sets of contrasting groups for cross-validation purposes. The first set consisted of seventeen college freshmen, nine of whom were intending to major in science and whose mathematical aptitude scores exceeded their verbal aptitude scores by 100 points. The other eight freshmen were a fairly miscellaneous group intending to major in either the social sciences or the humanities (largely the former), whose verbal aptitude score exceeded their mathematical aptitude score by at least a few points. The second set consisted of graduate students and young instructors at a Midwestern university, thirteen of whom were physicists, ten chemists, and twelve language students and teachers (largely in the field of English). The average liking for the various nature metaphors was computed, and correlations run among the various groups of subjects to determine whether the science groups agreed sufficiently with each other to enable one to think in terms of a stable preference by scientists for particular metaphors. The rank order based on the average liking for the fifty-nine descriptions by the freshman science group correlated $+.57$ with the combined rank order made by the physicists and chemists. The physics and chemistry rank orders correlated $+.61$, whereas they correlated with the language group rank order on the average $+.48$. Finally, the freshman nonscience group showed a preference for the metaphors which correlated only $+.34$ with the graduate language group, indicating that there was less consistency between the nonscience groups than among the scientists. One reason for this probably lies in the fact that the freshman nosncience group was composed largely of people oriented toward the social sciences, whereas the graduate nonscience group was oriented toward languages and the humanities. Since the primary concern is to discover how scientists differ from the "generalized other" rather than from social scientists or language teachers as such, the preference scores for the two nonscience groups were combined and each of the two science groups (college freshmen, and graduate physicists and chemists combined) was compared with the same standard. Table 1 presents the results in terms of the rank orders of the differences in prefer-

159

ences by the two science groups as compared with the combined nonscience group. For example, Item #49 ("A pillar of strength

TABLE 1. Rank Orders of Metaphors for Nature Most and Least Preferred by Scientists over Nonscientists

Item	College Freshmen	Graduate Students and Instructors	Most preferred by Scientists (Relative to Nonscientists)
#49	1	5.5	A pillar of strength and virility
#12	2	11	A perfect woman nobly planned
#59	5	7	The nurse, the guide, the guardian of my heart and soul
#46	10	4	A grand and inspiring father
#39	3.5	12.5	Lady of silences
#18	15.5	1	A banquet of delights
#27	11	8	A stern and loveless master
# 7	7	14.5	Glens of brightness
#42	6	17	A vineyard to be reaped for pleasure
# 5	18	5.5	Something certain and infinite
#45	8	18.5	Fairest among women
			Least Preferred by Scientists (Relative to Nonscientists)
#35	57.5	58	The desolations of many generations
#15	57.5	55.5	A tyrant despite her lovely face
#40	56	57	A great cave that encompasses us and swallows us up like atoms
#34	53	47	A spring whose waters will not do our bidding
#57	51	49.5	A Titan waiting terribly to break forth
#41	50	49.5	An arrogant master who likes to rule and dominate

and virility") showed the largest difference in the direction of greater preference by the freshman scientist group over the non-science group; it also tied for fifth and sixth place (out of fifty-nine) in the size of preference shown it by the graduate science group over the nonscience group. Included in the upper portion of the Table are only those metaphors which ranked in the top ten for one of the two science groups, as contrasted with the control, and in the top eighteen for the other. In the lower half of the Table have been listed the descriptions of nature least preferred by the scientists (or most preferred by the nonscientists). For example, Item #35 ("The desolations of many generations") was relatively much less preferred by both of the science groups than by the nonscience group.

Table 1 shows that there is considerable agreement in the preferences of the two science groups. Over two-thirds of the descriptions above the median in preference in one science group were also above the median in preference in the other science group. The agreement is highly significant (Chi-square $= 8.36$, $p < .01$). Considering only the descriptions on which the science groups show greatest agreement, we arrive at three main conclusions. First, scientists prefer metaphors describing nature in idealized human (male or female) terms. There are eleven such metaphors on the test (counting "Lady of silences" which is somewhat less definitely positive than the other ten), and nine of these appear in the top half of the scientists' preferences in each of the two groups (Chi-square $= 5.79$, $p < .05$). Or, to put it another way, the average rank of the eleven positive human images was significantly higher than for the remaining items, being 13.1 for the college freshmen scientists and 15.6 for the graduate physicists and chemists ($p < .002$ in both samples, by the Mann-Whitney U test). Most of these images rank very high in both groups, as Table 1 illustrates (Items #49, #12, #59, #46, #39, #45).

Secondly, scientists reject images of nature as threatening. Five of the seven items so classified (#35, #15, #40, #57, and #41) appear at the bottom of Table 1, and the average rank for all seven items was 49.1 in each of the two science groups, which is significantly below the average rank for the remaining items ($p < .002$ in both samples, by the Mann-Whitney U test).

Thirdly, there is little or no support for the hypothesis the experiment was conducted to test—that nature represents for scientists either a sexualized or pre-Oedipal mother image. It is true that positive female images are more preferred by the scientists, but so are positive male images; and there is almost no evidence that scientists see nature as having even symbolic sexual connotations. Unfortunately, the data do not permit a clean rejection of the hypothesis which they were collected to test; they can still be interpreted as consistent with the hypothesis. It may be

161

argued that the male images for nature are liked by the scientists because they arouse subjective feelings of male potency (e.g., "A pillar of strength and virility," "A grand and inspiring father," "A stern and loveless master"). In support of this point, the three male images not so highly preferred by the scientists ("A thing of manly power and beauty," "A young boy's first hero," "Symbol of manhood") are perhaps not so evocative of male potency, but represent nature as a male *thing* or symbol. The positive female images preferred, on the other hand, are all clearly of nature as an object and three are suggestively pre-Oedipal in nature ("Lady of silences," "Glens of brightness," "A banquet of delights"). Could it be that nature serves as a cue which serves simultaneously to remind them of their own male potency and of a female object for that potency?

Oddly enough, the one female image which is ranked far below the other four positive ones in both science groups is the one description in the test which uses the word mother ("The mother of us all"). Could this be because the direct reference to "mother" arouses the anxiety which the test is seeking to get around by less direct allusions to mother? Finally, the six phallic images are not particularly preferred one way or the other by the science groups, but there is a striking exception in each case. For the freshman group one phallic image, #42 ("A vineyard to be reaped for pleasure") actually showed the sixth largest preference over the control group, whereas in the graduate science group #47, another phallic image ("A mystic thing to meet and fuse with") ranked second in order of preference over the control group. Could it be that the highly symbolic, "oral" character of the phallic image for the younger boys has given way to a more realistic sexual image of mystic union for the older more experienced men? It may further be argued that none of the other phallic images are quite as directly suggestive of the sexual act as these two (cf., e.g., "A dizzy rapture," "A place for daring and boldness," "Beauty, burning with flames of ecstasy," "Wild flesh").

But proper scientific caution must brand all such speculations as strictly *ad hoc*. The fact is that the images used are all so suggestive that no matter how the results had come out, they could, by special pleading of this kind, have been made to support the hypothesis. Here, as always in scientific research, one must make a judgment concerning whether the data confirm the hypothesis sufficiently to make it worth further investigation, or infirm it to the extent that it is more profitable to think of alternative hypotheses. In the present instance it is my judgment that the reasoning necessary to support the sexual explanation of scientists' interest in nature is sufficiently tortuous to render the explanation highly unlikely and to suggest that alternative hypotheses should be entertained. Nevertheless, the data and their possible interpretation in terms of the original hypothesis have been spelled out in detail so that others who judge differently may pursue it further if they feel my judgment is incorrect.

So again, as in any good detective story, we are back where we started. An initially plausible explanation of the facts has turned out to be inadequate in several ways. Once again let me challenge the reader—who may not have liked all this Freudian "nonsense" anyway—to have another try. After all, the Metaphor Test has yielded some new facts.

Let us begin there. In a way it is quite remarkable that scientists prefer to conceive of nature in positive *human* terms. It is especially surprising because there are at least ten abstract descriptions of nature in the list which are not particularly positive or negative and not expressed in human terms at all, which one might have supposed in advance that objective scientists would have liked, when forced to make a choice. Of all these only one ("Something certain and infinite") appears high on the list of those preferred by the two science groups over the control group. Why should the scientist pass by these safe, "neutral" images and show such definite preferences for conceiving nature in idealized human terms? One possible explanation is that early in life scientists have had difficulty in their relationshps with people (since we know they consistently avoid people), and have found in nature a symbolic substitute for the idealized people they could not find in real life. The hypothesis is actually a restatement of the sexual one in a more generalized form. That is, the sexual hypothesis assumed that a particular sexual conflict of the boy led him to find in nature a substitute for his mother whom he had renounced in life, whereas the more general hypothesis is that the sexual problem is not necessarily the central one in his relationship to people, since there is no special evidence that nature is conceived in feminine sexualized terms.

If the scientist's difficulty in human relations does not lie in the sexual sphere, where does it lie? Maybe it is different for each scientist. Need we assume more than that each scientist has had some particular kind of trauma in his interpersonal relations early in life which has turned him away from people toward nature? Perhaps not, but such a pluralistic explanation runs squarely into two facts: men are more likely to become scientists than women, and boys brought up in a radical Protestant background are more likely to become scientists than other boys. If becoming a scientist is strictly a matter of miscellaneous traumas, why should these not occur as often in one population group as another?

Putting the question in these terms suggests another possibility. There is another problem peculiar to the male sex, and perhaps particularly so to males in radical Protestant households: the problem of aggression. A key characteristic of radical Protestantism is its emphasis on asceticism, on the necessity for curbing impulses early in life. "Give the devil a little finger and he'll take the whole hand," is the maxim in terms of which many such parents operate. They identify the devil with sex in any of its forms, with aggression, and with general willfulness or disobedience. According to wellknown facts (Dollard and others, 1939), severe frustration of all such impulses should produce strong instigation to aggression in children. Yet direct expression of aggression is one of the impulses most severely controlled in such families. So a conflict should often arise in the children of such families between the strong impulse to aggression and an equally strong fear of expressing it. The problem should be even more acute and more prevalent among boys than girls, since for boys controlling aggression is more of a problem because of their innately greater strength and destructive power.

A common solution to such a conflict is to convert the aggressive impulses into a more socially acceptable form, such as arguing or participating in strenuous physical activity. Still another common solution dramatized by the authors of *The Authoritarian Personality* (Adorno and others, 1950) is for the boy to identify with his strict father and to behave aggressively toward persons beneath him who are younger or less powerful. But in the case of the future scientist, another solution appears to be adopted. He simply "goes out of the field" and attempts to avoid interpersonal contacts, since they are the most likely to arouse the impulse to aggression and the anxiety over expressing it. It is a fact that scientists are low on aggressive themes in the TAT, and when faced by a problem in aggression typically solve it by minimizing it or attempting to avoid it altogether. There is very little guilt in their TAT stories because there has been very little expression to be guilty about. In fact, one might almost say that the only time a scientist can manage to express aggression is when he is morally indignant. For then, and perhaps only then, are his moral values, which normally frustrate his expression of aggression, in actual support of his aggressive impulses. It is difficult to be very precise in such matters, but it is clear that scientists can get involved in some extremely heated scientific controversies, especially when they suspect that moral values of the scientific code (e.g., honesty, full publicity) have been transgressed.

As was pointed out above, scientists in their personal lives are upset by human emotion, perhaps particularly by aggression, so that their withdrawal from people can perhaps be viewed as a mode of defense against conflicts over aggression. Their avoidance extends even to their own parents (see above), and to art and poetry, which contain many cues that might arouse their aggression-anxiety. What, then, normally becomes of their impulse to aggression if it does not express itself, as it does for most people, in the area of human relationships? To some extent it may simply be decreased in intensity because situations which arouse it are avoided, but what is left may be sublimated into an attack on nature. It is certainly part of the folklore of science that it represents an attempt to *conquer* nature, to dominate it, and bring it under man's control. Social theorists have noted that the view that man could be more powerful than nature is by no means a

165

common one in history. In fact, the usual belief among the peoples of the world, even today, is that nature is much more powerful than man (witness floods, droughts, earthquakes, and so forth), and that man must somehow placate the gods who control nature. It may not seem too far-fetched to assume that it took an unusual psychodynamic situation to create in some men the apparently irrational belief that they could conquer nature. The blocked aggressive needs of a few scientists, diverted toward nature, may well have fulfilled such an important historic function.

On a more personal level, we have noted that the scientist is intensely analytic in his approach to experience. His response is to freeze the flux of reality, to ask what it is, to take experience apart and see what makes it tick. It is no mere metaphor to say that analysis represents a form of aggression. To take something apart is to destroy it in a very real sense. Of course the creative scientist attempts to put reality back together again on his own terms, but even he would admit that the model he constructs of reality is a poor substitute for the richness of human experience.

But why are scientists so intensely masculine? How can this fact be fitted under the hypothesis that they have adopted a unique method of handling aggression-anxiety? Earlier we pointed out that one of the common methods of handling the aggression problem is for the boy to identify with the aggressor (usually the father), because he gets some gratification in behaving in a similar powerful fashion. The same mechanism may be operating in the case of the scientist, but there is evidence that it does not follow its normal course. According to Terman's (1954) data, physical science research subjects report least understanding and affection from their fathers, while the subjects who were undergraduate science majors but did not pursue research careers report the most understanding and affection from their fathers. In other words, the research group, like the nonresearch group, takes the initial step in dealing with the aggression problem of strongly identifying with the male role. After all, the male is the image of power and aggressiveness. But the next step, of behaving aggressively like a powerful male, is further discouraged by a distant, unaffectionate, real father in the research group and promoted by an understanding father in the nonresearch group.[5]

Direct confirmation of the hypothesis appears in the fact that the nonresearch group maintains a high interest in outdoor sports (Terman, 1954), whereas the research group has a low interest in sports. That is, while scientists are definitely masculine, they do not express their masculinity in the aggressiveness of outdoor sports as more "normal" males do, but may satisfy it more indirectly through scientific analysis.

So the new hypothesis is that scientists work so hard and love their work so much to satisfy not sexual but aggressive needs. Such a notion has the further advantage that there is no consistent evidence in the literature for sexual difficulties among scientists. One might reasonably expect that if they have so much anxiety over their sexual love of their mothers, more of them would never have married, like Leonardo da Vinci, or at least would have shown a history of homosexual or other perverse sexual outlets. But such is not the case. Scientists as a group appear to be heterosexually normal, although somewhat delayed in their approach to women, probably because of their general avoidance of interpersonal contacts.

What *direct* evidence is there that scientists are satisfying aggressive urges in their interest in nature? Unfortunately, the Nature Metaphor Test was constructed so that it contained no images at all of man as conquering nature. One would certainly have to predict in terms of the new hypothesis that scientists would prefer such metaphors. However, the test did contain a number of the reverse type of metaphor in which nature is depicted as threatening to man. Most of them appear in the bottom of Table 1, and the scientist rejected them more than any other type of metaphor. In other words, the one thing he rejects most

[5] It is particularly interesting that, in fantasy, scientists portray fathers as understanding but report their own fathers to have been distant and unaffectionate. It is as if they have interiorized the positive male image but are somehow blocked at the level of *behaving* like a normally aggressive male because of ambivalent feelings toward their own fathers, of incomplete identification with him because of his distance, or of other sources of aggression-anxiety mentioned above.

167

compared with the nonscientist is the notion that nature threatens him. It is not unreasonable to assume that this is because he thinks he is capable of dominating or "threatening" nature, although there might also be other reasons why scientists would not see nature as threatening. Still, the finding makes the hypothesis a little more probable and encourages one to explore it further.

One slight bit of evidence in its favor is the fact that Stein's creative chemists averaged somewhat higher in nPower [6] (mean $= 4.05$, SD $= 3.14$) than his uncreative chemists (mean $= 2.74$, SD $= 2.50$, difference $= 1.31$, $t = 1.52$, $p < .15$). Unfortunately the really crucial comparison between scientists and nonscientists cannot be made with these data.

But there are still some important loose ends. Why should research scientists like music so much? Why should they conceive of nature in terms of idealized human figures, rather than, for example, in terms of adversaries to be conquered? Why the interest in "fusing" with nature or "reaping it for pleasure?" There is certainly a hint here of a relationship to nature which is more than a conquering, dominating one. It is almost as if the scientists felt themselves "one with nature" or conceived of it as a pleasurable extension of their fantasy life. One of the characteristics of music is that it is an "objectless" form of art. It seems to come from everywhere, and the person as he listens can, so to speak, "melt" into the environment or lose his sense of being in a particular time or place. It is interesting to note in this connection that Fisher and Cleveland (1958) report that scientists alone among their successful professional groups have low body boundaries as measured by the Rorschach, indicating that they maintain a more "open" relationship to the environment and do not conceive of their bodies as having a hard protective shell which separates them from the world. They do not develop as much as most people do a percept of themselves as distinct individuals interacting with other distinct individuals. Instead, the environment appears to remain as a "part of themselves" long after most people have withdrawn themselves more distinctly from the environ-

[6] Based on stories to TAT cards #7, #13MF, #17BM, the blank card, and two laboratory scenes especially constructed by Stein.

ment. So music may appeal to scientists because it promotes a feeling of "oneness" with the environment. Up to now we have stressed the negative reason for scientists being interested in nature. They turn to it because interpersonal relations have proved so frustrating and anxiety-provoking. But there appears to be a positive attachment to nature, too, which in a certain sense they simply fail to outgrow in order to enter into more conventional human relationships.

Confirmation of this tendency may be found in a new approach to the Rorschach developed by Paul Stern (1958). Taking his cue from European existentialist psychologists, he has developed a method of coding Rorschach responses to yield an Index of Existential Pathology. The Index has five dimensions: Primitivity of Object Choice, Alienation from the Environment, Dissolution, Primitivity of Object Relations, and Spatiality. The first of these dimensions is the most important, accounting for between 45% and 60% of the total score. In general, responses are coded under the heading of Primitivity of Object Choice if they suggest primitive percepts of people—in other words, humanlike figures, primitive or young humans, monsters, and so forth. Examples of responses which would be included under this heading are: witches, a statue, Chinese image, leprechaun, two elfish characters, gnomes, Pan, Dionysius, cherubs, Gargantua the ape. Stern's method of analysis was applied to the Rorschachs from thirty-one of Roe's eminent scientists [7] and the results compared with two other populations as shown in Table 2. The comparison groups are by no means ideal, consisting of a group of normal and a group of neurotic college students all much younger than the scientists in question, but the differences are so striking and meaningful that it seems unlikely that correction for age differences would wipe them out. The neurotics are clearly differentiated from the normals (this difference was Stern's primary interest), but the scientists fall neatly in between. Sixty-one per cent of them could be classified as displaying a moderate amount of Existential Pathology as compared with only about a third of the normal subjects. Furthermore, since their means are comparable to the

[7] I am much indebted to Dr. Stern for coding the protocols according to his new system.

TABLE 2. Frequencies and Percentages of Eminent Scientists and of Normal and Neurotic College Students Who Are High, Middle, and Low on an Index of Existential Pathology (IEP)

	Normal College Students	Eminent Scientists	Neurotic College Students
Low IEP (2.0–3.9)	11 (50%)	6 (19.4%)	0 (0%)
Moderate IEP (4.0–5.9)	8 (36%)	19 (61.2%)	12 (37.5%)
High IEP (6.0–11.0)	3 (14%)	6 (19.4%)	20 (62.5%)
Total	22	31	32

Chi-square, normals vs. scientists = 5.46   (df = 2) $p < .07$
Chi-square, normals vs. scientists, low vs. moderate categories, = 5.35   (df = 1) $p < .05$
Chi-square, scientists vs. neurotics = 14.87   (df = 2) $p < .01$

means for the normal group on the other four dimensions, their deviation from normal is located exclusively in the "Primitivity of Object Choice" dimension.

Here is one authentic case where "genius is next to insanity." The scientists are a little more primitive in their percepts of people than the normals, but by no means so much so as the neurotics. In Stern's terms, the scientists' preferred method of seeing people has not developed to the normal human adult level. They still live to a moderate degree in the world of witches, gnomes, fairies, and ogres—a rather surprising fact if one is used to thinking of scientists as the most objective, dispassionate, and realistic of men. But it may be the very childlike quality of their imagery which enables the best of them to be creative in imagining new ways in which the world can be understood in abstract terms. Stein (1956) discovered in a relaxed moment in an interview with one of his creative chemists that "he sees atoms and molecules moving around like friends of his and he works with them as friends." It is apparently only in off-moments and through subtle psychological tests that one discovers the childlike imagery of the scientist, but it is undoubtedly present and may well be an important factor in their creativity.

Why do they remain childlike in perceiving humans? Why does nature appear like an extension of themselves? Again we may turn to the asceticism of many of their parents for an answer. Impulses denied expression in real life, if they are urgent enough and the person is intelligent enough, may work themselves out in childish fancies that give a great deal of pleasure. In other words, we need only assume that the young scientist has enjoyed his fantasy life as a means of expressing blocked impulses, to discover a reason why he continues to pursue such "immature" fantasies when he is confronted by anxiety in adult interpersonal relations. So his interest in nature not only represents a flight from people and a turning of aggression into new channels; it also permits him to continue indulging childlike fantasies originally developed out of a frustrated impulse life. His goal may ultimately be power—dominion over nature—but the means to the goal—the continued pursuit of childhood fantasies in which nature is a kind of extension of the self—is in itself pleasurable. It is my guess that among the "pioneer" scientists pleasure in imaginative play is the more important determinant of scientific interest, and that for the "colonizing" scientists who build on the explorations of the pioneers, pleasure in the conquest of nature is the more important determinant.

Many questions remain unanswered. It would be particularly interesting to know why withdrawal, as contrasted with other defenses, is the method of handling aggression adopted by people who become future scientists. Two possibilities seem worth further consideration. First, Roe (1953b) found that many of her eminent scientists had had a serious illness when young, and having been in bed for a long time, out of normal contact with normal human relations and masculine pursuits, should certainly provide the opportunity for development of a rich fantasy life and for the discovery that withdrawal may solve many problems. Secondly, I have pointed out in another place (McClelland, 1956) that one of the paradoxes of history is that radical Protestantism produced not only more than its share of scientists but also more than its share of business entrepreneurs. The paradox arises from the fact that on nearly all tests like the Strong Vocational Interest Blank, scientists and businessmen are diametrically opposed in their interests and attitudes toward life.

How could two such negatively correlated character types

have been produced by the same family type? The answer may lie in the typical mode of adjustment adopted by the two groups— the scientists *withdrawing from* and the businessman typically *entering into* the field of human relationships. Rosen and D'Andrade (1959) have demonstrated that the parents of boys with a high need for Achievement, which predisposes individuals to business entrepreneurship (McClelland, 1955) set high standards for their sons, but also show a good deal of warmth in praising them for their efforts at achievement. We also know that scientists report that they were distant from both parents and therefore in all likelihood did not receive the parental warmth and support that future entrepreneurs get. It may not be pushing credulity too far to infer that warmth should encourage boys to enter into interpersonal relationships whereas coldness should discourage them. So while the future scientist and the future entrepreneur may both have been exposed to high standards, the former, being treated indifferently by his parents, tends to retreat from people, while the latter, being encouraged by his parents, moves out more confidently into the world of adult human relationships. Similarly, high standards plus coldness make frustration and aggression the chief problem for the scientist, while high standards plus warmth make achievement the chief concern of the entrepreneur.

Many facts appear to be falling into place, but it is time for the analytic side of the scientist to show itself and to remind us that many of these supposed interrelationships have not been firmly established by any means. Fantasy is fun, but it must also be checked and disciplined. After all, the scientist's fancy differs only a little from the normal and very much more from the neurotic in poor touch with reality.

What has been accomplished? If I have succeeded in displaying both the "play" and the disciplinary "aggressive" interests of the typical scientist, I will have managed to illustrate with my own work the main points that I have been trying to make. Yet caution must have the last word. Half-way through our investigations, we thought we had a good explanation of the psychodynamics of the scientist. It certainly sounded reasonable. But further checking showed that it was hardly tenable. We have now ended with a new hypothesis. Further research will un-

On the Psychodynamics of Creative Physical Scientists

doubtedly show that it too is defective in some ways. So the truth the scientist seeks always just eludes his grasp, and he must gain his satisfaction from his faith that in unravelling the secrets of the universe his attempt to untie the first knot may make it easier to untie the second.

REFERENCES

Adorno, T. W., E. Frenkel-Brunswik, D. J. Levinson, and R. N. Sanford, *The Authoritarian Personality* (New York: Harper, 1950).

Cattell, R. B., *Personality and Motivation: Structure and Measurement* (Yonkers, N. Y.: World Books, 1957).

——, and J. E. Drevdahl, "A Comparison of the Personality Profile (16 P.F.) of Eminent Researchers with That of Eminent Teachers and Administrators, and of the General Population," *Brit. J. Psychol.*, 46 (1955), 248–261.

Dollard, J., L. W. Doob, N. E. Miller, O. H. Mowrer, and R. R. Sears, *Frustration and Aggression* (New Haven, Conn.: Yale University Press, 1939).

Fisher, S. and S. E. Cleveland, *Body Image and Personality* (Princeton, N. J.: Van Nostrand, 1958).

Freud, S., *A Psychological Study of an Infantile Reminiscence* (New York: Moffat, Yard, 1916).

Knapp, R. H., "Demographic, Cultural and Personality Attributes of Scientists" and "Personality Committee Report," ed. C. W. Taylor, *Research Conference on the Identification of Creative Scientific Talent* (Salt Lake City: University of Utah Press, 1956), pp. 204–212, 229–241.

——, and H. B. Goodrich, *Origins of American Scientists* (Chicago: University of Chicago Press, 1952).

Kubie, L. S., "Problems of the Scientific Career," *Amer. Scientist,* 41 (1953), 596–613.

McClelland, D. C., "Some Social Consequences of Achievement Motivation," *Nebraska Symposium on Motivation* (Lincoln: University of Nebraska Press, 1955).

——, "The Calculated Risk: An Aspect of Scientific Performance," in *Research Conference on the Identification of Creative Scientific Talent,* ed. C. W. Taylor (Salt Lake City: University of Utah Press, 1956), pp. 96–110.

Merton, R., "Puritanism, Pietism and Science," Chapter XIV, *Social Theory and Social Structure* (Glencoe, Ill.: Free Press, 1949).

Roe, A., "A Psychological Study of Physical Scientists, *Genet. Psychol. Monogr.*, 43 (1951), 121–239.

————, "A Psychological Study of Eminent Psychologists and Anthropologists, and a Comparison with Biological and Physical Scientists," *Psychol. Monogr.*, 67, No. 2 (1953).

————, *The Making of a Scientist* (New York: Dodd, Mead, 1953b).

————, *The Psychology of Occupations* (New York: Wiley, 1956).

Rosen, B. C. and R. D'Andrade, "The Psychosocial Origins of Achievement Motivation," *Sociometry*, 22 (1959), 185–218.

Shipley, T. E. and J. Veroff, "A Projective Measure of Need for Affiliation," *J. exp. Psychol.*, 43 (1952), 349–356.

Stein, M. I., "A Transactional Approach to Creativity," *Research Conference on the Identification of Creative Scientific Talent*, ed. C. W. Taylor (Salt Lake City: University of Utah Press, 1956), pp. 171–181.

Stern, P. J., "The Dimensions of Psychopathology: An Existential Approach," unpublished Doctoral dissertation, Harvard University (1958).

Taylor, C. W., ed., *Research Conference on the Identification of Creative Scientific Talent* (Salt Lake City: University of Utah Press, 1956).

Teevan, R. C., "Personality Correlates of Undergraduate Field of Specialization," *J. consult. Psychol.*, 18 (1954), 212–218.

Terman, L. M., "Scientists and Nonscientists in a Group of 800 Gifted Men," *Psychol. Monogr.*, 68, No. 7 (1954), 44.

Veroff, J., A. Cooper, G. Heckler, and R. H. Knapp, "A Factor Analysis of Thorndike's Ratings of Eminent Men" (Middletown, Conn.: Wesleyan University, mimeographed, 1957).

6

RETROSPECT AND
PROSPECT

ROBERT B. MacLEOD
Cornell University

My task is to comment critically on the previous chapters and to attempt an answer to the question, "Where do we go from here?" To do full justice to these five presentations is manifestly impossible. Each stands by itself as a significant contribution, thoughtful and literate, and would gain nothing from the pallid paraphrasing of a commentator. To chart the future at this stage in our inquiry would be foolhardly, and I have no intention of trying to do so. The various contributors have, however, converged on a number of central problems which might bear re-emphasis, and the discussion has revealed some areas of uncertainty which invite further exploration. The best I can do is attempt to identify a few of the common problems and a few of the gaps in our understanding. If we have learned anything from

175

this discussion it is that, to quote the climactic sentence of the sophomore's term-paper, "There is much work to be done."

All of us who have contributed to this book are empirical and experimental in our orientation; most of us have been influenced, directly or indirectly, by the thinking of Max Wertheimer; none of us, so far as I know, is a professed mystic, an out-and-out Freudian, or a "mental tester." Nevertheless, we must not forget that there are approaches other than the strictly experimental, and that if we are to have a proper psychology of creative thinking we must tap all possible sources. Bruner and Henle have quoted extensively from "intuitive" reports. A thoroughgoing mystic might challenge all our laws of evidence, and insist that only through intuition can we understand the process of creation. He may be right, but I think that Bruner and Henle have made the best compromise in their acceptance of the evidence of intuition as empirical fact, to be assessed in accordance with the standards of empirical science. An out-and-out Freudian would push the problem of creativity back into the unconscious. Perhaps we should have had a Freudian among us, but McClelland has helped to fill the gap by playing freely with a Freudian hypothesis. Freud and the Freudians raise questions about the motivation and the personality structure of the creator. Both McClelland and Crutchfield, without being orthodox Freudians, have made us think about the nature of the person who creates. A strict associationist of the nineteenth century variety— and there are still some vocal defenders of this position—might have urged us to seek for the secret of creativity in the varying combinations of elementary ideas or reinforced S-R linkages. Herbert Simon is far from being a nineteenth century associationist, but he keeps reminding us that through the clever combination of elements we can produce behavior that looks amazingly creative. We could certainly have profited from the presence of a Cattell or a Guilford, with the rich store of information their factor analytic studies have yielded; and we might even have learned something from Harlow's monkeys and Köhler's apes. This book may be a bit overbalanced on one side, but I don't think it has done serious injustice to the topic.

For generations psychologists have been going through contortions to avoid the use of words like "mind," "mental," "idea," and so forth. I forget who it was—but it was probably Woodworth—who condensed the history of psychology into a few concise statements. It was originally the science of the soul. First, it lost its soul—presumably in the eighteenth century. Then it lost its mind, at the hand of the nineteenth century associationists. Early in the twentieth century it lost consciousness, because of the Freudians and the Behaviorists. What is left is behavior, of a sort, defined in terms of S-R connections in the brain. But a recent commentator has suggested that we have now disposed of the brain and replaced it by a computing machine. This book has brought the computer to the forefront of the stage. Is it a tool? a liberator? a creator? a master? a monster? We may have reason to be frightened of it, but we cannot evade its challenge. I shall have more to say about the electronic computers later, but may I momentarily remind you of a passage from William James? James was playing with the idea of the perfect automaton, a machine which could replicate perfectly human appearance and human behavior. In characteristic Jamesian fashion the automaton was presented as a young lady, perfect in her beauty, exquisite in her manners, but without a soul. Could you, James asked, fall in love with a beautiful automaton that had no soul? He thought that you could not. We now have the answer to James. During these discussions it became amply clear that it *is* possible to fall in love with a computing machine. Don't be confused by our frequent use of the masculine pronoun. We may speak of the machine as "he," but we really think of her as "she"; we are merely suppressing the sex reference.

An interesting inference from this book is that some psychologists seem to have lost their fear of old-fashioned terminology. We have talked lightly of "mind" and "ideas" and "mental combinations." We are not ashamed to speak of "the self," and, in a very timid sort of fashion, we have almost reintroduced "the soul." This reflects, I think, a growing sense of security. It may be that the computing machine has so frightened us that we are scurrying back to the cloudy terminology of a

177

bygone age. I prefer to think, however, that, far from being frightened by the machine, we feel ourselves liberated by the machine from the task of demonstrating that we have a science, and free to take a fresh look at phenomena with which a bygone methodology could not cope. We, as experimental psychologists, believe in the unity of nature. It is our faith that even the least tangible of human experiences will ultimately be intelligible as evidences of natural law. Hence our willingness to play with the possibility that that least tangible of all human phenomena, creativity, may eventually yield to the methods of science.

THE CENTRAL PROBLEMS

Our discussion has raised three major questions, about which cluster a great many subsidiary questions. (1) Is it possible to study creative thinking scientifically? (2) What are the criteria of creativity? (3) Under what conditions do people become creative? I shall comment briefly on each of these. We have not found a satisfactory answer to any of them. Nevertheless, *prudens quaestio dimidium scientiae*. Even the attempting to formulate a question clearly can in itself yield a substantial measure of understanding.

Can We Have a Science of Creative Thinking?

It is easy to state our faith that all human phenomena conform to the laws of nature; it is less easy to find cold propositions that state brute facts and unequivocal relations. The psychologist who insists that creativity can be studied scientifically must bear the burden of proof in the face of centuries of testimony from mystics and artists, and even from ordinary people, who claim that at least in his moments of inspiration man is not subject to the laws of nature. And this is no mean testimony. Coleridge recording his *Kubla Khan* and Poincaré at the end of his now familiar journey from Caen to Coutances were not behaving like the machines we study in the physics laboratory. Could anyone have predicted, much less controlled, what was to happen? The psychologist will have to work hard if he is to

178

demonstrate that man at his best can be reduced to statements of cause and effect. Indeed, the psychologist must work hard to prove that even on his most humdrum level man behaves in a scientifically predictable way.

Nevertheless, my answer to the question is "yes," if you permit me to define "science." Science is sometimes regarded as an orderly array of facts, derived from observation, tested by experiment, capable of yielding secure predictions. Sometimes the emphasis is less on factual content than on the methods of observation, verification, and prediction. Both are important, but they constitute only a part of science. The essence of science, it seems to me, is an attitude—an attitude of disciplined curiosity. Both words are to be emphasized, "curiosity" and "discipline." Curiosity is natural in human beings. Our educational system is frequently successful in suppressing it, but if we need reassurance all we have to do is to look at any normal child. Our children, until we ruin them, are bundles of curiosity. But the child is not yet a scientist, not until his curiosity has been disciplined by methods that have stood the test of experience. A scientist who is worthy of the name is forever questioning, forever observing, forever raising and testing hypotheses. No true scientist ever believes that he possesses the truth; there is always the lure of the unexplored and the challenge to develop methods that will make further exploration possible.

In this sense, and only in this sense, we can have a science of creative thinking. We have the curiosity—we can be curious about the nature of curiosity. We have a certain amount of discipline—discipline in observation and inference. What we are fumbling for is method, or perhaps even technique—ways in which the creative process, about which we are curious, can be brought under controlled scrutiny. In this symposium a number of different approaches have been suggested, e.g., the purely descriptive, the cultural-historical, the individual-historical, the statistical-analytical, the experimental. It is evident that all are rewarding and that at this stage of the inquiry all should be explored.

Our common bias is, I think, in the direction of the experimental approach. We shall not be happy until we have pinned

179

down the processes of creation in such a way that we shall be able to generate them, control their course, and predict their outcome. I agree; but at the risk of appearing disloyal I should like to argue that experimental psychology is not yet ready to assimilate all the phenomena of creativity. It is my faith, and I think my colleagues share it, that ultimately there will be a single science of nature that will encompass all that now seems to be uniquely human. My misgivings are about premature attempts, limited by available methods, to squeeze the intangibles of behavior into existing molds.

There are some who would discard the experimental approach because it cannot at present do justice to all the phenomena. This attitude we all reject as unworthy; there was a time, not long since, when pessimists were saying similar things about the possibility of a complete science of physics or of biology. How wrong they have proved to be! There are others at the opposite extreme who claim that the existing methods of physics or of biology are quite capable of dealing with all the phenomena of mind. All we need to do, they suggest, is drastically simplify the psychological problem to the point at which existing methods can be made to work. It might appear at first glance that Herbert Simon has advocated this approach to the study of creative thinking. He has focused on "problem-solving" as the best example of the creative mind in action, and has demonstrated that properly instructed machines can solve problems pretty much as humans do, and often very much more efficiently. It may be that by concentrating first on miniature samples of thinking we may be able to recognize essential principles which are obscured when we attempt to observe thinking on a more global level. No one really quarrels with this procedure; it has been followed by experimental scientists since the beginning of history. The danger, as Simon has explicitly recognized, is that in reducing our problem to convenient dimensions we may unwittingly trim away the very dimensions which make it interesting and challenging. The history of psychology is studded with instructive examples.

It may be that the alternatives we face are really reflections of differences in scientific temperament. There are some, like Lewin, who approach a fuzzy problem with exuberant abandon, slashing about with improvised tools and leaving to others the less exciting task of measuring precisely and testing rigorously. There are others, like Hull, who prefer neat and orderly work with razor-sharp instruments, postponing the attack on the fuzzy problems until appropriate instruments have been developed. Freud had a word for each of these types. I suspect that the world needs both. Would we be richer or poorer if Lewin had become compulsively concerned about confidence levels and Hull had been seduced into phenomenology? So far as creative thinking is concerned—that fuzziest of all fuzzy problems—my judgment is quite firm. Let us, by all means, sharpen the tools we have; let us carefully dissect every miniature sample of creativity that we can bring into the laboratory; but let us also keep on looking at the fuzzy phenomena in all their complexity, trying out different descriptive languages, searching for hints about dimensions and variables that may later yield to experimental control. At this stage in the game, it seems to me, our greatest need is for a better phenomenology of thinking.

The Criteria of Creativity

I have just mentioned the need for a better phenomenology of thinking, but I promise not to inflict on you a wearying discussion of phenomenology. For present purposes all we need to know is that the phenomenologist is intensely curious about all the phenomena of direct experience, that he accepts the observation of experience as the starting point for any psychological inquiry, that in observing and describing experience he attempts to suspend the biases that have been imposed on him by his culture and his individual upbringing. It is conventional to define psychology as the science of behavior *and* experience. The phenomenologist begins with direct experience, and he approaches the study of behavior initially as a form of experience. Phenomenology is not a science but an approach to science; there never was and never could be a complete phenomenologist, but in psychology at least the *attempt* to be phenomenological has yielded rich rewards.

The term "creative thinking" is extremely fuzzy. When we begin to discuss it we are sure that we have a community of mean-

ROBERT B. MACLEOD

ing, and then it dawns on us that each of us has his own slightly different conception of it. This is not an unusual situation in psychology, and it need not perturb us too much. Our linguistic tradition hands down a word to us, a word which we cannot define precisely but which seems to carry a certain face validity. There is a survival of the fittest in linguistic as there is in biological evolution. Many words and expressions appear suddenly on the scene, enjoy a fleeting popularity, and then gradually sink into oblivion as they fail to prove their right to continued existence. Others are tough and resistant. They may yield to phonetic change or lose their birthright through one of the accidents of semantic change, but where identity has apparently been lost we find a few synonyms popping up to re-establish continuity of meaning. In opposition to Professor Bruner's "unregenerate Nominalism" I am prepared to defend, rather tentatively, a modified form of Classical Realism. Granted that many of our linguistic structures are arbitrary, flimsy, and sometimes evidences of nothing more than cultural lag, I should still argue that the persistent attempt to clarify linguistic meaning may lead us to the discovery of things, processes, relationships, and ideas that possess the attributes of "reality." Socrates followed this procedure with some success in his search for the meaning of "justice." Whether "creativity" will survive the same sort of scrutiny remains to be seen.

At any rate, we have been presented with the term "creative thinking" and have been asked to explain what it is. We might, of course, following the associationist tradition, define creation as a recombination of previously existing elements and conclude accordingly that it is merely an illusion. This would be to impose a structure of theory on the phenomenon before the phenomenon has been really inspected; just as illicit as it would be to assume at the outset that creativity is a statistically isolable personality factor or is the expression of an unconscious life-urge. And, indeed, we may find ourselves led to any of these conclusions; but, please, not before we have first looked at the phenomena.

The phenomenologist's first question would be: What phenomena in experience and behavior *invite* the term "creativity"? I use the word "invite" advisedly. The conceptualizations

182

we achieve are by invitation from a world that offers possibilities of categorization; the situation which we apprehend as a problem invites us to do some exploring; the traditional categories of psychology which irritate us today (like perception, feeling, will) would not still be with us were there not phenomenal distinctions which invite them.

What then are the phenomena we find ourselves invited to look at? The contributors have given us a fairly impressive array, although with regrettable modesty they have withheld one important block of evidence, namely, the memories of their own creative moments. If a Poincaré or an Einstein is willing to share his experience, why shouldn't a Bruner or a McClelland? It seems to me that it is with old-fashioned self-observation that the inquiry should begin. Fortunately Bruner and Henle have combed the literature for significant examples of self-revelation and have found many, some more articulate than others. Few of the reporters were trained in observation and we have no adequate controls. Nevertheless, the impressive fact is that so many of the reports ring true. Even the ordinary, uncreative person, peering through the metaphors of the mystic or the poet, dimly recognizes something similar in his own experience. He remembers the odd instance when he, too, felt the startle of a discovery or the glow of a new insight; and he begins to have a feel for the meaning of creativity. Introspection and retrospection may not give us secure criteria, but without the intuitions derived from direct experience our inquiry would be formal and barren. Just as the sensitive psychiatrist understands his patient in part through the memories of his own moments of irrationality, so the psychologist must seek for criteria of creativity in the memories of his own creative moments.

So much for phenomenology. Given a "feel" for the meaning of creativity, the psychologist's real task still lies ahead. It is that of examining the varied situations in which human behavior invites the term "creative," of dissecting out the essential from the accidental, the relevant from the irrelevant, of applying the tools of criticism and experiment to determine whether or not there really is something in behavior that corresponds to his intuition. Intuitions must always be accepted at face value as facts, but their

183

usefulness is limited if they cannot be meaningfully related to more readily observable phenomena.

The situations to be studied seem to fall into four categories: creative periods in history, creative groups, creative persons, and creative acts, and all four have been discussed. If we can find something common to all these we shall be well on our way toward the identification of a criterion of creativity. I cannot honestly say that we have succeeded, but I feel that we have made a moderately good start.

The creative period in history, as a psychological problem, is usually left to the literary historian, and in this volume it has not received the attention it deserves. All of us, as we look back over history, are agreed that certain periods stand out as significantly creative. One thinks of the scant three centuries of Athenian glory that left their stamp on all subsequent philosophy, art, and science, of the Italian Renaissance that was a birth as well as a rebirth, of the American Revolution that gave the world a new conception of the place of man in society, of the technological revolution that has occurred within our own lifetime. One could slice history in many other ways and find as many different examples of the creative movement or the creative period. What is important is that in retrospect we can recognize the difference between periods of stagnation and periods of creativity and can ask for the whats and the whys of these differences. Psychologists have done little with the problem, but McClelland, in studies not reported in this book, has obtained promising results from the application of the methods of content analysis to the cultural products of creative and uncreative periods.

I shall not review the studies of group creativity. Suffice it to say that it has been amply demonstrated that groups as groups can be creative or uncreative; but we do not yet know precisely under what conditions, working on what types of problems, composed of what types of people, a group can be most creative. Bruner has described one obviously creative group. With such a group it would be difficult to introduce controlled variations, and it may be that artificially contrived groups will never provide the conditions that foster group creativity at its best. In due course, however, it will be possible to accumulate records of wider and wider arrays of "natural" groups which show varying degrees and kinds of creativity and thus a posteriori to fill the cells of what ideally would have been a designed sample. Group creativity is certainly a field that deserves to be ploughed and cultivated.

When we come to the problem of the creative person our criteria tend to be confused. McClelland has assumed that recipients of the Nobel Prize are creative, and has plunged into a deep analysis of their motivation and their personality structure. The Institute for Personality Assessment and Research has selected a long list of supposedly creative individuals for study, but Crutchfield has not told us precisely why they were rated as creative. One cannot quarrel too much with such selections. Most of us have a "feel" for the difference between a creative and an uncreative person, and we are likely to place in the first class the scientists, the poets, and the inventors who have won the respect of their colleagues. The fact remains, however, that we would still like to find a criterion by which we can distinguish the scientist who discovers by accident from the scientist who discovers by design, between the inventor who merely is a developer and the inventor who really presents us with something new and useful. Certainly there are people who may be judged as creative; but two facts stand out clearly, namely, that the behavior of creative people is not uniformly creative and that acts of creation may emerge from people who would ordinarily be regarded as utterly uncreative.

This leads us to the creative act itself, and here the experimental psychologist ought to have something to say. The interesting fact is that although the experimentalists have painstakingly examined the conditions of creative behavior they have for the most part dodged the question of criteria. The exceptions, however, are notable. The Würzburgers, even within the framework of their tedious experiments, were able to report the "Aha!" of discovery. Köhler's apes, and the many other apes and children who succeeded them, often behaved stupidly but also showed that, when presented with a situation that they could "see into," they could apprehend things in new relations that opened up new possibilities. The best was, of course, Max Wertheimer, whose book

Productive Thinking might just as appropriately have been entitled "Creative Thinking." Wertheimer distinguishes clean from ugly thinking, thinking that is more than merely repetitive, that goes to the heart of the problem, that grasps inner structural relations. Even these characterizations, however, appealing as they may be, are descriptive rather than analytic. They leave us with a feel for what we are trying to identify but with no explicit criteria.

Perhaps this is as much as we can hope for at our present stage. Certainly, our discussions have not left us with a set of firm criteria on the basis of which we can design our research. We have, however, moved toward some conclusions about which there seems to be a fair measure of agreement. We have found nothing, for instance, to suggest that creativity is a simple, unitary trait of personality. There may be identifiable trait clusters which predispose the individual to act creatively, but there are also determinable social and other conditions which facilitate or inhibit the emergence of the creative act. Nor may we equate creativity to productivity, at least in the quantitative sense of the term. Our judgments are always based, of course, on some sort of product, but it is the kind of product and not its amount which interests us.

Whether or not creative thinking and problem-solving are the same thing is a more difficult question to answer. Simon has made a strong case for the usefulness of the problem-solving experiment as a way of observing and replicating the processes that go on when a person thinks creatively. His case becomes even more impressive as he demonstrates the evident parallel between the human processes and those of an "intelligent" computing machine. One cannot quarrel with his initial selection of "tidy" problems, like those of logic and chess, for which the machine is a peculiarly appropriate instrument; one should always begin with an experiment which has some chance of success. The fact remains, however, that the machines show improvement "with experience," and that they are now showing modest promise in fields, like the composition of music, which are not so tidily logical. There is no reason to doubt that before long the machines will be replicating human problem-solving on levels of much greater complexity.

For the time being, however, it seems to me that a note of caution is in order, and this has to do with the meaning of the word "problem." Psychologists have not always been precise in its use. In one sense everything we do is a problem, and every decision we make is consequently an example of problem-solving. This is obviously too amorphous a concept to have any scientific value. More commonly, in our laboratories, we have tended to limit "problem-solving behavior" to what is observed under certain specified conditions of experimental control; and this is equally unsatisfactory. Neither the very broad nor the very narrow meaning provides an adequate distinction between problem-solving that is creative and problem-solving that is uncreative. A skilled technician who knows his tools can efficiently but routinely solve a great array of problems, provided some creative person has already invented the right tools. Perhaps this is what our machines are doing, although Simon is optimistic enough to think otherwise. Most of us fumble our way through life's problems fairly successfully, with seldom a spark of the creativity that transforms the meaning of life. Evidently the "problem of the problem" must be thought through before we can know which kind of problem-solving is creative.

This leads to the criterion which appeals to me as most nearly satisfactory, namely, novelty. Must an act yield something new if it is to be considered as creative? Bruner and Henle lay a good deal of stress on the importance of novelty, but each is careful to point out that much that is novel is utterly trivial. Obviously we cannot consider as creative any act which accidentally yields something new. How then are we to qualify the criterion of novelty to make it acceptable? I suggest that we can do so if we dwell for a moment on the meaning of "trivial" and the meaning of "accident." Again, I shall resist the temptation to be phenomenological, but we cannot avoid the questions "new to whom?" and "new in what context?". The newness, I suggest, must be newness to the thinker; the context must be the world as he understands it. It may well be that what is new to him is familiar to everyone else, and that which is perfectly routine for him is new to everyone else. These are irrelevant considerations. The magician may have been creative when he invented his new trick,

187

but there is nothing especially creative about the act that flabbergasts his audience.

And now for our qualifications, "not accidental" and "not trivial," both of which refer to the world of the thinker. Many a discovery has been made by accident—the appearance of an unexpected precipitate in a test tube, the uncovering of a skeleton in a gravel pit. The creativity is not in the observation itself but in the recognition of its significance. The creative mind sees something new in it, something that is not trivial. Bruner's "effective surprise" is not the startle that comes from the sudden slamming of a door; it is the startle that comes with the seeing of a set of new and important relations. The Würzburgers reported "Aha, I've got it!" They might quite as properly have reported "Aha, that's something I had never thought of before!"

Two things about the "Aha!" experience must not be forgotten. In the first place, we tend to think of it as something sudden; and it is true that the more glamorous examples of insight are the flashes that bring sudden illumination. But they are not always sudden; the dawning of insight may be as gradual as the dawning of day, with facts ordering themselves into new relations so slowly that no one moment in time is remembered as the precise moment at which everything became clear. And, secondly, the "Aha!" can have no meaning except in the context of a search that is actively going on. It may be the search for the solution of a very specific problem or a dimly apprehended, perhaps even unconscious, search for a satisfying philosophy of life; without motivation there can be no true surprise. What is new in creative thinking must be something apprehended as significantly new in the context of something that is important for the thinker.

Wertheimer, Duncker, and other Gestaltists have talked about the "restructuring of the cognitive field"—a cumbersome expression perhaps, but less unsatisfactory than many. When we think creatively we shake ourselves loose from our old assumptions, we see the problem as imposing new requirements, we see old instruments as capable of new functions—the rigid structure of the field has been broken down so as to permit new configurations. From this point of view it is obvious that wherever restructuring takes place there is the possibility of creative thinking.

There can consequently be degrees of creativity. This I agree to. I should be inclined, however, to include a value dimension and to reserve something like "true creativity" for the act which has resulted in a radical restructuring of a major cognitive or motivational system. The "truly" creative person is the person who has "seen the light," has experienced a flood of illumination on a problem or a concern with which he is deeply involved, and has thoroughly reoriented his thinking as a result. "Wissenschaft," said the German philosopher, "ist das Wissen mit dem Wissen der Grenzen und Weisen des Wissens." The creative act, if one may be permitted to paraphrase, is "truly" creative when it carries with it an awareness of how and within what limits it has yielded something new.

The Conditions of Creativity

We have not established a firm set of criteria of creativity, and one might argue that until we have done so we cannot hope to specify the conditions under which creativity emerges. The logic of science tells us to define the effect we wish to explain before we try to determine the cause. This would seem sensible but the apparently logical pattern of scientific progress is for the most part a *post hoc* interpretation. Archimedes may have known precisely what he was looking for before he shouted "Eureka," although I doubt it, but certainly the quest from Galileo to Newton for the laws of gravitation did not begin with a clearly defined concept of "mutual attraction" which had to be explained. The very fact that the problem was stated as that of "falling bodies" indicates that the scientists knew only vaguely what they were looking for. In struggling to define the criteria of creativity I have found myself slipping into a discussion of conditions. Now, as I try to review the conditions of creativity, I find myself tempted to go back and say something more about criteria. We shall probably have to oscillate back and forth many times before we really know what we are talking about.

In our discussion, it seems to me, we have been focusing on two sets of conditions which are really inseparable from one another. On the one hand we have the cognitive field of the thinker, on the other his motivation and personality structure.

189

Bruner and Henle have dwelt particularly on the former, Crutch-field and McClelland on the latter. A third set of conditions, namely, the social and cultural settings that foster creativity, we have touched upon only incidentally. This topic belongs, presumably, to the historian and the sociologist, but the psychologist ought also to have something to contribute.

There is no need to review in detail the points about cognitive organization made by Bruner and Henle. The impressive fact is that the two speakers are in substantial agreement. Creation is perception as well as action; to know the way in which people apprehend the world is essential to an understanding of what they do about it. When I use the word "cognitive" I realize that I am inviting a misinterpretation. The classic distinction of knowing from feeling and willing has embedded itself deeply in our vocabulary, and has left us with the impression that states and processes of knowing are pallid things, devoid of feeling and force. We might escape from the bonds of faculty psychology by inventing a new jargon, but it seems to me that it will be more profitable in the long run if, at the risk of initial confusion, we insist that the meaning of "cognitive" be broadened.

John Locke defined an idea as "whatsoever is the object of the understanding when a man thinks." Not a bad beginning, so long as we don't let the word "object" trick us into excluding its traditional opposite, "subject," from the field of cognition. The cognitive field includes not only all the things, events, and relations as they are apprehended, but also the self which is the crucial anchorage point of all apprehension. Perceiving is a special kind of relation between self and object; remembering and imagining are slightly different kinds of relation. To assert that desiring and willing, hating and fearing, are coordinate relations between self and object is not to reduce motivation to perception; it is merely to recognize that processes which have been traditionally assigned to different faculties belong together in a single psychological field. The self is "something there," or more properly "something here," and its properties and dimensions are no less objects of the understanding than are the squareness and the brownness of the table.

190

If we grant this one point, namely, that the self is a cognitive fact, we may find that we can sharpen our questions about the cognitive conditions of creativity. Even when we speak of self and object as different structures in a single field, possessing many phenomenal properties in common as well as properties which differentiate them, we still run the risk of treating them as two different kinds of existent. The fact is that there are degrees of subjectivity (selfhood) and degrees of objectivity (thinghood), but that some differentiation along this dimension is necessary for all mental life. James' hypothetical "blooming, buzzing confusion," or the state of Nirvana reported by the mystics, would represent a state of utter de-differentiation in which no thinking could take place. The cognitive conditions for thinking, then, must be sought in certain special self-object relations.

One way of dealing with these would be to plot something like a set of Lewinian diagrams and transform them into moving pictures; this I shall refrain from attempting. Bruner and Henle have used the much more appealing language of common sense, richly besprinkled with literary metaphor. This is probably at present a far better means of communication. It is interesting that both authors found themselves stating the conditions of creativity in the form of antinomies or paradoxes. The creator is both detached and committed, free and yet ensnared, concerned but not too much so; it is difficult to quantify these, but we know what they mean. In no case is the condition exclusively subjective or exclusively objective; it is always a self-object relation. If motivation is too strong the person is blinded; if the objective situation is too tightly structured the person sees none of its alternative possibilities. Obviously, if we are to identify the conditions of the field which contribute to creativity, we cannot deal with subjects and objects in isolation.

Our temptation, of course, is to concentrate on the subjective end of the relation, and to seek for the "traits" and the "attitudes" of the self which seem to be essential to creative thinking. "Traits" and "attitudes" are, however, weasel-words. Traits are not phenomenal data; they are inferred from the consistent attitudes which people adopt. Nor are attitudes phenomenal data; we infer attitudes from people's responses to objects. Since phenomenological observations do not warrant a radical separation of self from object, the physicalist will have the burden of proof if he is to demonstrate that the contributions to creativity of "organism" and "environment" can be divorced from each other. This problem we must examine.

First, another quick look at the phenomenology of creativity. The creative moment, the creative impulse, the experience of "Aha! Now I have it!" all have a distinctly subjective flavor. It is the "I" that does the seeing and experiences the thrill; the "I" feels itself the agent, and not merely the recipient. The dominating "I" has mastered its world and made something new of it. But there is also the humbler "I" that looks at the world, and looks again, and then says, "Here is something I had only dreamed of, but it's true." In the field of the recipient creator the self is very small and the world is wide-open; to him the world has disclosed something new.

In the examples offered by Bruner and Henle the honors seem to be fairly equally divided between the dominating creator and the recipient creator, but for both there seems to be a combination of insistent curiosity, unfettered by personal concern, and *Weltoffenheit,* disciplined by rules of critical thinking. In this sense Plato was a creator, and so were Galileo, Shakespeare, Beethoven, and Goethe. Each was open to the world, infinitely curious, but each bowed to certain rules that were not of his own creating.

Let us now translate our problem into the quasi-biological and quasi-sociological language of "organism" and "environment," but without forgetting the leads we have received from phenomenological analysis. From this point of view capacities, traits, attitudes, and our deeper motives are treated as dispositions of a behaving organism, which can be independently studied in the context of an independently definable environment. I can see nothing illegitimate in the treatment of attitudes, for instance, as intervening variables, the characteristics of which are deduced from observed behavior. This approach has led to such practically useful constructs as intelligence, authoritarian tendency,

192

and empathic ability, which in turn can be progressively refined through analysis to provide us with an array of less immediately intelligible but more reliably predictive indices. We observe creativity in behavior; we ask whether or not there are specifiable conditions in the organism which predispose it to be creative and under what environmental conditions it is most likely to be creative.

Similarly, I consider it quite legitimate and frequently very rewarding to trace the developmental history of a particular disposition. We may ask whether or not there is any correlation between observed creativity in behavior and particular types of organism-environment relation at earlier stages of development. This was, of course, the emphasis of the Darwinians, and later of the Freudians. The results of predictive tests have not always been impressive, but this is no reason for a disparagement of the genetic method.

The focus on dispositions and origins might be condemned by a Lewinian as an Aristotelian rather than a Galilean mode of thought. It is indeed Aristotelian in many respects; but so was Lewin's field theory. Within the psychological field one may reject inherent properties in favor of relational determination; but the outer boundaries of the field must, if only for practical reasons, be described in class-theoretical language. The danger which Lewin was combatting is the tendency to reify dependable and consistent sets of relations, to treat intelligence, for instance, as an inherent property of an individual rather than as a characteristic of behavior. There seems little likelihood that anyone contributing to this book will attempt to reify creativity.

At any rate, Aristotelian or not, McClelland and Crutchfield have asked the questions: What are the personality characteristics of a creative person, and how does he get that way? Neither one has reified creativity: in fact both have been loyal to the data of phenomenology, and both have contributed richly to our picture of the creative act. What I find most challenging about their approach is that they bring us back into contact with real people. What they want to know is why one person is creative and another person is not.

193

Is there such a thing as a creative person? If so, is he born or bred? There are some who believe he is born, and I don't think this idea should be discarded too lightly. It has been said that "genius will out." This is obviously untrue, because genius can be throttled, literally or figuratively; but we should not overlook the possibility that whatever underlies creativity may be lodged in the genes. McClelland did not bother with this question, and I don't blame him. What McClelland is concerned with is the conditions of early experience which may predispose the individual to become creative. Even if there are genetic differences in potentiality, there must also be nongenetic influences which will decide whether or not the potential becomes actual. The self is a growing thing, battered into shape by all sorts of forces. It is important to know which forces foster creativity and which inhibit it. McClelland has played with one set of hypotheses, more or less Freudian in character. To say that I am not fully convinced is to say nothing more than he would say himself. His is an adventurous mind, and tomorrow we may find him playing with some of his alternative hypotheses.

Crutchfield's cross-sectional type of analysis is perhaps more precarious. Without denying the relevance of early developmental history he assumes, quite correctly, that all factors which enter into the determination of creative behavior must be lodged somehow or other in the present structure of the creator; even "probability of novel response" can be translated back into dispositional terms, some sort of "attitude" perhaps. It was a difficult task to translate the properties of intelligent behavior into measures of intelligence; to do the same for creative thinking is even more difficult. Every possible sampling difficulty is present in the selection of things to be tested and of techniques of testing, and there is the additional problem of sampling the population of creative people to whom the tests are to be administered. It need not be mentioned that Crutchfield is fully aware of the hazards, and that his conclusions are almost excessively modest. He finds certain clusters of dispositions which seem to be characteristic of people who are judged to be creative, and these suggest interesting hypotheses about the relation between creativity and conformity;

194

it would be quite out of character for him to assert at this stage that there is a creative type, much less a trait of creativity.

Bruner and Henle have helped us particularly to understand the field-conditions of the creative act. McClelland and Crutchfield have added to our understanding, but what excites me about their presentations is the hope they hold out that we may eventually be able to identify creative people and to determine what makes them creative. It is not beneath the dignity of the scientist to have a concern for the welfare of his society. Of all the scientists, none should be more concerned than the psychologist that society be enabled to identify potential creators and provide conditions that will foster their full development.

RETROSPECT

How does our present interest in the psychology of creative thinking fit into the story of man's age-old quest for an understanding of his own mental processes? This could easily be a chapter in the history of psychology, but I shall limit myself to a few variations on a single theme, namely, that of the constricting assumptions that have prevented psychologists from making a frontal attack on the problem of creativity. All thinking is governed to some extent by its implicit assumptions, and the history of ideas is in part an attempt to identify assumptions that have given shape to ideas. It seems to me that we can identify four sets of assumptions in the history of Western thought that have tended to direct, and possibly to constrict, our thinking about creativity.

1. Man is uniquely rational. This was Plato's conception, and Aristotle clothed it with flesh when he characterized man as a "rational animal." If we are rational beings who think at our best in accordance with the laws of logic and mathematics, then creative thinking is an orderly exploration of what may follow from certain premises. The best disciplined thinker produces the best ideas; but he does not really "produce" them, he merely "deduces" them. Creation may have its aura of originality, but the real crea-

tor is he who has thoroughly mastered the techniques of inference. Our electronic machines are the best rational animals we have yet seen.

2. Man does not belong to the natural order. His bodily processes may conform to natural law, but reason and will are not subject to the laws of nature. There can be no creation apart from God's creation and no discovery apart from the revelation of what was already in the mind of God. Whether God reveals the truth through the ecstasy of the mystic or through the struggle of the soul in agony, the truth is outside the order of natural events. Only God creates: man can only discover.

3. Man is a part of physical nature, and his mind behaves consequently in accordance with the laws of physical science. This was the view that was gaining ground in the eighteenth century and that found its neatest expression in the mental mechanics of James Mill. If the physical universe can be explained in terms of the behavior of material particles, existing in space and time and propelled or constrained by force, why cannot we reduce mind to analogous elements and explain its behavior by the same laws? James Mill's theory was obviously patterned after Newtonian mechanics, which at that time was the accepted model of Science. John Stuart Mill's addition of the chemical analogy challenged in no fundamental way the principle of explanation by reduction. If to explain is to reduce to elements and their combinations, then anything that appears novel can be nothing more than an unfamiliar combination of already existing elements. For the associationists, consequently, and for those contemporary students of behavior who cling to the Newtonian model, "creation" can mean only "recombination." There can be nothing in the mind that was not previously in the senses, nothing in the whole that was not previously in its parts.

4. Man is an adaptive organism, constantly adjusting itself to its environment. Darwin's thinking was essentially Newtonian: variability is the result of chance combinations of elements, survival the result of mechanical selection. Certain non-Newtonian analogies were, however, unavoidable. The "struggle for survival" almost implies that survival is a goal rather than a mere outcome; and the temptation is almost irresistible to interpret structures in

terms of "what they are designed to do" rather than to think of function as an accident of structure. Darwin's disciples soon began to stray from the Newtonian fold. When man began to look at the animals, at his children, and at the mental aberrations of himself and his fellow-man, he found the associationist model altogether too cumbersome. Herbert Spencer strove valiantly to make associationism evolutionary; Charles Lloyd Morgan, having struggled to maintain the Law of Parsimony, finally conceded a principle of "emergence" in evolution; McDougall quite frankly espoused the cause of purposivism; Freud, less frankly, did the same thing. The outcome of Darwinism was a psychology that looked for its explanations to the past and to the future, but seldom to the present.

No one of these four sets of assumptions can be idly dismissed. It may be that man has a uniquely rational faculty, the characteristics of which can be teased out, possibly by the methods of factor analysis. We may finally decide that the answer to the problem of human creativity lies outside the realm of empirical science; our difficulty in deciding what it is we are really talking about tempts us to take this position. It is the other two, the Newtonian and the Darwinian models, which I think we should explore a bit further before we yield to the mystic or to the rationalist psychology's most fascinating set of problems. My thesis is that both the Newtonian and the Darwinian models, useful as they have been and still are in some contexts, are incapable of dealing satisfactorily with the phenomena which we are now inspecting.

Newton symbolizes one of the great revolutions in the history of modern science, as did Copernicus before him and Darwin subsequently. Newton gave us a vision of a science of physical nature which would ultimately explain, without residue, all the phenomena of the material universe in terms of natural law. He gave us mathematical tools and explanatory constructs; and one of the greatest tributes to his genius is the fact that, with only minor modifications, his system still provides a perfectly satisfactory basis for a great deal of physical analysis. Newton's prestige in the eighteenth and nineteenth centuries was enormous; and physicists of today are less inclined to say that Newton was wrong than that the physics of an expanding universe requires a broader conception of natural law. What is important for us as psychologists to recognize is that at the time when psychology was beginning to be a science the conception of science was essentially Newtonian. Science in its essence was the reduction of the complex to the simple, of quality to quantity, and the quantification of cause-effect relations in such a way that they can provide a basis for prediction. Newtonian science in the nineteenth century was not only a set of laws; it was a *Zeitgeist*. The scientist of the nineteenth century had to reduce to elements, had to quantify the relations among elements.

I have mentioned James Mill as the prototype of the Newtonian psychologists. He did not attempt to quantify—although Herbart did—but he at least tried to reduce all mental contents to elements and combinations of elements. When psychology began to be experimental, with Fechner, Helmholtz, and Wundt, the reductive principle was never questioned, and the focus of attention was on quantification. The elements were sensations rather than ideas, and quantification was sought in precise psychophysical and psychophysiological correlations. Although William James had some reservations about the value of psychophysics, there is no question that psychology gained much from its Newtonian associations. It gained at least a respect for careful observation and meticulous measurement, and it gained something of the physicist's faith in the universality of natural law. What it lost, I believe, was something of the spirit that pervaded the new science of the Renaissance, the spirit that impelled Galileo to look for a new law when he found that the accepted laws of Aristotle could not account for the facts of observation. In the same spirit physicists of recent generations have allowed the facts of observation to lead them beyond Newton.

Psychology, as a science, has understandably been overpowered by the achievements of its elder brother. All too frequently, however, psychologists seem to have assumed that because a method has proved fruitful in physics it is therefore universally applicable. The method that psychology has borrowed from Newton is that of reductive analysis. Today we have the almost amusing picture of a psychology that is still trying to pattern itself after nineteenth century physics, while the physicists of today have long since left the nineteenth century behind. If psychology is to imitate the physical sciences, which is not such a bad idea, it should imitate not the methods and the constructs of a particular era but the openness to facts and the willingness to challenge assumptions that have been the hallmarks of science in the modern world.

At any rate, the psychology of thinking in the Newtonian tradition has had a sad history. Newtonian principles were fine for the elementary psychology of sensation. They could be made to work, as Helmholtz showed, for the simpler forms of perception, provided one were willing to dispose of all the tricky problems by assigning them to a central, unconscious, inferential process. They could even account for memory, as Ebbinghaus so painstakingly demonstrated, if one limited one's tests to the recognition and recall of nonsense syllables. Give us time, said the Newtonians; once we have mastered the elements we shall be able to deal with their combinations. But the "higher thought processes," even the thought processes just one notch higher than those of sense-perception, never really yielded to analysis. Wilhelm Wundt, perhaps the best Newtonian of them all, conceded that human thought could not be studied in the experimental laboratory; it can be understood best, he argued, through an analysis of cultural product, especially language. Oswald Külpe, a disciple of Brentano rather than of Wundt, claimed nevertheless that the higher thought processes could indeed be analyzed and that their analysis reveals elements not found in simple sensation. The controversy over "imageless thought," in which the introspectionists of Würzburg were pitted against those of Cornell, was perhaps the final *reductio ad absurdum* of Newtonian psychology. The question was, "Is there a unique 'thought' element over and above those of sensation, feeling, and image?" Cornell's answer was "no," Würzburg's "yes." The decision was not even a draw; the spectators left the arena before the battle was over. The controversy over imageless thought made it clear that the search for "thought" elements was getting us nowhere.

It remains to be seen whether the Newtonians of today, namely, those who substitute S's, R's, and their combinations for

199

the "ideas" of Mill and the "sensations" of Titchener, will get us any further. My own impression is that so far the translation of old-fashioned "mentalistic" concepts into terms of verbal behavior has given us little more than a new, and possibly more cumbersome, language. It sometimes happens, of course, that a new language helps to sweep away some of the cobwebs, and it may be that sustained self-stimulating and automatically self-reinforcing verbal behavior will be easier to explain than is creative thinking. We shall eagerly await the demonstration, but I fear that the piano will be as difficult to play with the new pair of mittens as it was with the old.

Darwin, as I have mentioned, did his best to remain loyal to the nineteenth century ideal of science, but the Darwinian movement could not be so confined. The Aristotelian teleology, which the Newtonians had tried so hard to expel from physics, began to sneak its way back into biology and psychology. "Force" in the Newtonian scheme had no inherent direction. The ebullient Darwinians, who spent their spare time looking at animal behavior, could not escape the conviction that force is not only "directed," but even "upward directed." Man's descent from the apes was in due course interpreted by the theologians as an "ascent," directed by God's purpose.

The psychologists fought valiantly against the reintroduction of Aristotle's "final" causes, and even of his "formal" causes; but it was a losing battle. The new psychology of adjustment, sparked by Darwin, contained a teleology only thinly concealed by Newtonian mechanism. Adjustment to what? To the environment, of course. And for what? Obviously, for survival, but possibly for something more than survival. Darwinian psychology transmuted Newtonian "force" into a *vis a tergo.* Bergson called it the *élan vital,* Freud the *libido.* Others used words like instinct, drive, need, and their synonyms. What was common was the conception of life as actively pushing forward, of man as not only coping with but also as seizing control of his environment. Darwinian psychology, perhaps best represented by American functionalism, was a psychology of motivation rather than a psychology of cognition. It talked of process rather than of content, of "perceiving" rather than of "percepts," of "thinking" rather than of "thoughts." It insistently raised the question, "Why do we do what we do?" For the psychology of thinking the question was not "What is the nature of thought?" but rather, "Why do we think, and why do we think in this particular way?"

According to the functionalists, we think when the built-in machinery of adjustment is incapable of coping simply and smoothly with constantly changing internal and external conditions. The spider does not have to think, at least not very often, because of his highly developed repertoire of instincts. Man guards himself against thinking by developing habits, but his habits are seldom fully adequate. As James Rowland Angell (1904) put it, "If the reflexes and the automatic acts were wholly competent to steer the organism through its course, there is no reason to suppose that consciousness would ever put in an appearance." Thinking, then, is an evidence of maladjustment, and the creative thinker must be very maladjusted indeed.

I have suggested that the Newtonian model, useful as it has proved in some contexts, has constricted our freedom to think about thinking. The Darwinian model is better, in that it permits us to conceive of thinking as directed activity. If I had to choose between the two I should certainly argue in support of Darwin. But the Darwinian model is still a bit fuzzy. The formula that was so popular in the heyday of functionalism—Stimulus-Adjustment-Response—leaves the three crucial terms only vaguely defined. A stimulus can be anything that evokes a response, a response anything that happens as a result of a stimulus, and an adjustment anything that intervenes between the two. Woodworth struggled with the formula in the successive editions of his textbook, moving from S-R through S-A-R and S-O-R (O for organism or organization) to W-S-O-R-W (W for world), which might be simplified to W-O-W, a broad enough formula to satisfy anyone. Woodworth did not seem to find any magic in the final formulation, but it helped to put the problem in better perspective. Thinking is a response to a challenge from the world (which includes the thinker's own constitution) which produces changes in the world, which in turn produce new challenges. It is an endless spiral.

One of the virtues of Darwinian functionalism is, possibly,

201

the very fact that it leaves its crucial terms undefined and invites the investigator to explore all possible relations among them. The passion of American psychology during the past few decades has been to correlate something with something else; and the results have not been completely inconsequential. In the psychology of thinking, the findings have been interesting but not always exciting. If we conceive of thinking as adjustment to a changing environment, we are tempted—and we usually yield to the temptation—to require our subjects, rats and college sophomores, to adjust themselves to a changing environment which we control. We set the problems, and we observe how our victims attempt to cope with them. From studies of this sort have come the principle of trial and error, the law of effect, and the like, and we have gained some understanding of the conditions under which some organisms meet our criteria of adjustment and others do not. We conceive of intelligence as a capacity of the organism which enables it to adjust as we think it ought to adjust.

All this is very useful and enlightening, especially when we are concerned with the practical problems of predicting and controlling behavior. But how much does it tell us about the nature of thinking as such, and especially about the kind of thinking that seems to break the rules and yields something unexpected? The adjustment theory is strictly pragmatic. The individual is motivated to survive; he has certain tools (reflexes, habits, skills) which are ordinarily adequate; the environment changes in such a way as to present a new problem; he tries the old tools, and they don't work; then he thinks, and either adjusts himself to the new situation or succumbs. There is nothing really wrong about this statement; it is merely incomplete. Most of our creative thinking is probably instigated by pressures from without, by crises, by decisions that have been thrust upon us, even by publishers' deadlines. We can learn much from the observation of organisms forced to adjust. But this is only part of the story. How about the kind of creation that invites the word "spontaneous"? A Navajo Indian is weaving a basket. He has woven hundreds of them, and he knows exactly how a good basket should be made. He possesses the materials and the skills; he has no problem. But this particular Indian adds a curlicue to his basket, perhaps

202

merely to escape the monotony of basket-weaving. He may learn later that the additional frills increase the sale value of his baskets, in which case he will become frantically productive of more and better curlicues; but the initial creation was not an adjustment to a problem set by his environment.

Here, I think, is where the Darwinian model begins to show its weakness. The theory of evolution gives us the picture of upward-striving species, slowly adapting themselves in varying ways to the demands of a changing environment, and generating in the process all sorts of structures and functions, including those that we label as mind. As a global picture, I think it is correct; my main criticism, as it was of the Newtonian scheme, is that it, too, has proved too constrictive. Let us examine this a little more closely.

Darwinian psychology has focused our attention on: (1) the adjustment of the individual to his environment; (2) the genesis of behavior; and (3) individual differences in capacity, aptitude, and so forth. All are fruitful fields, and none has been properly cultivated by the Newtonians. I have some complaints about all three.

1. Adaptation, in the Darwinian sense, refers to progressive changes in species in response to changes in an independently definable physical environment. Darwin made his case, and we need not quarrel over his specific hypotheses. The adjustment of the individual to his environment suggests an alluring analogy, but I don't think that the analogy holds. We can plot changes in physical environment (climatic, nutritional, and so forth), and see how organisms adapt themselves in successive generations. But for the individual organism the situation is not really analogous. The individual selects from its physical (and cultural) environment that to which it will respond. It is thus not only shaped by but also a shaper of its environment. This fact was clearly recognized by Darwin, but its implications have been too lightly overlooked by Darwinian psychologists. It implies that mere adjustment is not enough, unless the term is to be used in such a broad sense as to be meaningless.

2. Darwinian theory leads us to seek for explanations by tracing back to origins. First was the backward look to earlier stages of evolutionary history; and the reconstruction of the de-

velopmental stages of various structures, and even of certain functions, was truly impressive. Then came, by analogy, the suggestion that ontogeny must recapitulate phylogeny, with the accompanying thought that the principle of evolution might even account for the structures and functions of society. This was not an unhealthy movement. In psychology it lured students into fruitful studies of animal behavior, child development and the mental processes of people in cultures widely different from our own. Where it has been constricting has been in its almost exclusive emphasis on explanation by reference to origins. "Why" is answered by "How he got that way." Again, there is nothing essentially wrong with this; it is merely incomplete. We have, perhaps too soon, set the instincts aside as explanatory constructs, but we are still under the weight of Freud, who would have us interpret the present in terms of early childhood experience; and there are still some who would follow Jung away back into the racial unconscious. Genetic accounts can be enlightening, but all too frequently they "explain away" without really explaining.

3. Spontaneous variation was one of Darwin's central concepts. The analogue in psychology is individual differences. However the differences come about, whether from nature or from nurture, they are there as regulators of behavior. In the Darwinian example the precursors of giraffes who happened to have longer necks were more likely to survive and produce long-necked offspring. For human survival the possibilities are more varied, but the most important characteristic is intelligence. Psychologists in the Darwinian tradition became fascinated by the problem of identifying and measuring human capacities, first intellectual capacity, and then more special abilities, aptitudes, interests, skills, and so forth. The tools of statistics were quickly sharpened, and from their use there has emerged what is almost a new science. Harking back to the faculty psychology of a bygone era, we now see behind every individual's performance a measurable factor, or usually a cluster of factors, which will explain it. Whether or not factor analysis will tease out a factor of creativity, or even a cluster of factors, remains to be seen. What is to be noted at this point is that factor analytic methods, ingenious as they are, have not yet approached the heart of the problem.

204

I have accused Newtonian psychology of having wasted our time with a fruitless search for elements, and Darwinian psychology of having become overly concerned with genesis. These are unduly harsh judgments, for Newton and Darwin symbolize the two great movements in modern psychology, and both have been richly productive. They have not, however, contributed much to our understanding of thinking. Is there an alternative? I shudder at the thought of being termed an eclectic, but I think that we have the beginning of a sort of Hegelian synthesis. I find that beginning in Einstein and Wertheimer.

My physicist friends tell me that Einstein should not be credited with the post-Newtonian revolution in physics. This I am prepared to accept; but for us, psychologists and other ordinary people, Einstein is a satisfactory symbol of the current revolution in our thinking about the universe. The "Einsteinian" revolution will rank in the history of science with the revolutions of Darwin, Newton, and Copernicus. The man who grasped its implications for psychology most fully was, I think, Max Wertheimer. Wertheimer was a perceptionist to begin with, but from the beginning he had an interest in thinking. The Newtonians had stressed the analysis of mental content; the Darwinians had focused on acts. Wertheimer, perhaps with a prod from Husserl, and certainly with a prod from Einstein, began to do what the physicists were doing, namely, to bracket existing assumptions and look at the phenomena. Einstein formulated a theory of relativity, which went far beyond Newtonian mechanics. Shortly afterwards Wertheimer presented his Gestalt theory; and the two were not unrelated.

It would be untrue to the facts, however, to identify the new movement in the psychology of thinking with Gestalt theory. Wertheimer and his colleagues were merely its best and most persuasive interpreters. European psychology in general was moving away from the Newtonian, and to some extent from the Darwinian, tradition. The movement was most evident in the German-speaking world where the Gestalt psychology of the Berlin group was paralleled by similar developments in Hamburg, Göttingen, Leipzig, Vienna, and other centers; but it was evident too in the work of such men as Michotte in Louvain and Piaget in Geneva. The emphasis was on wholes rather than parts, on functional rather than structural analysis, on behavior in natural rather than artificial contexts. It is characteristic that terms like field, vector, and relational determination—all borrowed, of course, from physical science—began to replace the traditional elements and their connections. Wertheimer's laws of organization may not be laws in the stricter senses of the term, but they represent at least useful descriptive statements of the ways in which psychological fields become organized and reorganized.

Wertheimer maintained the faith, with the Newtonians, that the laws of physics and of psychology belong to a single realm of nature whose laws will eventually be unified; but Wertheimer, like Einstein, no longer felt constrained to accept one set of constructs and one mode of analysis. The traditional scheme could not deal adequately with familiar phenomena such as apparent movement, much less with the equally familiar but more complex phenomena of perceptual constancy. A Newtonian like Helmholtz had to superimpose on his primary sensations certain hypothetical unconscious intellective processes. Wertheimer inverted the traditional procedure. The phenomena are there, he said; instead of trying to explain them away, let us observe their regularities and conditions, and then formulate laws that accord with observation. This approach seems so obviously right that one wonders why it should be considered revolutionary. Yet, as Wertheimer's studies of thinking showed time and again, it takes a great wrench on the part of the thinker to become aware of and to challenge assumptions that are implicitly there.

Wertheimer's approach to thinking was as deceptively simple as was his approach to perception. The first, and persistent, question was: What occurs when, now and then, thinking really works productively? It was an invitation to observe and describe, without reference to hypothetical elements or hidden motives, what happens when people think, trying always to identify what is really going on in the psychological field and then to contrive situations which will bring these processes into clearer focus. *Productive Thinking* is full of examples which need not be repeated. Suffice it to say that Wertheimer finds the essence of thinking in the reorganization of the psychological field. This is an

active process, for the field is not a static array of contents or connections but a reflection of the on-going life of a goal-directed individual. With this approach the traditional distinction between
cognition and motivation breaks down; we are dealing with
cognitive structures, but with structures that are dynamically
related to one another.

I must confess that I have always found Wertheimer's book
somewhat disappointing. There is nowhere a richer source of
descriptive material, of brilliant insights, of penetrating comments
that make one sit up and exclaim "Aha!" It is an exercise in
the descriptive analysis of processes of thinking, with only too
infrequently a lifting out and a systematic scrutinizing of principles. Were another volume to have been written it might have
contained a more formal critique of the psychologist's thinking
about thinking, with an examination of alternative assumptions
and interpretations. Perhaps such a task would have proved too
dull for the mercurial Wertheimer. Lacking such a study, however, we must regard his book as essentially a brilliant foray
which has revealed all sorts of exciting possibilities; but there is
still ample room for adventure. What I find most invigorating
about the movement Wertheimer represents is its affirmation
that the data of experience and behavior can be accepted as valid
in their own right, worthy of interpretation in accordance with
their own dictates. Granted that psychology has learned much
from the older sciences, and that we all look forward to a closer
integration of the sciences, it is high time, it seems to me, for
psychology to discard its subservience to physics and biology and
to insist on the dignity of its own field of phenomena and its right
to its own methods and constructs.

PROSPECT

Having expressed some misgivings about psychology's current obsession with prediction, I shall certainly not attempt a
forecast of future developments. What I am inclined to say by
way of extrapolation from the past and present is more likely to
sound like moralizing than like prophecy. One of the many

Titchenerian legends that still float about Morrill Hall at Cornell is that back in the 1920's, some years before his death, Titchener predicted that in another fifty years the task of psychology would be complete. At that time such a prediction could make sense. The structural psychology had a clear conception of its problems, its data, its methods, and its explanatory constructs. Anything that could not be included within this framework was simply not psychology. The fifty year period is almost up, and the task is not nearing completion; not, however, because it proved too difficult but because there are no Titchenerians left to complete it. Titchener's was perhaps the neatest, cleanest system of psychology ever devised. It failed to survive because, like a Darwinian species, it was too rigid to adapt itself to a changing environment. Psychologists simply could not limit their energies to a Newtonian type of analysis of the content of consciousness. Functionalism, Gestalt theory, and Freudian psychoanalysis were infinitely sloppier, but they asked new questions, looked at new phenomena, devised new methods, and played with new ways of explaining. Fifty years hence the psychology of today may be almost unrecognizable in retrospect, but, unless we allow ourselves to become rigid again, the new psychology of the twenty-first century will still express man's curiosity about his own nature.

The moral, of course, is: Let us not be rigid! This book has amply demonstrated, I think, that creative thinking is a researchable problem; but it has not pointed to any one approach as uniquely good. One of the lessons of history is that the creative spurts in science have taken place when scientists have broken free from a tangle of constricting assumptions and begun to look at their problems in a new way. This, we have also learned, is one of the essential conditions of creativity in the individual. This lesson we should take to heart as we proceed with our psychological study of creative thinking.

If I may be permitted to "view with alarm," may I express some anxiety about psychology's present enthusiasm for theoretical models? Not that theoretical models are bad; they are potentially very productive, and they are always fun. Even a bad theory, it has been said, is better than no theory at all. The obvious danger, however, is that we may become so enamored of our models that we may either (1) exclude from consideration any phenomena which cannot be encompassed by the model, or (2) allow our research to degenerate into a mere linguistic exercise in which it is tediously demonstrated that the phenomenon can be "taken care of" by the jargon of the model. Both S-R theory and Freudian theory, it seems to me, are open to these criticisms. Gestalt theory might also be criticized, certainly on the second count, for it threatened to develop a horribly pedantic jargon, were it not for the fact that it has ceased to be a theory; perhaps it never really was a theory. Gestalt psychology's great contribution was twofold: it challenged traditional assumptions, and it pointed to phenomena which every theory must take into account. Both the challenge and the invitation need to be constantly restated, but the fact that we no longer think of a Gestalt "school" is perhaps an indication that the Gestalt contribution has for the most part been absorbed into general psychology. This is the way science should progress.

Of all fields of psychological study, that of creative thinking must not be hedged in by theoretical models. By all means, let us try out existing models, and let us construct new ones; but let us happily tear them to shreds when we find that they do not fit all the facts. What I am arguing, I suppose, is this: we think we know what we mean by creativity, but we have no firm criteria; we find people flailing away with all sorts of instruments at what may or may not be the same problem; we cannot ask them to suspend activity until we are all agreed; better, we think, to encourage them all and to live in hope that various lines of inquiry will eventually converge. But, we say, let us all remain flexible! This may sound like strange counsel. Science ought to proceed in cool, orderly fashion from initial problem through observation, hypothesis, and experiment to final conclusion. But science has seldom proceeded in precisely this way, and in this particular field there should certainly be no premature freezing of methods and models.

One thing I am quite sure of, however, is that the task of sheer descriptive analysis, i.e., phenomenology, will never be complete. Even the simpler forms of perception, in which the phenomenon is anchored to a specifiable set of physical stimuli, constantly reveal fresh nuances to the sensitive observer—which in turn set new problems and invite new theories. When we turn to the infinitely more complex phenomena of thinking, the need for careful description becomes correspondingly more insistent. Thinking may have tenuous anchorage points in the laws of logic, but even the best disciplined mind is never *bound* by logic. Thinking ranges in all directions, expresses itself in the language of literature and the arts as well as in the language of science, assumes different forms at different ages and in different cultures. If the psychologist is to discover order in this rich array of phenomena he must indeed be flexible, and he must have a mind that is always open to facts.

And now for a word about the problem that has gripped us all with a fascination that almost approaches fear, namely, the thinking machine. Herbert Simon has made a most persuasive case for it. Is the thinking machine going to render all our psychologizing irrelevant? This does not disturb me particularly; the world might be a sweeter place without psychologists. Will the machine, however, rob man of his freedom and responsibility by demonstrating that they do not exist? This is a thought that might well give us pause. To explore it fully, however, would require a long dissertation. Let me merely suggest very briefly why as I contemplate our future life with the machine I feel a thrill of excitement but not of anxiety.

Simon has told us an entrancing story of the machines that solve logical problems, play chess, and even compose music, and every day we read stories of other fantastic accomplishments. The layman has no grounds for questioning Simon's belief that in another few years these will seem almost picayune. Let us assume that we have a machine that can simulate perfectly all the products of human thinking. Would this give us a correct theory of thinking? No, we are agreed, not until the simulation includes process as well as product. But Simon's experiments have shown a striking similarity of process when both machines and logically trained men solve a problem. From this we can conclude that some logically trained men can think like machines and that some machines can think like logically trained men. I see no rea-

210

son for not assuming that, so far as logical processes are concerned, the simulation will eventually be perfect. Now let us assume further that in due course all the characteristics of human affect will have been built into the machine, that it will cringe in terror, groan in agony, and leap with a joyous "Aha!" when it has solved a problem; in other words that James' perfect automaton has been created. Should not this cause us anxiety? Certainly not; we should shout "Eureka!" for it would mean that we had synthesized a human being and at long last had discovered the laws of human nature. But how about freedom and responsibility? No problem; or, rather, precisely the same old problem, for our synthetic man would present all the familiar phenomena of experience and behavior that now lead us to believe that we ourselves are free and responsible.

So much for romancing. The machine-builders are not now trying to synthesize man. For the most part, they are not even trying to replicate human thought processes. Their interest is in the product and in the ways in which it can be obtained most efficiently. The machinery of the electronic computer bears no more necessary resemblance to that of the human mind than does the machinery of a jet-propelled plane to that of a bird. In his attempts to fly, man learned a great deal from the bird, but if he had limited himself to the replication of birds he would not now be flying. The fact that we have learned to fly in a nonbirdlike way, however, has not diminished our interest in the study of birds.

The machine-builders have given us fantastically efficient tools which now permit an attack on all sorts of problems hitherto beyond our reach; and this in itself is exciting. Even more exciting, however, is the possibility that what we have learned in the designing of superefficient machines may enable us to reproduce in machine models more and more of the processes that actually go on in behavior. Simon and his colleagues may be pardoned for having concentrated first on the simulation of clean, logical thinking. Thinking in its clearest form is easier to reproduce than is the ordinary muddy thinking in which most of us indulge. Machines can make mistakes, as Clever Hans did; when the machine can accurately replicate human stupidity in all its profundity, then we shall have a model that will enable us to test a theory of thinking as thinking actually takes place.

So far as the psychology of thinking is concerned, it seems to me, the machine's most immediate promise is the possibility of hitherto impossible tests of theory. The simple trial-and-error model has been built into the machine, and it works; machines can simulate something like Bruner's "strategies"; and there are machine analogues of "cognitive reorganization." The machine can now determine whether or not a theory is self-consistent. For some time to come, however, it will be the psychologist who, having endlessly observed and thought about the phenomena of human behavior, will present the theory to be tested and will decide which of the various self-consistent theories is true: we still have something to do.

INDEX

INDEX

Bibliographic references are in *italics;* references to footnotes are indicated by *n* following the page number.